# IN THE FOOTSTEPS OF
# ALEXANDER
# THE GREAT

To Martyn and Amanda
with lots of love as ever
from Mike
Sept '98
('Sogdian Rock? Don't know that
one... how about the Ubangi Stomp?')

# IN THE FOOTSTEPS OF
# ALEXANDER THE GREAT

## A JOURNEY FROM GREECE TO ASIA

# MICHAEL WOOD

BBC BOOKS

*To Mum and Dad*
*who first inspired me with a love of history*

Frontispiece: Roman marble bust of Alexander the Great
copied from a Greek statue of 338 BC

———————————

This book is published to accompany the television series
*In the Footsteps of Alexander the Great,* produced by Maya Vision
for the BBC and first broadcast in 1997
Producer: Rebecca Dobbs  Director: David Wallace

First published 1997
© Michael Wood 1997
The moral right of the author has been asserted

ISBN 0 563 37144 7

Published by BBC Books, an imprint of BBC Worldwide Publishing
BBC Worldwide Limited, Woodlands, 80 Wood Lane,
London W12 OTT

Picture research by Frances Abraham
Maps by Line & Line

Set in Bembo by BBC Books
Printed and bound in Great Britain by
Butler & Tanner Limited, Frome and London
Colour separations by Radstock Repro Limited, Midsomer Norton
Jacket printed by Lawrence Allen Limited,
Weston-super-Mare

# CONTENTS

li aparuſt en macedone en
la ſamblance quil li deuſt
aidier·quil peuſt recorner
ſain et ſauf a ſon peuple
non mie por luy·ayes por le

ſauuement deaus·Lors
A ombia la uertu diuine·
Coment alixandres ſe fer ca
tie en la mer ſpi·i·tonnel
...

# PROLOGUE

BUMPING AND JARRING OVER FROZEN ROADS, slewing through great cuttings of hardened snow drift, it took us twelve hours to get over the Lowari Pass and into Chitral. Then, just as the sun disappeared, the last valley in Pakistan's North-West Frontier came into view. Ahead, still lit by the setting sun, was the great wall of the mountains of the Hindu Kush. At Chitral we had black tea under a spreading plane tree and then pushed on. We still had two or three more hours to go, up the steep gorges which lead to Rombur, the valley where the last of the Kalash live, the 'black pagans' of the Hindu Kush. Above us now, tipped pink by the last light, loomed the snowy peaks of Afghanistan. At the bottom of the darkening valley a stream rushed over boulders, roaring in our ears; our headlights lit up a waving field of wheat and a graveyard planted with a clump of intense purple irises.

It is a land so remote that Islam only penetrated it in the last hundred years; its valleys so inaccessible that, until a dirt-track was blasted through terrifying over-hangs a few years ago, the only way in was on mule paths along vertiginous cliffs. All the early explorers agreed that this was a place where ancient legends and customs had been particularly tenacious. Here in Victorian days ragged chieftains produced Hellenistic bowls for British administrators, which they claimed had been given to them by Greek kings and proved their right to rule; such stories their ancestors had told to Marco Polo in the thirteenth century – and they are still told today.

It was pitch dark before we finally stumbled into Rombur, a tiny cluster of rubble and beam houses with wooden verandas. The electricity had failed and Engineer Khan came down to greet us waving a torch. We had last met in Peshawar in the North-West Frontier five months before, and I had no idea whether any of our messages had got through to him since. 'Welcome to the land of the Kalash,' he beamed. 'So you finally made it. I got your letter. We've been awaiting you for two days!'

Up the dirt street we heard the distant sound of drumming and chanting. Above us, against a full-moon sky, the dark shape of the open-air temple stood over the village; dying

---

In later legend Alexander enjoyed an extraordinary afterlife
as a combination of superman, magus and prophet. In this medieval
painting he plumbs the ocean depths in a diving bell while the
fishes crowd around to pay homage.

7

flames licked the sacrifice stone, and in the shadows were the carved wooden effigies they use in their religion. (Astonishingly, alone in a surrounding sea of Islam, the Kalash pray to the ancient gods, in particular Di Zau, the great sky god, brother to the Greek Zeus.) The women's dance was almost over. Shuffling and swaying in a long line, young and old together, arms around each other's waists, sprays of walnut leaves in their hands, austere in black embroidered dresses and elaborate cowrie shell headdresses topped with pompons of crimson and marigold, their strange ululating wordless song echoed around the mountain sides.

That night, after the dance, we sat by the fireside and drank sweet white wine (unlike their Muslim neighbours the Kalash harvest and ferment the grape, which they revere). Then the tale-teller began his tale. His name was Kasi Khushnawaz, 'the bringer of happiness'. A tiny bird-like man, with a pinched face, and a pair of old boots several sizes too big, he commanded instant respect from the big crowd of men all around. TV has not yet reached the Kalash valleys and here the story-teller is still an entertainer, a kind of magician. He has hundreds of tales and they have never been known to run out. We had come for one in particular:

> *Long long ago, before the days of Islam, Sikander e Aazem came to India. The Two Horned one whom you British people call Alexander the Great. He conquered the world, and was a very great man, brave and dauntless and generous to his followers. When he left to go back to Greece, some of his men did not wish to go back with him but preferred to stay here. Their leader was a general called Shalakash. With some of his officers and men, he came to these valleys and they settled here and took local women, and here they stayed. We, the Kalash, the Black Kafirs of the Hindu Kush, are the descendants of their children. Still some of our words are the same as theirs, our music and our dances too; we worship the same gods. This is why we believe the Greeks are our first ancestors.*

I looked round at the faces in the flickering fire light. At such a moment in such a setting it is easy to suspend disbelief. It was an extraordinary idea that we were staring at the descendants of the last survivors of the Macedonian army which had burst across Asia like a meteor between 334 and 324 BC. And yet it was not so implausible: after all, 2000 years ago the Greeks did enter these obscure valleys on the edge of Nuristan. Indeed some had stayed on to found their own Raj, and these Indo-Greek kingdoms had lasted here for centuries after Alexander's day. Their language died out here only in Muslim times; their coins which proudly blazoned their petty dynasts as invincible maharajahs are still for sale in the bazaars of Kabul and Peshawar. A legend it may be, but the Kalash tale is still an extraordinary testimony to the enduring power of the tale, the myth of one of history's greatest conquerors, Alexander the Great.

It was by common consent one of the greatest events in the history of the world, opening up West and East for the first time; an extraordinary tale of bravery, and cruelty, endurance and excess, chivalry and greed; a journey of ten years and 22,000 miles all told, enough to circle the globe. Behind it, like the wrack of a receding tide, it has left strange and glittering debris: lost cities, blue-eyed Indians, exotic treasures, ancient manuscripts, and a great harvest of amazing stories, songs, poems, myths and legends.

The legend spread to every corner of the old world: Alexander appears in the apocalyptic visions of the biblical Book of Daniel as The Third Beast who unleashes a bloody tide on humankind. In the Muslim Koran he is the mysterious 'Two-horned One' who built a magical wall to keep out Gog and Magog, the evil ones who, in the Apocalypse, will ravage the earth with Satan in the last days. The Greek Orthodox Church by contrast turned him into a saint, a latter-day St George.

There are over 200 different Alexander epics and poems in medieval European languages alone, surviving in literally thousands of manuscripts: for example, in Russian, Polish, Old French, Czech and Serbian. In Jewish tradition Alexander is nothing short of a folk hero. There is a medieval German Alexander epic, an Icelandic Alexander Saga, and an Ethiopian Alexander Romance. By the mid fourteenth century the tale had even reached Mongolia, where Alexander appears as an almost supernatural predecessor of Genghis Khan. You will find him depicted as one of the four kings on the standard French pack of playing cards; you will find the map of his empire on every Greek school map, and every taverna wall; he's on Sicilian carnival carts, Ethiopian bridal cloths, Byzantine church murals, and on paintings from Moghul India. His tomb is claimed in Egypt, Pakistan and Uzbekistan.

His tale has been reinterpreted by every generation since his day. Jews told how he punished the ten lost tribes of Israel and found the wonderstone in the earthly paradise; Muslim poets told how he found the tree of everlasting life, plumbed the deepest sea in a diving bell, and rose to heaven on a magic chariot pulled by griffons. In Europe in the Middle Ages he was the 'perfect knight' and the philosopher king, and the legend of his ascent to heaven, carved on cathedral stalls from Somerset to south Italy, became an anticipation of glory in the hereafter. In India, legend said he had found the Speaking Tree which had foretold his destiny: 'to die young but win eternal glory'.

This century the fascination shows no sign of dying out; rather, there has been an unparalleled outpouring of books and films on the king. Modern people, of course, have sought and found something different again in Alexander's amazing career. In the latter

10

days of the British Empire, imperial historians saw him as a visionary idealist, a benevolent empire-builder in their own mould, pursuing the dream of uniting mankind under one rule, irrespective of race, creed or colour. Conversely in Hitler's Germany the greatest Alexander scholar (who had himself embraced Nazism) portrayed his hero as *Ingenium und Macht,* intellect and power, the Superman as real-life hero and model, the embodiment of manifest destiny.

Now, at the end of our troubled century, another Alexander is being disentangled from the sources. Indeed never before, perhaps, has he been subject to such detailed investigation. Now the dark deeds of his reign are being investigated in the way that modern journalists have attempted to uncover the truth behind war crimes in Vietnam, Cambodia, and the Bosnian war. The Macedonian conquest of the world as far as India, which has always been seen through Greek sources exclusively, is now being illuminated for the first time by native sources, newly discovered oracles and prophecies on papyrus or clay tablet.

In this light the Greek adventure in Asia is being reconsidered in terms of modern ideas on colonialism, orientalism, racism. So, too, are the king's power-politics now being seen in the light of modern history: his purges and massacres, his reliance on intelligence spies, secret police, his control of information, use of torture, manipulation of images, his state propaganda, his use of terror against civilian populations – all attested in our sources. They have taken on new meaning in our own time which has lived through the great communist utopian tyrannies.

On the king's sexuality there are new insights, too, as more becomes known about Greek male attitudes to women, and to homosexuality. Others have attempted to look into the king's mind, in particular the psychology of leadership and the pitfalls of absolute power. A new study has suggested alcoholism as the root of his downfall. The most recent survey has found suggestive parallels with Cortés and the conquistadors, emphasizing his dark side: 'murderous and melancholy mad' as one hostile contemporary remembered him. It is all a far cry from the golden boy we have known for so long; it may, perhaps, be nearer to his truth – it is nearer to ours, no doubt.

---

Above left: The spring festival at Brumboret village, Chitral, in the North-West Frontier of Pakistan, home of the last of the Kalash who claim descent from Alexander's army.

Left: 'Two-Horned Alexander' on a silver coin of c. 300 BC, wearing the diadem and the ram's horns of the Egyptian god Ammon.

The result of all this ferment of ideas is that a new and much richer picture is now emerging, all the more fascinating because of its apparent contradictions. The final word on Alexander, of course, will never be said. But it is an exciting time to look again at his story. This account of Alexander is based on the texts of the Greek and Roman historians which have come down to us, and which I carried with me in my rucksack. But its special interest is that it takes the form of a journey in Alexander's footsteps, perhaps the first time this has been done in full since Alexander's day.

It involved a journey on the ground even longer than Alexander's – his journey through Iran, for example, we did in its entirety twice. In Egypt, we, too, crossed the desert to Siwa to find the oracle of Ammon (and moreover we undertook the hazardous return across the trackless wastes of the Great Sand Sea). In Iran we, too, asked local guides to take us through the Zagros Mountains to find the lost site of Alexander's epic battle at the 'Persian Gates' which has never been securely identified by scholars. There, in an unknown and unvisited corner of Persia, we slept out in the open for three chill November nights surrounded by a sea of golden poplars, as we attempted to uncover his secret route.

That same glorious autumn we crossed from war-torn Kabul to North Afghanistan, walking as Alexander did over the Khawak Pass in the Hindu Kush, with packhorses carrying our gear and gunmen by our side to ward off bandits. The following spring we came down off the Khyber and retraced Alexander's steps up the inaccessible heights of Mount Pir Sar in the North-West Frontier; we sailed Mohanno boats down the Indus just as the furnace heat of the hot season started to clamp on the plains, and finally we took a train of twenty-three camels across the Makran Desert in an effort to experience for ourselves what might have happened to Alexander's army during their disastrous retreat.

Popular legend imagines film-crews ensconced in air-conditioned luxury in between their brief forays into the real world. But this was not a journey like that. Nowhere did Hilton Hotels beckon for us – except the little known 'Hiltan Hotel' on the Afghan border near Chitral (five rooms, no beds, no running water, but that night no lodging could have been more welcome). Indeed, there were times when the crew was too ill to carry on, and we simply had to stop. Often we stayed in the houses of ordinary people whose hospitality was invariably unstinting, even in war-ravaged Afghanistan. We slept in Iranian station waiting-rooms and Afghan stables, on sail boats on the Indus, in a mosque in the North-West Frontier, and on desert dunes by the Arabian Sea under a starlit sky crossed by comet Hyakutake. We travelled light as we could, and did not always plan ahead as well as we might, waking to chill dawns in the Great Sand Sea and the Desert of Death, grateful for a few dried dates and cup of water. After such days, steaming green tea flavoured with cardamom and hot coarse bitter bread on the snowy heights of the Hindu Kush seemed simply heaven.

As we journeyed it was astonishing how much more came out of the ancient texts when read on the ground. The words of the Greek historians came alive in a way in which even their authors could not have foreseen – for they had no more seen these sites than most of their modern counterparts. Often solutions to Alexander riddles were instantly apparent when one stood on the ground where these events had actually taken place. But even more than that, there was the sense of a continuing history: a realization that Alexander's tale still reverberated across eastern Asia, especially, strangely enough, in the Muslim world, where he is regarded as a great folk hero, whether as 'The Two Horned One', the 'Great' or the 'Devil'.

We saw his story retold by Greek and Turkish shadow players, and by tale-tellers in Isfahan and Tehran cafés. We saw the king come alive in an epic Hindi movie banned by the British occupiers in World War II. We saw one of the last of the travelling one-man shows in Iran, complete with painted backdrop showing the death of Darius in epic style, 'cutting a passion to tatters' like Hamlet's player king. We heard stories of Alexander from professional bards in Turkey and Central Asia; we crouched in a Tajik cave by the mummified body of Alexander's greatest foe, to hear his tale recounted by Muslim pilgrims; nearby at the blue mirror of Iskander Gol we heard of the dam of gold which he left behind which still gives up gold at each flood time; we heard about Greek medicine from the doctors of Kandahar who claim descent from Alexander's medical team; we sat in a felt yurt on the Turkoman steppe to hear the story of his devil's horns and his two-week sex romp with an Amazon queen (as the tabloid newspapers would put it today: and, beware, such mythical creatures still exist out there by the Caspian Sea and still carry off unsuspecting young men for use as studs before they kill them – or at least so the Turkomans say!).

In Pakistan we listened to Sufi singers on the river boats, telling tales of Alexander's encounter with Indian holy men. And all along the way, in chance meetings, we heard from ordinary people who had their own stories: a civil servant in Kabul, an Afghan horse-handler, an Uzbek mullah, and a Luri farmer in the Zagros who said Alexander's tale had been handed down in his village 'from chest to chest'. And the more we heard, the more we came to realize that, although our goal was to try to find the real historical events, the legend was almost as powerful and fascinating (and far more pervasive and long lasting). As John Ford, director of the film *The Man Who Shot Liberty Valance,* said, 'When the fact becomes a legend, print the legend!'

So this book, then, is both the story of Alexander's expedition and a record of our modern-day journey which followed as far as humanly possible the track of Alexander's journey from Greece to India. Only in one part, at the time of making these films, did it prove impossible for me to travel in his footsteps. Since the Gulf War I have been involved in publicizing the atrocities done by the Iraqi regime of Saddam Hussein against the population of southern Iraq, especially the tragic fate of the Marsh Arabs. Because of this I was strongly advised by Iraqi friends in exile that it would be unwise for me to return to Baghdad; so, although I was subsequently able to journey through Free Kurdistan to Irbil, the description in this book of the journey from Irbil to Babylon, and of the cities and landscape of southern Iraq, is based on diaries of my journeys there before the Gulf War. One day I hope to return to a free and democratic Baghdad.

Alexander's expedition was a turning point in human history. It opened up contacts between East and West, Europe and Asia, and laid the foundations for much of what followed. Like the European conquest of the Americas, it involved gigantic cruelty and destruction, and yet unleashed astonishing historical energies: in particular the interaction of Greek with Egyptian, Jewish, Iranian and Indian cultures, whose effect is still felt today in the lands between the Mediterranean and the Himalayas. Through the Romans and their successors the fruits of this great opening up were bequeathed to the Western world, too. As we shall see, the aftermath still affects us today in our ways of thinking and seeing.

And at the heart of this amazing and terrible story is the enigmatic character of Alexander himself. Only thirty-two when he died, there is still the widest disagreement on his true nature and motive, and no doubt there always will be. There is an old rhyme still repeated by Greek fishermen in the Aegean Sea. It can happen any time, they say, whether the sea is calm and sunny, whether squalls or a storm are coming up. A mermaid appears in the water by the boat searching for her lost brother, Alexander, and asks this question:

'Where is Great Alexander?'

On the answer your life depends. Say he is dead and, in her rage and anguish, she will call up the storm and you will be engulfed and drowned. The answer is:

*Great Alexander Lives. And Still Rules!*

---

Our film crews. Top: at Dasuya in the Punjab.
Below: on the Khawak Pass in the Hindu Kush Mountains of
Afghanistan, where Alexander stood in the spring of 328 BC.

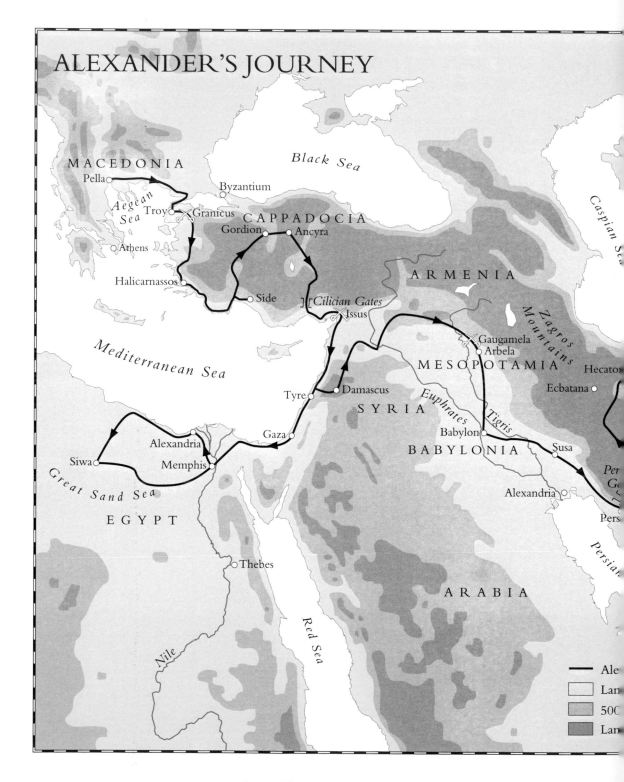

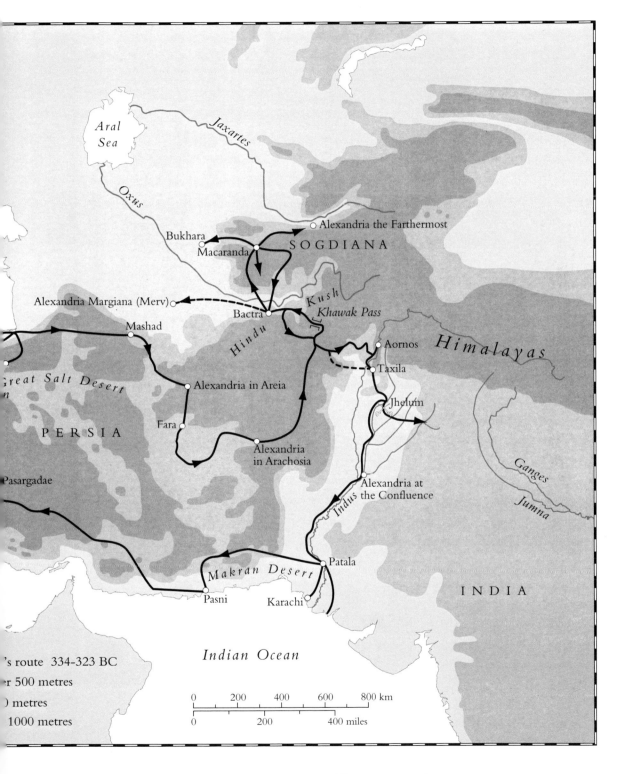

Aral
Sea

Jaxartes

Oxus

Bukhara

Macaranda

○ Alexandria the Farthermost

SOGDIANA

Kush

Alexandria Margiana (Merv) ○

Khawak Pass

Bactra

Mashad

Hindu

Aornos

Himalayas

Taxila

Alexandria in Areia

Great Salt Desert

Jhelum

Fara

PERSIA

Alexandria
in Arachosia

Pasargadae

Alexandria at
the Confluence

Ganges

Indus

Jumna

Patala

INDIA

Makran Desert

Pasni

Karachi

's route 334–323 BC

r 500 metres

) metres

1000 metres

Indian Ocean

| 0 | 200 | 400 | 600 | 800 km |

| 0 | 200 | 400 miles |

# PRELUDE

## THE YEARS BEFORE ALEXANDER'S BIRTH

THIS STORY OF ALEXANDER THE GREAT is the tale of one of the most extraordinary people in history. He ascended the throne at twenty, conquered much of the known world before he was thirty, and was dead by the age of thirty-two. But it is also a tale of enmity between two great and ancient civilizations. The story begins long before Alexander's lifetime – begins with the events of ten dramatic, never to be forgotten years in the fifth century BC – events which still loom large in the Greek myth of themselves and their historical destiny. At that point the Persians (today's Iranians) had created a great empire, stretching from Central Asia to Ethiopia, and from the Indus to the Aegean. The mainland Greeks, meanwhile, were just a group of tiny warring states occupying most of today's Greece, and only brought together by the threat that the Persians would attempt to conquer them and extend their empire into Europe.

The Persian King, Darius the Great, made the initial trial of strength. In 490 BC, at Marathon near Athens, a small Persian expeditionary force was defeated by the hoplites, the heavily armed footsoldiers of democratic Athens. Ten years later came the great invasion, led by Darius's son Xerxes. With a huge army, drawn from the forty-five nations of the Persian empire, Xerxes marched on the Dardanelles. Twelve hundred galleys accompanied the force by sea. At Troy, Xerxes sacrificed to the dead of the Trojan War (the Greeks had invaded Asia nearly 1000 years before – such are the long memories in this story!). At the narrows between Sestos and Abydos, the Persians had built two great bridges of boats and there the Great King scourged the waves before crossing. What happened next would be etched forever on Western minds: for, in Europe, since the Renaissance and the Enlightenment, these events have always been seen not only as the salvation of Greece but also, in some sense, as the foundation of the West.

Confronted with the Persian invasion, the Spartans and Athenians buried their differences and joined forces. The Spartan king with his élite troops, the Three Hundred,

---

Right: Contemporary marble torso of Alexander, with little horns, as the god Pan. How far he actually saw himself as divine is still an open question.

Inset: Persian cavalry of Darius the Great. Detail of a Greek vase, fifth century BC.

attempted to hold back the Persians at the Pass of Thermopylae, but was killed in an heroic last stand against overwhelming numbers. The Persians then marched on towards Athens and, in desperation, the Athenians asked the oracle at Delphi what to do. In a memorable response the prophetess told them not to defend their city, but to 'forsake the land and rely on wooden walls'. In the nick of time the entire population was shipped over to the island of Salamis, just offshore in the Saronic Gulf. The Persians burned the deserted city of Athens, pillaged and desecrated her temples, and cut down the sacred olive tree of Athena. With the Greek fleet apparently trapped behind Salamis the Persian fleet closed in for the kill

Xerxes, seated on a golden throne, prepared to watch from a vantage point on the shore. But, the night before the battle, the Greek Commander Themistocles used an informer to spread a false rumour to the Persians. Xerxes was told that the Greek fleet would attempt to escape next day. Before dawn the Persians pushed their fleets into the narrow straits between Salamis and the coast of Attica. There, suddenly jammed into a narrow space and unable to manoeuvre, they were attacked by the Greek ships and suffered a catastrophic defeat. The poet Aeschylus, who was an eye-witness, reports Themistocles's rousing cry: 'On, on, sons of Greece, your wives and families, your temples, the graves of your ancestors: now everything is at stake'. The straits around Salamis became a swirling mass of debris, wrecked ships, and drowned warriors. Although the Persians were able to extricate a part of their fleet, they were finished; the superior naval power of the Greeks forced them to withdraw. Xerxes left a large army of occupation on Greek soil, but this was decisively defeated the next year at Plataea in a combined effort by the usually divided Greek city states. So ended the Great Persian War.

From then on the Persians set the limit of their empire at the Aegean Sea, on what is today the western shore of Turkey, where rich Greek-speaking cities, such as Ephesus and Miletus, paid tribute to the Persian 'King of Kings'. On the walls of the palace at Persepolis we can still see their ambassadors represented bringing gifts to the annual durbars. Opportunities were great in such a land. The Persian kings employed Greek sea captains, mercenaries and doctors, and Greek contractors, stone-cutters and sculptors worked on their palaces. For the next century or so the Persians ruled the Near East, including the commercial and maritime city states of Phoenicia, and the richest and oldest country in the Eastern Mediterranean, Egypt. With efficient land communications linked to the great

---

Greek hoplites (heavy infantry) on the Nereid monument from
Xanthos (c. 400 BC). The grave demeanour of these men vividly
suggests the spirit of the heroes of Marathon and Salamis.

Persian Royal Road from Sardis, in Turkey, to Susa, in Iran, theirs was the first world empire.

The Greeks, though, never forgot. Above all, they never forgave Xerxes's sacrilege in destroying their holiest shrines. In Athens the Acropolis was rebuilt with magnificent temples whose roofless remains can still be seen today. But the fire-burned column drums of the old Parthenon, which Xerxes destroyed, were set into the wall overlooking the city so all could see them (they are still there today – perhaps the oldest war memorial in the world). The memory of the Great Persian War would remain etched in the Greek psyche. When the poet Aeschylus died a generation later, it was not his dramas which found pride of place on his tombstone, but his pride in being a veteran of Marathon. What also lingered in Greek minds was the idea that one day they would take revenge; that one day the Greeks would mount a crusade against Persia.

## THE RISE OF MACEDONIA

It was, however, the Macedonians not the Athenians who finally put the anti-Persian crusade together. The fifth century BC had been the heyday of classical Greek civilization with Athens as the undisputed cultural and political leader of Greece. But the century ended in a disastrous war with Sparta and the destruction of the Athenian empire. The middle years of the fourth century saw the rapid rise of a new power: Macedon. Who the Macedonians were, though, is today a very contentious issue. With the present troubled mix of races and religions in the Balkans there is much controversy now about Macedonian origins, with some questioning whether they were Greek at all. The creation of a new Slav state called Macedonia to the north of Greece has only fuelled the argument. Everywhere in Greece these days, from supermarket checkouts to roadside hoardings, you see the sign 'Macedonia is Greece'. But scholars still debate whether the Macedonian language is actually related to Greek. Moreover, it is clear that, in Alexander's day, they were viewed as barbarians who, although they spoke Greek, were not fit to be called Hellenes, that is, true bearers of Greek civilization.

Politically and militarily, however, the Macedonians were masters of their world. In the 350s and 340s BC, under Alexander's father, King Philip, Macedonia became a kind of Prussian state, geared to war. At the core of its standing army was a new and highly disciplined fighting machine, the infantry phalanx. Inevitably, Philip turned his New Model Army on to the older city states of the south which had banded together in the face of the threat from the northern upstarts. In 338 BC, at a bloody battle at Chaeronea, the

Macedonian phalanx overwhelmed the hoplites of the southern Greek states. In this battle the teenage Alexander won acclaim for his courage and tenacity, and for his tactical acumen. Democracy was effectively abolished; the Macedonian monarchy now ruled Greece. The following year, Philip was assassinated in the theatre at Aegeae, and his young son Alexander became king. The stage was set.

## ALEXANDER'S BIRTH AND PARENTAGE

*Intimations of greatness: 'Through my father Philip I was born of the line of the deified Heracles, grandson of Zeus, and born of the line of Achilles through my mother Olympias …'*

CHIGI RELIEF, ROME

Left: Gold medallion with the head of Alexander's father, Philip,
whom Alexander claimed bore him 'ill will and jealousy'.
Right: Onyx cameo portrait of Alexander with his mother Olympias,
c. 278 BC. It was widely believed that the couple were implicated
in Philip's murder.

Alexander was born in 356 BC, possibly on 20 July, which would make him a Cancerian for those who see significance in horoscopes. His father was Philip, King of Macedon, who had single-handedly created the Macedonian kingdom out of disparate tribes and principalities. Alexander's mother, Olympias, was a young princess from Epirus, the mountainous region bordering Albania. Philip had allegedly fallen in love with her when he saw her, aged about fourteen, at the celebrations of the mystery cult on the island of Samothrace. Later writers portray Olympias as eccentric and intense, devoted to strange mountain cults, and snake-handling, a devotee of Dionysus, the god of ecstasy and possession.

Alexander clearly owed some of his characteristic traits to both his parents. Like his father, he was a ruthless and practical politician. But he also exhibited a strong penchant for oracles, cults and omens which we might guess he inherited from his mother, along with her volatile and emotional temperament.

The relationship between his father and mother was never easy. It was said that Philip shunned Olympias after he saw her one night in bed with a snake – a tale which gave rise to legends that she had been impregnated by a god, and that Alexander was not the son of a mortal father. Later it was not in the interests of mother or son to deny such tales. Olympias developed an intense and perhaps obsessive relationship with her son. As was the custom among Macedonian royalty, Philip practised polygamy, and when Olympias was in her mid-thirties, he abandoned her for a younger wife. The young Alexander sided with his mother and went home to Epirus with her for a while; when he returned he had to endure taunts about his father's second marriage and a new heir. (Later, Olympias and Alexander had their revenge; the child and its mother were mercilessly put to death by Olympias when Alexander attained power. Such savagery within the royal house needs to be borne in mind when we see the ruthlessness with which Alexander would liquidate erstwhile friends who crossed him; evidently he had learned the hard way in adolescence.)

## ALEXANDER'S EARLY YEARS

For all the veneer of Hellenic culture, then, Alexander was brought up in a semi-barbaric world, in a hard-drinking hard-living court, torn by ferocious feuds. As we would expect with such a person, many stories are told of the young Alexander which anticipate his later fame. One tells of a visit to Pella by Persian ambassadors who found themselves being questioned in detail by the boy prodigy about roads and distances in their own country; it is said they left deeply impressed. The famous tale of Alexander's taming of the horse Bucephalus is in the same vein. The horse had been brought to Philip by a Thessalian breeder and was named after his distinctive brand mark: 'Ox-head'. It was a fine animal, and a fine price, too, but no one could master it. To everyone's amusement Alexander bet his father that he could, and facing the horse into the sun (so it would not be disturbed by its own shadow), he walked it round, calmed it down, then jumped on and rode off. King Philip laughed 'Get yourself another kingdom, my boy, for Macedonia is not big enough to hold you!'

When Alexander was thirteen or fourteen, his father sent him to study in the 'Gardens of Midas' at Mieza, under the greatest philosopher of that, or any other, day, Aristotle of Stagira. It is an extraordinary fact that two of the most significant figures in world histoy should have come together in this way, and if Alexander is politically the father of the Hellenistic Age, Aristotle can be seen as its spiritual or philosophical founder. Aristotle inspired in Alexander a life-long devotion to philosophy, and we would dearly love to know more about this relationship. Alexander is said to have looked up to Aristotle 'like a father'. Many of their letters to each other survive, some of which may be genuine. Others are even now being discovered in Muslim libraries in India. Aristotle is said to have given Alexander his precious copy of the *Iliad*, the story of the Trojan War, and this was the book which Alexander carried with him to India. Seldom can any teacher have had the opportunity to see his theories put into practice on such a stage; and seldom can a teacher have ended up fearing his pupil's potential so much. Aristotle's nephew, Callisthenes, would accompany Alexander's expedition as historian, but, as we shall see, he fell out with the king in the most dramatic circumstances, and in the end this led to the breakdown of Alexander's friendship with Aristotle.

## ALEXANDER'S SEX LIFE

Alexander's sexual orientation is still the subject of great speculation, with the King portrayed across the spectrum from family man to gay icon. His key relationship with a woman was evidently with his mother. He was apparently twenty-three before he had a sexual relationship with a woman, and, although he developed warm relationships with some older women (whom one might hesitantly call mother-figures, for example Queen Ada of Caria, and the Persian Queen Mother Sisygambis), his attitude to younger women is impossible to determine. If the Greek historians are to be believed he ostentatiously avoided contact with Darius's captive wife Stateira, who was said to be the most beautiful woman in Asia, calling her beauty 'torture to my eyes'. But this sounds rather strange for a

Above: The philosopher Aristotle whom Alexander 'treated like a father' until their falling out. Roman copy of a Greek bronze.

Left: Among Greeks, the Macedonians had the reputation of being violent, boorish and great drinkers. Detail of a Greek vase, fourth century BC.

man of his time. He is known to have fathered one child by his mistress Barsine, and two by his wife Roxanne, but his deepest emotional ties were apparently with men. So, when Alexander spoke of sex as one of the things which 'reminded him of his mortality', it is unclear whether he meant sex with men or women – or both. Such conundrums, however, may have seemed irrelevant to his contemporaries, who, unlike us moderns, were not concerned with making heterosexual relationships the norm.

His most intimate friendships were certainly with men. He lived in a thoroughly male society, and his friends were drawn from the upper crust, many of whom were his companions on the expedition to Asia. His closest relationship in the tight-knit circle of young companions was with Hephaistion whom he may have known from childhood. Later stories portray Hephaistion as Alexander's alter ego, sharer of his heroic dreams, 'another Alexander' who, pointedly, loved the king 'for himself'. On a funerary monument created soon after the king's death, the pair are portrayed almost like divine twins, smooth-faced androgynes in association with the goddess of fortune, Tyche. Real evidence for their friendship, though, is surprisingly scanty in our sources. Perhaps the key clue remains the king's extreme grief at Hephaistion's death – grief which speaks of a most powerful, even obsessive affection. Their youthful occupations were those of any military aristocracy: riding, games, gymnastics, and hunting (at one point, during rest and recreation at Samarkand, a game reserve of several thousand animals was wiped out in a day's hunt). Another all-male occupation was drinking. The Macedonians were famed throughout Greece for their prodigious consumption of wine which shocked visitors to their court. Alexander was better able to handle these heavy drinking sessions at twenty-two with the world at his feet, than at thirty-two when fate was closing in.

## WHAT KIND OF MAN WAS ALEXANDER?

His looks have been reproduced in a thousand images. These usually portray wavy leonine hair and quiff (*anastole*), tilted head and uplifted faraway eyes. It is the conventional ancient portrait of the ideal man – a dreamer with a lion's spirit. But whether he really looked like that is uncertain. Such images were first and foremost created to convey a political and cultural message, just as official portraits are today. But we have TV and photographs, so we all know what the President of the USA looks like. In Alexander's time, when so few people would have seen him in the flesh, the picture created by his artists for propaganda need only have had a very general resemblance to his real face. What counted above all was the idea. We know he was short (his father, Philip, was only about 5ft 2in), stocky, and that he had a reddish complexion which flushed when he was angry. In the only early representation we have of him in colour, the Issus mosaic now in Naples museum, his hair is shown as brown and unkempt. The same picture gives him a big chin, bulbous eyes and a prominent straight nose (like his father). This may be the nearest we can hope to get to his true looks, but ultimately they continue to elude us because, while all the Alexander images have the same general feeling, they are not much alike in detail. It remains a paradox, then, that, although Alexander was one of the most famous people who ever lived, we don't really know what he looked like.

What is clear though is that Alexander grew up as an exceptionally tough young man with great stamina and mental resource; capable of rapid and ruthless action, adept at seizing the moment – one of the keys to his generalship. As to his psychological make-up, there was – and is – the widest divergence of opinion. He is portrayed as one of the noblest souls who ever lived, and as a murderous conquistador who waded through blood to rape Asia.

Many tales are told to illustrate his nature; some perhaps true. Plutarch, who had access to early histories, puts it well. At times, he says, 'his society was delightful and his manner full of charm beyond that of any prince of his age', but at others (especially when drunk) 'he would sometimes become offensively arrogant and descend to the level of the common soldier, not only allowing himself to give way to boasting but also to be led on by his flatterers'.

Alexander was, evidently, a man of extremes and contradictions. His story is full of chivalrous gestures, especially towards women, such as those of Darius's family. And yet he exhibited an almost sadistic malevolence towards those who crossed him. He was capable of intense spurts of energy, then long sulks; of ferocious self-denial, and then prodigious self-indulgence; of extreme generosity and murderous cruelty against former friends. At heart, if we guess it right, there was perhaps a deep insecurity in him which must have originated in his childhood, and especially in his relationship with his father. This insecurity was not assuaged by becoming the most powerful man in the world, indeed it was only exacerbated. In one sense his is a parable of the loneliness of power. But that is to anticipate the story …

---

Overleaf: Princely pursuits – the contemporary Lion Hunt mosaic
from the palace at Pella. The young prince on the left may be
Alexander; on the right is perhaps Hephaistion, the king's favourite.
Theirs was a society where men learned early how to kill.

## ALEXANDER BECOMES KING

When Philip was assassinated in the theatre in Aegeae in June 336, the integrity of the kingdom he had created was instantly thrown into doubt. There were whispers that Alexander and his mother were implicated in Philip's murder, which, although it has never been proved, is not impossible. At any rate, Alexander, at the age of twenty, became ruler of a kingdom which, at that moment, was beset by formidable tensions and jealousies, 'with external dangers on every side'. To the north, Balkan tribes rose up in rebellion, and Alexander drove up as far as the Danube to overcome them in a lightning campaign. Then, in what was to prove a most horrific event, Thebes in central Greece, revolted against the Macedonians. Although one of most famous and ancient Greek cities, Thebes was sacked and its population massacred or enslaved (though, in one of those characteristic gestures which mark his career, Alexander spared the descendants of the great Theban poet Pindar). The Athenians made peace.

At twenty-one years old, Alexander was the unopposed leader of the Greek world, or the 'tyrant of Greece' as his enemies said – a jibe which angered him more than any other.

## CRUSADE AGAINST PERSIA

He then turned his attention to Persia. The previous year a congress of Greek city states, held at Corinth, had passed a vote that they would join forces with Alexander in an invasion of Persia, and that he would be the Commander in Chief. Alexander already had an expeditionary force in Asia Minor, across the Dardanelles, under his father's right-hand man Parmenio, an experienced general in his mid-sixties. Now Alexander would follow with the main army supported by a fleet raised from his Greek allies.

First he visited Delphi to consult the oracle over the expedition. Consultation of oracles was something Alexander did obsessively in the early part of his career. In that he was very much a man of his time. He went on an inauspicious day when the prophetess did not deliver replies. When she refused to officiate he sought her out and tried to drag her to the shrine. Impressed by his persistence, she said 'You are invincible, my son'. That was all he wanted to hear. The crusade was on.

The army assembled at Amphipolis in North Greece: 32,000 men, with another 12,000 in the advance guard which had already crossed the previous year. It was one of the toughest and most professional armies in the ancient world – by the end literally invincible.

Its mobile élite was Alexander's Companion Cavalry, drawn from the cream of the Macedonian aristocracy; its backbone was the phalanx, six highly-drilled infantry brigades, capable of fighting different kinds of warfare, but specializing in set-piece battle in an eight-deep hedgehog formation with 5½-metre-long spears. There were also specialist units: skirmishers, archers, light infantry with mountain training (the thousand Agrianians – often described as the Gurkhas of antiquity – used in many of his most daring enterprises). There were also units from non-Macedonian Greeks (rather as in Operation Desert Storm the United States roped in forces from many Muslim countries so it would not appear a purely Western operation). The best of these units were the high-quality cavalry squadrons from Thessaly. For Alexander, the presence of troops from southern Greece helped to justify his claim to be the 'General in Chief of the army of the Hellenes'.

Many other specialists formed the back-up units. The army, for example, carried a siege train (under Alexander, sophisticated siege technology was developed for the first time in history with mobile siege towers, stone-throwing catapults and javelin throwers). There were engineers, bridge-builders, sappers, surveyors, along with a supply corps. Medicine, too, was an important consideration for the High Command: we have accounts of tonnes of medical supplies being sent out to the expedition in India, and the names of several of Alexander's doctors have come down to us. In addition, a large number of non-combatants accompanied the force, whose presence must sometimes reflect the king's own interests: scientists, botanists, astronomers, philosophers, seers, and the official historian or propagandist Callisthenes who self-importantly announced that he was joining the expedition 'to make the king's name' for posterity.

In spring 334 they marched for the Dardanelles, which the Greeks called the Hellespont, the great divide between Europe and Asia. The world would never be the same again.

# PART ONE

# The INVASION of ASIA

## GREECE AND TURKEY

### 334 – 333 BC

*Alexander crosses the Dardanelles into Asia and sacrifices to the heroes of ancient Troy; first blood: the battle at the Granicus river; Alexander at Ephesus; the strange tale of the oracle at Didyma; the siege of Halicarnassos; the march along the Lycian shore; the legend of the Gordian Knot; Darius the King of Persia enters the war; the battle of Issus*

I T WAS A MAY MORNING. Although our sources do not say so, strong winds would have been gusting as usual down the Dardanelles and on to the Trojan shore. In the middle of the straits a flotilla of ships was cutting across from Gallipoli, buffeted by the powerful steel-blue current of the Hellespont. On the flagship a bound bull, decked in flowers, struggled as its throat was cut; seers poured a libation from a golden bowl which they then threw into the sea. In the bow of the flagship stood a young man in full parade armour, with greaves and shield, on his breastplate the image of a gorgon's head whose gaze was said to turn onlookers to stone. As the prow ground into the sandy beach, he was the first to leap shore. Wading through the waves he hurled his spear into the beach and, in a harsh high-pitched voice, claimed Asia his by right, 'spear won'. The avenger had come.

Above the shore at Besika Bay was a conical tumulus which tradition said was the grave of Achilles, the hero of the Trojan War. Here Alexander and his friend Hephaistion stripped naked, cutting off locks of hair, and ran round the tomb. Their vistas were long, not just the 150 years back to the Great Persian war, but far beyond that to mythical times, when the Greeks had invaded Asia for the first time to avenge the seizure of Helen by sacking Troy.

Later they rode up to the city, a small walled town on a steep hill over a windswept plain. On the tiny acropolis they entered the archaic temple of the goddess Athena. There in the light of oil-lamps they were shown pitch-covered weapons hung on the wall, which their guides told them had belonged to Achilles and been dedicated by the Greeks after the city was sacked, its menfolk killed, and its women and children enslaved. (These were the grim conventions of heroic warfare which Alexander would apply across Asia.) The king took the shield down, replacing it with his own; he would carry it all the way to India where, years later, it would save his life in the sweltering plains of the Punjab. At the same time, perhaps, he made a promise (which only comes to light after his death) that, if successful, he would return to little Ilion and build a gigantic temple to Trojan Athene, the biggest in the world, in gratitude for her help.

Alexander's visit to Troy was not just a propaganda stunt, the ancient equivalent of a press call; nor was it merely a youthful lark, or even a religious pilgrimage. To Alexander and his contemporaries, this was a holy place soaked in the blood of heroes, and inhabited by their ghosts. Now the spirits of the ancients had been co-opted for the war against Asia.

---

Previous pages, left: The shield of Achilles, the ultimate hero, on a Greek vase. Alexander carried the shield to India where it saved his life.
Right: Young Alexander: tilted head, upward glance, melting eyes, leonine hair. This second-century BC fantasy image is everyone's Alexander. What he really looked like we cannot be sure.

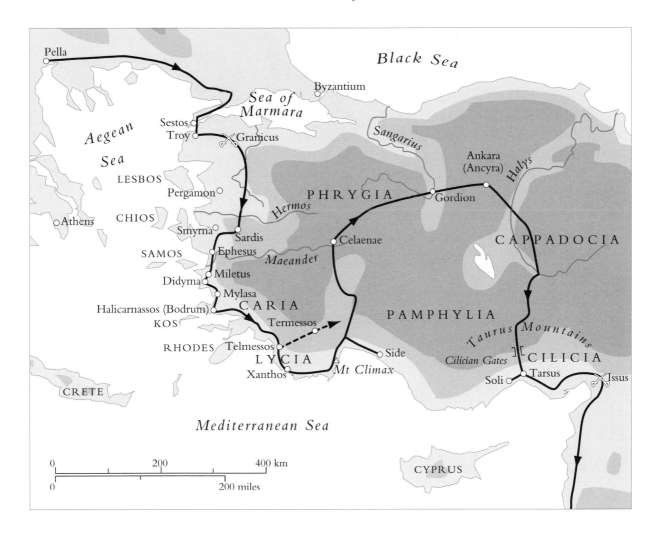

The army crossed at the narrows from Sestos to Abydos with 160 ships, covered by Parmenio's advance guard. Alexander swiftly rejoined his troops and the Macedonians set off into the plain which runs along the Sea of Marmara. The Persians had failed to stop the disembarkation; how would they respond now? They had known, of course, what was coming. They had many spies, allies and friendly sources in Greece, where smouldering resentment against the Macedonians was so rife that many were willing to co-operate with Darius to see the young upstart put in his place. Darius had stationed a strong army near the Dardanelles. Its backbone was several thousand Greek mercenaries who had no reason to love the Macedonians. There was also a big Persian fleet operating off the Aegean coast. Their empire was so huge, its resources and gold reserves so great, that it could afford to raise army after army against Alexander and even to foment risings behind him. But at

this moment, perhaps, before the first clash of arms, the situation did not appear to Darius as serious as it would later. As the Athenians jibed, Alexander was 'just a boy, a *margites*, a mad-hatter'.

The Persian high command held an urgent war council at Zeleia, now the little country town of Sarikoy just off the main Bursa-Cannakkale road south of the Sea of Marmara. The Persian field commander in the west was the local governor, the satrap of Phrygia, but the leader of his Greek mercenaries was Memnon of Rhodes, one of the most difficult opponents Alexander ever faced. Married to a Persian royal lady, Memnon came from an influential military family and had probably met Alexander in Macedonia. He understood the young king's impetuous and somewhat manic disposition and argued that it was better to frustrate him rather than play into his hands by doing what he wished. In any case, the Persian front-line troops were not strong enough to beat the Macedonian phalanx. So, best not fight him in a pitched battle. As Memnon saw it, scorched earth was the best tactic; denying Alexander supplies by devastating the countryside. The Persian leaders, however, balked at the thought of burning their own fields, and, against Memnon's advice, they decided to fight. This was the fatal error on which the whole campaign hinged. With hindsight, Memnon's plan might have saved them and their master.

## FIRST BLOOD

In the early summer dusk there was a slight dust haze over the river plain, and the rolling fields of sunflower and corn. We found the mullah in his shirtsleeves in the tea shop at the little hamlet of Cinar Kipru, 'plane tree bridge'. Before evening prayers he led us up the narrow steps of his minaret to show us the lie of the land. 'There is the river Koçabas Çay which the ancients called the Granicus,' he said, 'the Greeks came from this side, the Persians were drawn up across the river. The battle was fought right there in front of you.'

From the minaret we could see the river fringed with trees meandering away to the Biga hills. Beyond were yellow fields and then the low ridge on which the Greek mercenaries had lined up. Known to the ancients as the Gates of Asia, this was one of those crossing points which have been used by travellers and armies throughout history. Just here the ancient Roman and Greek road along the Sea of Marmara joins the route which cuts

---

Natural born killer: Alexander at the Granicus, aged twenty-two.
The Alexander Sarcophagus from Sidon, now in Istanbul (c. 310-300 BC).

south to Sardis. Close by, an intact Roman bridge marks the old crossing. The river could be quite an obstacle; today it is about 25 metres wide with steep banks, broken in places by shallow slopes down to beds of fine white and grey gravel. In the winter it fills right up, often 6 metres or more deep, but it is usually shallower in spring, and by May it is easily fordable. This was the scene of Alexander's first battle in Asia.

At dusk on that May day, Alexander approached the river in battle formation. Ahead, on the other side, the Persians had lined the banks with cavalry, about 10,000 strong, among them élite squadrons from as far away as Bactria, northern Afghanistan. They also had some 4000 Greek mercenaries and other infantry levies which they placed on the low rise a kilometre or two back from the river, clearly not expecting them to be involved. The Persian plan was simply to hold Alexander off, prevent him getting across, and though it was a strange way to use cavalry, evidently they were confident they could do it.

In the Macedonian ranks Alexander's senior general Parmenio counselled that they should postpone the battle. It was too late now, almost sunset. Alexander, though, would have none of it. They had given him the initiative, and it was not in his character to decline the challenge; he decided to strike now. The later Greek historian Arrian preserves a powerful and moving image of that moment. The first blow, he says, was preceded by a deep silence, 'as if both sides were reluctant to start the whole thing' – not just the fight in that place, perhaps, but the whole great war which would be carried as far as India and involve numberless deaths and the fall of empires.

The silence was broken by blaring trumpets and a tremendous roar, the Macedonians calling on their war god. Then it all happened very fast. Alexander launched a feint attack with 1000 cavalry and 500 light infantry to draw them down into the river bed, making them think the main attack had begun. The Persians were nervous and immediately fell for it; the Persian left-wing surged forward loosing all their javelins and crashed in on the advance guard. A great melee developed on the bank and in the stream bed. Once the Persians had committed themselves, Alexander then led his élite cavalry squadrons down into the river, pushing them obliquely out to the right 'against the current of the stream' so as to outflank the Persian line and fall on them from the side. Against all expectation, Alexander had forced his way across in the face of his enemies.

Now, in a last-ditch attempt to kill Alexander himself, several of the leading Persian officers closed in on the king. One got close enough to hit him on the helmet, but, in a desperate struggle, Alexander was saved by the quick thinking of one of his cavalry officers, Black Cleitus, whose sister had been the king's childhood nurse. Eight of the Persian commanders were cut down in the scrimmage, including Darius's son-in-law. It was all over in a few minutes.

The Greek mercenaries, meanwhile, who were among the Persians' best troops, were in for a nasty shock. Standing back on the ridge in dusk-light they had watched the melee at the river, all dust and confusion. Then suddenly they saw Persian cavalry retreat and Alexander and his companion cavalry emerge from the river bed and head straight towards them. Arrian says the mercenaries were 'simply astonished at the course the action had taken'. In the grip of battle-rage, Alexander launched a fierce attack in which he lost several companions and had a horse killed under him. The phalanx was then brought up and a bitter infantry battle went on into darkness, by which time half of the mercenaries had been massacred. Alexander, though, refused anything but unconditional surrender. With the moon rising, the surviving mercenaries finally laid down their arms and were sent in chains to hard labour for life in the silver mines of Thrace, where some of their manacled skeletons have been found by modern archaeologists. It was a grim message to any Greeks thinking of taking the Persian king's shilling.

The victory opened up the Ionian coast.

For us, it was easy to follow Alexander's route in the early stage of our journey. Some cities in western Turkey surrendered and welcomed him, chief among them Sardis – the main centre of the Persians' western empire – on its tremendous acropolis towering above the valley under Mount Tmolus at the end of the Royal Road from Susa in Iran. Then he cut down the valley of the Hermos river to the coast at Ephesus, whose gigantic temple to the goddess Artemis he promised to rebuild.

Some Greek city states did not find the prospect of Macedonian rule congenial, and were prepared to resist, relying on support from the Persian fleet. Miletus was one, the self-styled 'metropolis of Asia', whose immense ruins lie along a silted promontory, where the great theatre looks over the grass-grown Lion Harbour. When resistance collapsed, Alexander treated the city leniently, as he could afford to at this stage. Meanwhile, the Persian fleet watched him warily from afar, making the occasional foray, black ships hugging the horizon.

South of Miletus you can still pick up Alexander's trail on the ground. We know that on his way south he made a detour to visit the famous oracle shrine at Didyma, and modern archaeologists have now uncovered the Sacred Way which joined the two places. He must have come this way. It is a very atmospheric walk of 20 kilometres, up into hills covered with thorn and asphodel and drenched in the smell of sage. You pass the remains of several ancient wayside shrines, and a couple of ruined Greek chapels before coming down to the sea at the ancient harbour of Panormos, now hideously disfigured by holiday developments. Turning inland again, you walk along a final stretch of the Sacred Way still paved with white marble, until you catch sight of the three giant surviving columns of the

Right: The huge temple to Apollo at Didyma. Alexander came
here in autumn 334 BC to visit the oracle whose sacred spring,
long dried up, promptly burst into life. Like some modern presidents,
Alexander was exceptionally skilled at making things happen to suit
him. The oracle prophesied that he would become Lord of Asia.

Above: The Gorgon's head at Didyma. Alexander wore this image
on his breast to turn enemies into stone. It worked.

temple of Didyma, among the most spectacular remains surviving from the classical Greek world.

Didyma played a strange and significant part in Alexander's story. In 494, when the Ionian Greeks had risen in revolt against the Persians, Miletus had been sacked and its temple at Didyma desecrated and looted, the cult statue of Apollo carried off to Susa. At that time, its priestly clan, the Branchidae, had collaborated with the Persians and were subsequently resettled in Central Asia. Then the oracle had fallen silent and, according to Alexander's propagandist Callisthenes, the sacred spring which was the source of the oracle prophecies had dried up. However, when Alexander came to Didyma the spring miraculously flowed once again. At least, that was the story circulated by Callisthenes. The oracle was reconstituted with a new priestess who soon spoke for her new patron, foretelling his victory in Asia and Darius's death. As for the original priesthood, a terrible fate awaited their descendants much later in the tale, when, by an astonishing coincidence, Alexander met them on the road to Central Asia and exacted revenge for the ancient sacrilege (see page 152).

Alexander now took the extraordinary and still controversial decision to disband his fleet. Like Cortés burning his boats on the shores of the Yucatán, he would win the war on land. Only enough transports were kept to take the siege-engines by sea from Miletus to the Halicarnassos (Bodrum) peninsula.

We now followed him by sea, too, on a local gulet (sailboat) out from Panormos. We soon left behind us the great rounded hump of Samos and the double peaks of Mykale where the Persians had their fleet base. All afternoon we passed along a jagged empty coast, with the dark shape of Kalymnos ahead. We coasted the promontory of Iasos, where a strange legend told of a boy who had befriended a dolphin and who was adopted by Alexander. Tacking past Wreck Rock at dusk, we entered the narrow mouth of Myndus (a city which closed its harbour to Alexander), and anchored in a still lagoon as the sun set over the sea between Kalymnos and the peninsula of Miletus.

We weighed anchor at dawn and passed Kos off our starboard beam, sailing into the still waters of the Ceramic Gulf to make our first sighting of the great castle of the Knights of St John at Bodrum, at the entrance to the ancient harbour of Halicarnassos from where, as the ancients said, the town still rises into the hills like a Greek theatre. This was the scene of Alexander's first siege.

He had pushed on south with the army on the old road to Mylasa (now Milas), the former capital of Caria. There, the deposed queen, Ada, offered him her help (her tomb, recently found at Bodrum, revealed a gold-wreathed skeleton of a woman in her late forties with a strong characterful face). She adopted Alexander as her son, and sent him gifts and sweets. More important, she ensured supplies for his army on the barren and waterless promontory of Bodrum. Then he began in earnest his siege of Halicarnassos, the Persians' main base in south-western Anatolia. Their HQ was in the Carian palace (where the castle of the Knights of St John stands today) which looked out over the town and the Mausoleum – the immense tomb of King Mausolus which was one of the Seven Wonders of the World.

Here, Memnon had concentrated his forces; now Darius's commander-in-chief Western operations, he was, as the Macedonians admitted, a man of 'great courage and deep understanding of strategy'. Memnon had sent his Persian wife Barsine with their children to Darius for safekeeping. With him were the Athenian mercenary commanders Ephialtes and Thrasybulos, two men who had been on Alexander's wanted list since the Theban revolt. There was no love lost between them and Alexander and they had massively bolstered their defences in preparation for his attack. The town was strongly fortified with a huge wall, which still survives in places, winding up into the rocky hills above Bodrum. It had two or three main gates and in the low ground was protected by deep ditches; in addition there were forts on the promontories above the harbour; out in the bay was a fleet of 400 ships. It was a tough nut to crack. Here at Bodrum, Alexander's siege-technology was tested for the first time and his assault was remembered as 'ferocious and energetic'.

Alexander chose to attack on the flat ground on the east side of the town. There his sappers soon filled up the ditch and demolished a stretch of wall, but, in the meantime, the defenders had built a new curved wall, a demi-lune, behind the breach and the Macedonians could progress no further. The siege settled into a period of night attacks and tit-for-tat raids. Then Memnon took the initiative and a massive dawn commando raid was launched in an effort to burn Alexander's siege-towers. It almost worked, and for a moment the Macedonians were rocked back on their heels. But Alexander's reserve, veterans of his father's campaigns, eventually threw them back inflicting heavy losses, and Ephialtes was killed.

Memnon had now had enough. He had judged his man right, though, playing him as long as he could. Finally, when things had got too hot and casualties too great, he decided to pull out. In the middle of the night, leaving garrisons in the forts, he evacuated his forces by sea to Kos, setting fire to his arsenals and those military supplies he could not take with him. At dawn the next day, from his HQ up on the heights towards Milas, Alexander would have seen a pall of smoke hanging over the bay and the town, in the middle of which the immense tomb of Mausolus stood intact, its gilded finials catching the early light. Memnon had gone.

Bodrum citadel, the castle of the Knights of St John, built on
the site of the Carian palace which was the Persian HQ during
Alexander's siege.

Alexander had won, but not conclusively. He had suffered losses, and would have to
leave troops behind to reduce the remaining forts. Memnon had been able to withdraw
his forces with hundreds of ships. It was, perhaps, slightly ominous: if Memnon continued
to resist him in this cunning fashion, Alexander might never get out of Anatolia, let alone
engage the Great King Darius himself. And what if Memnon decided to try to take the
war by sea to Macedonia and Greece? That didn't bear thinking about.

## THE LYCIAN SHORE

That winter Alexander stuck with his plan and marched along the south-west coast of Turkey through the beautiful scenery of Lycia with its high forested citadels whose magical remains still dot the landscape: Xanthos, Tlos and Termessos. At this point, he allowed the army's newly-weds, including his general Coenus, to go home for the winter to their wives: 'nothing gained him more popularity than that', says Arrian. The army must have split up here: with the main force perhaps cutting inland on the old caravan road from Kaş past Termessos. Following that route, we had a memorable meeting one morning with villagers at a little place called Susuz, 'No water', in a wide dusty yellow plain between barren hills; 'There is the path taken by Buyuk Iskandar,' they said, pointing to a distant column of hundreds of goats being moved to higher pasture, 'As our elders told us, that is the Old Baghdad Road!'

Alexander himself pushed along the coast with a smaller force to Mount Climax, which rears dramatically 3000 metres above the seashore. Here he split again: the choice was a very rough path over the mountains or a march right along the beach. Some went over the mountain on a route hacked out by Thracian pioneers; Alexander took the short cut along the seashore. But this was wintertime and he set out while the weather was stormy and the sea still high. For much of the day the troops had a wet, cold and uncomfortable march. His path must have led right below Climax, along Beldibi beach where today, to walk in his footsteps, you must negotiate serried ranks of lilos, parked windsurfers and all the beach paraphernalia needed by well-heeled European tourists.

I tramped through with rucksack and hiking boots, splashing round headlands, sometimes chest-deep in water, and trekking under broken orange cliffs with old dwarf pines bent by the winds like trees in a Japanese miniature. Beyond, up hazy valleys I could just make out the course of the ancient path over Climax, where the serrated edges of its ridges disappeared into cloud. Alexander and his men fared no better. They marched chest-deep most of the day, says the geographer Strabo. But, finally, the wind slackened and shifted offshore and they were able to dry off, enabling Callisthenes to turn bad planning into a propaganda coup: 'the sea bowed to Alexander' he announced. The story was greeted with jeers and guffaws in Athens, where all were hoping to hear that the young 'mad-hatter' had come unstuck.

## THE GORDIAN KNOT

In early spring, after taking the surrender of over thirty cities in Lycia, Alexander moved up on to the Anatolian plateau, to make the long loop to Ankara. The first part of the route has to be followed on foot; you only have to go a few kilometres from the holiday beaches of Antalya to pick up the old road heading towards the mountains which fringe the Mediterranean. Ruined caravanserais mark the beginning of the path out of the plain and up to the bottom of Dosheme gorge. Then it's a steep climb of 5 kilometres where much of the paved road is intact, with the Roman and Byzantine surfaces running in parallel. At the top are the remains of a way-station and customs post, with a gate and walls and a Hellenistic tower, a cistern and a ruined Byzantine church. From the crest, the road winds down into a deserted valley sparkling green with mimosa, myrtle and olives. At sunset the valley shone with a velvet sheen, crossed by the whitened cobbles of the road, still neatly edged. Beyond the hills the ancient road passes through wide wheatfields rimmed by distant mountains; then on into the bleak uplands of Anatolia.

After about three weeks' march they reached the ancient city of Gordion. This famous place stood on a mound circled by the Sangarius river, its deep-cut bed fringed by reeds, mallow, wild olives and willow. All around are dusty rolling plains, burned yellow in summer, which are dotted with tumuli, the greatest of which covers the tomb of Midas, the oldest wooden structure in the world. The citadel in Alexander's day was about 700 metres across and you approached it on a ramp which went up a steep glacis of stepped stones 10 metres high. At the top a huge gate flanked square towers which led to an inner-courtyard where three strange megarons, or halls, stood whose function is still unknown. The temple of Zeus, mentioned by the Greeks, was never identified by the archaeologists – the site of the strange myth of the Gordian Knot.

Alexander came here for strategic reasons – Gordion was the key-road junction in central Anatolia – but also for a weird legend which he must have been known from his boyhood in the Garden of Midas. Gordion was the city of Midas whose father Gordius was believed to have migrated from Macedonia centuries before in a wooden cart. His arrival fulfilled a local prophecy, and Gordius became king of the place, which was henceforth known as Gordion. As a thanks offering he left the cart within the enclosure of the temple of Zeus, King of the Gods. It was an 'old inexpensive' farm cart, which must have looked very much like the wooden-wheeled farm carts which one may still see in the Anatolian countryside, where the yoke is held to the shaft by a leather knot and fixed by a wooden pin. But Gordius's cart had a knot of extraordinary complexity, made of cornel bark, whose ends were invisible (the kind we call a Turk's Head). A local legend said that whoever undid the knot would become ruler of all Asia.

Alexander went up to the acropolis. Perhaps the whole thing was set up, rather as politicians today will have a photo-opportunity stage-managed for them by their handlers. Perhaps, though, this was slightly less controlled. There are hints that the king's entourage were nervous. Alexander clearly had to have a go, or be accused of ducking the issue. But what if he failed?

'He stood silent in thought for a while but he couldn't work out how to undo it.' What happened next we'll never know for sure. Even Arrian was hesitant: 'I can speak with no confidence on this'. According to the earliest source, he pulled out the pin which goes through the knot holding yoke to shaft. Others, though, more romantically perhaps, say Alexander suddenly muttered 'It doesn't matter how the knot is loosened' and, drawing his sword, hacked the knot open to reveal the ends inside (hence today we still speak

of 'cutting the Gordian Knot'). Whatever happened, Arrian says they left the acropolis believing the oracle had been fulfilled, and that night a storm with thunder and lightning burst over Gordion. Zeus had approved.

Back at the archaeologists' dig-hut in Gordion a tremendous wind came up after sunset, suddenly lifting eddies of dust off the tracks and fields and shaking the trees by the village mosque. As we made to leave, big drops of rain spattered the yard and a faint dark whirlwind hung like a shadow over Midas's tomb. It felt as if the spirit of Aristander, Alexander's interpreter of omens and signs, was by our side.

## THE KING OF KINGS

We pushed on in Alexander's footsteps by bus to Ankara, then south towards Tarsus. In the Aegean, events had developed as Alexander might have feared. After Alexander's fleet had disbanded, Memnon put his own into action, 300 ships with experienced crews from Cyprus and the Levant, and moved up through islands on the Anatolian seaboard reducing Alexander's allies. Chios and Lesbos, good bases for operations in the northern Aegean, were taken. But then suddenly Memnon fell ill and died. It was one of the biggest strokes of luck in Alexander's entire career, and it changed the face of the whole war.

In Babylon, 1000 kilometres to the east, the Persian King Darius was dismayed by the news of Memnon's death and hastily searched for a successor for his commander in the west. The historian Curtius tells the story of bitter argument in the royal council in Babylon where an Athenian mercenary commander Charidemos reiterated Memnon's plans, recommending Darius not to take the field himself. Bluntly, he told the king, the Persian forces were not up to it: 'Sir, the only way to beat the phalanx is by putting Greek troops against it: use your gold to buy the right kind of men. An army of a hundred thousand should do it, providing one third is Greek mercenaries'. But so disparaging were his remarks about the Persian forces, and the king's judgement, that a violent argument ensued; bitter insults were traded, and Darius had Charidemos executed, a decision he would regret. Lacking any other experienced general, Darius had no alternative now but to make himself the leader in the field.

---

The Sacred Way, south of Miletus, western Turkey. Alexander came
this way in autumn 334 BC on his way to Didyma, a visit which
strikes us today as a mixture of pilgrimage and press call. As so often
with Alexander, the truth probably lies half way between the two.

Darius has had a bad press. Defeated on the battlefield, he has suffered a second defeat, character assassination by later historians. The victors ensured that he was condemned after his death: 'as soft and unsound of mind in war as anybody ever was', is Arrian's uncompromising verdict. Seeing Darius's world from the inside has proved very difficult in modern times, not least because what we call the historical tradition on Persia is actually, in the main, the creation of her enemies. Finding the real Darius behind the dense smoke-screen of propaganda has so far proved an impossible task. So who was Alexander's great adversary?

He was in his mid-forties when Alexander invaded Asia. His name was Artashata – Darius III was his throne name (Daryavaush, meaning 'he who holds firm the good') assumed when came to the throne in 336 BC. He was a great-grandson of Darius II, but was only a distant member of the royal clan. In his twenties he had married his full sister, Stateira, reputedly the most beautiful woman in Asia, and was apparently devoted to her. They had three children, two teenage daughters and a young son.

Although Darius was condemned by the Greeks as an effeminate coward, incompetent on the battlefield, there are odd hints (even in the Greek sources) that that was not the whole story. Said by Plutarch to have been *andron kallistos kai megistos* (most handsome and tallest man in Asia), Curtius too talks of Darius's justice and clemency and his mild and placid disposition. Diodorus Siculus drew on a Persian source for his story that Darius was known in his younger days as an extremely brave man, 'bravest by far of the Persians'. Darius had once fought valiantly in single combat for his predecessor Artaxerxes when the champion of an opposing army had challenged any Persian to fight him – 'none dared accept but Darius alone, after which he was conceded first among them for bravery'. One of his first acts after becoming king was to retake Egypt which had revolted during the interregnum following his predecessor's death. The king who faced Alexander, then, was mature, personally brave and probably militarily resourceful.

But once he became 'Great King', Darius entered another sphere, circumscribed by a host of totems and taboos, and attended by a vast crowd of ritual specialists, hangers-on, court officials, and eunuchs. Leading his army, clad in white, blue and red, he was Viceroy of the great god of wisdom Ahura Mazda, symbolizing and defending the cosmic order against the three great enemies: The Great Lie, the hostile army, and famine. In Alexander – as is still asserted by the Iranian Zoroastrians – Darius faced the threat of all three.

Leading the Persian army westwards from Babylon (as portrayed by Curtius who used material from Persian eye-witnesses) Darius was no longer a mere war leader – he was a semi-divine being. His war tent, where the trumpets sounded at dawn, was crowned by the image of the sun enclosed in crystal – symbol of the light god Mithra, lord of sun and of just battles. The Procession was led by the holy fire on silver altars tended by Zoroastrian priests, magi, singing hymns, and 365 youths, as many as the days of the year. Drawn by white horses the empty chariot of Ahura Mazda was followed by a great white horse sacred to the Sun, with drivers in dresses of white and gold. Then came ten chariots embossed with gold and silver, and a mounted guard of twelve nations, their different weapons and customs, a symbol of the diversity of the Achaemenian commonwealth. Then, preceded by élite regiments, came the king himself: his royal chariot embossed with images of the gods in gold and silver; on the yoke images of the gods again. Darius, his cloak ornamented with golden hawks – divine birds of primeval legend – royal standard, always carried with Great King in war and peace, and symbol of the Tree of Life, the *axis mundi*.

Darius, then, had ceased to be a man, an ordinary mortal. He was no longer the noble Artashata, but had taken on the part of a cosmic king, symbolizing and defending the world order. He should not be killed, or fall into his enemy's hands, because he was ruler of the world. For all the great practical achievements of their empire, Persian kingship inhabited an archaic ritual universe which simply had not come to terms with the approaching time.

Alexander had come down from central Anatolia to Tarsus through the Cilician Gates, a deep and narrow defile which pierced the Taurus mountains carrying the ancient route from Anatolia into Syria – one of the great routes of history which has now been blasted away by a modern motorway. At Tarsus he fell ill after bathing in the icy waters of the Cydnus river. He was quite possibly suffering from malaria, for which the Tarsus region was – and is – noted. For a time his doctors thought him on the point of death, and rumours abounded of a plot in which Darius had attempted to have Alexander poisoned.

Alexander, though, recovered, and in late October moved down into the narrow gap between the Amanus (Nur) mountains and the sea, hoping to entice Darius to fight in a narrow space which would nullify his superior numbers. Then came a most surprising failure of Macedonian intelligence, which shows that Darius had not yet lost his nerve or understanding of strategy. In a daring strategic manoeuvre, Darius made a circling movement behind Alexander and cut off his line of retreat. Alexander was completely wrong-footed and had to hastily send a ship up the coast to find out if it really could be true. However, even though Darius had strategically outwitted Alexander, he could not profit from it. He still had to fight Alexander on ground which suited Alexander – a narrow coastal plain between the Amanus mountains and the sea. There, close to the little town of Issus, destiny waited.

## THE BATTLE OF ISSUS

When you go to Issus today, it does not look like a place of destiny. The modern age has dealt harshly with the once beautiful plain of cypresses and the fields of tobacco and wheat, which lay between the sea and the pine-clad slopes of the Amanus, a world so recently gone it is still remembered by the old shepherds who graze their goats in the hills. Issus, however, has been a strategic place throughout history, the main road from Anatolia to Syria and Egypt still comes through here today, and here the Iraq pipeline reaches down to the sea. Along the road is a jumble of lokantas, roadhouses and chai stalls, smothered in dust and pollution from factory chimneys. Stand today on the modern bridge over the Payas river where the armies met, and the slopes of the Amanus range are almost invisible most days in summer because of the smog. And your view up the river is obstructed by a web of power lines along the new superhighway, whose access-roads carve right up the river bed where Alexander and Darius met all those years ago. Yet, an older history is still there. The story can be traced on the ground starting by the ancient mound of Issus (Kinet Huyuk) near the oil terminal. This is where Darius stopped before the battle to mutilate Alexander's sick and wounded as a warning to the Greeks. Moving south to the Payas river, you see fragments of an Ottoman bridge, a lovely sixteenth-century stone caravanserai, and an ancient fort by the shore where fishing boats heave and settle in the warm brown swell.

The battle was fought in November 333 BC on the Payas river. It took place on a front of only 2600 metres (a figure given by Alexander's surveyors and now proved true by new surveys showing the aggradation of the plain since his time).

Once Alexander had confirmed that Darius had indeed encircled him, he turned on his tracks back along the coastal plain towards the Payas river and prepared for battle the next day. The size of Persian army was magnified by Greek propaganda to more than half a million men; no doubt it was bigger than the Greeks, but perhaps not by so much. Darius was facing south, his plan was to hold Alexander on the river-line and use his best cavalry on the right, along the seashore, to break through Alexander's left-wing under the old stalwart Parmenio. In the middle were Darius's best troops, heavy infantry including Greek mercenaries, in numbers at least equal to the Macedonian phalanx. Placed in the

---

The Issus battlefield today. In the left foreground is the steep
cliff which broke up the advance of Alexander's phalanx; Alexander's
cavalry charge came down from the right, on the slope in the middle
distance, where now a steel mill stands.

centre they had the steep sides of the Payas river in front of them, in places a precipitous little cliff 6 or 7 metres deep. During the long wait that day they had made it stronger, topping it with a rough palisade that stuck up above the Macedonians 'on the brow of the river', as Callisthenes (an eye-witness) described it. There was no chance the phalanx could tackle this in order – they would have to cross piecemeal.

If the Persian troops had been up to it, it would have been a good plan. But, as at the Granicus, it ceded Alexander the initiative and, as usual, he was not slow to seize the chance. Once he had confirmed where Darius was, Alexander went up into the hills to pray to the local gods. Then, at the third watch, 2 a.m., he began the march. At first the plain was too narrow for him to deploy. By the time he neared the Persians it was late afternoon, and their advance troops had the unnerving spectacle of watching the Macedonians change from line of march to battle in front of them. The dense mass of the phalanx spread out with parade-ground precision from a column thirty-two deep, to sixteen and finally to eight where the plain widened out in the last two kilometres, with the cavalry moving out to the wings. The whole thing must have been simply terrifying to the Persians.

Alexander assessed the situation from his customary position up on the right wing, near the hills. He saw that their heavy cavalry were concentrated on his left by the sea, and immediately switched his Thessalian cavalry over to the left, moving it behind his lines to bolster Parmenio. On his side he noted the weak Persian formation up against the foothills, where an inexperienced infantry division was covered by archers. This was a sure sign that Darius did not have enough confidence in his infantry to hold the line on its own (you don't protect infantry with archers unless you are worried). Moreover, as Callisthenes reported, the river banks directly in front of them, just where the river came out of the hills, were low and easily passable by cavalry. There Alexander decided to attack, leading the charge in person. It was around 4 p.m., November light closing fast.

Battle cries rolled round the gorges; then Alexander and his companions charged down to the river on the Greek right (the slope is still there, for about a furlong north of the new highway, below a small mosque). As Alexander had seen, the Persian infantry was not top notch, and the archers who were supposed to protect it failed to do their job, loosing their arrows pointlessly and then breaking line in panic. The Macedonian cavalry was now pouring across the river, and within moments it smacked into the Persian infantry line which collapsed, enabling Alexander to push it back and get round behind the Persian centre.

In the centre meanwhile, Darius's Greek mercenaries were holding their own easily against the Macedonian phalanx; in a severe battle there, 120 of Alexander's best phalanx troops were killed with their brigade commander. But suddenly the mercenaries, who were keeping an uneasy eye on events behind them, saw with alarm that they were likely to be surrounded, and knew all too well that their fate would be the same as their comrades' at the Granicus if they did not extricate themselves in time. Again the course of the battle had been decided in a matter of minutes. But the mercenaries had the discipline to pull back, and at least 12,000 of them survived, probably the majority. They were helped by the fact that it was nearly dusk, and because Alexander now focused his attack on Darius himself.

Now the whole thrust of Alexander's attack was to capture or kill Darius, and suddenly the two found themselves almost face to face. Several of Darius's leading kinsmen fell in a desperate hand-to-hand fight defending him, and then his own chariot horses were wounded and began to panic. Afterwards the Greeks said Darius had been a coward to flee at this point, but, seeing it from the Persian point of view, Darius's job was to stay alive; instantly he was pulled out by his bodyguard, took a fresh horse and fled. Behind him in his camp he left all the royal women and his children, along with the tens of thousands of ordinary soldiers who now jammed that narrow space between mountains and sea. As darkness fell the scene must have been one of total chaos.

We have an almost photographic image of this moment in the mosaic of Issus – one of the greatest of all war pictures. It is presumed to be a faithful copy of a late fourth-century painting perhaps done for a Macedonian king in Pella, but possibly made in a Greek environment in Syria or the Near East. Like all masterpieces it is full of ambiguities. On the skyline is a threatening hedge of phalanx spears; weapons and bodies are littered on the ground; in the middle distance is the single bare tree mentioned in one source, the drama heightened by foreshortened distances, riderless horses plunging and bucking. The picture depicts the famous incident told in all our sources: the moment of screaming terror when Alexander and his companions burst into the Persian centre round Darius: 'Then the carnage took on truly horrendous proportions', says Curtius, 'around Darius' chariot lay his most famous generals who had fallen to a glorious death in the eyes of their king and

---

Overleaf: The terror of war – Alexander at Issus. Discovered in Pompeii in 1831, this great mosaic (2.17 metres by 5.12 metres) is a second-century Roman copy of a painting done in Macedonia around 300 BC. Composed of minute stone and glass tesserae, perhaps no work of art has better captured the frenzy and confusion of battle. Alexander charges on Bucephalus; Darius, in the yellow Persian tiara, seems powerless to halt Alexander's remorseless impetus.

now lay all face down where they had fallen ...' All this, remember, was compressed into a few confused moments with an autumn dusk coming on. Curtius continues: 'Darius' horses by now had been pierced by lances and were distracted with pain; they had begun to toss the yoke and were on the point of hurling the king from his chariot. Fearing he might fall into his enemies' hands alive, Darius jumped down ...' In the mosaic all these images are here: Alexander spurring his horse, wild haired, an elemental force; Darius with his eyes wide open – not so much in fear, perhaps (though who would not have been frightened in his shoes?), but in distress, as if encountering an alien aggressor. In the picture two universes are in collision: the cosmic king, now all too human and vulnerable, suddenly drained of his numinous power; the murderous invader almost demonic in his force. Darius does not so much gesture in self-protection but in sympathy, powerless to help as one of his companions tumbles to his death, run through by Alexander's lance. Whoever he was, the artist evidently intended us to feel sympathy for the vanquished.

By complete contrast, as narrated by Arrian and Curtius, is the scene of calm in the royal tent afterwards. It is midnight; the battle is over; the incredible wealth of the king's regalia and furniture tumbled out on rich carpets for the victors to see. 'So this is what it is like to be a king', says Alexander ironically. Later still, Alexander enters the women's tent, drawn by the sound of wailing by the Persian eunuchs, courtiers and women, fearing the death of the king of the world. Appalled. Waiting their fate, like all women at the hands of victorious armies from the ancient world to Bosnia. The Queen Mother goes down on her knees before Hephaistion mistaking him for Alexander (he is the taller and more handsome of the two): 'Don't worry mother', says the king, 'he too is Alexander' – a significant acknowledgement that Hephaistion was in some sense Alexander's alter ego – if the tale is true.

Alexander had a way with older women, perhaps he was drawn to mother figures. His relations with Darius's mother (who must have been in her early sixties) were said to have become very intimate; the Greeks claimed she came to adore him like a son, and that she sickened and died of grief within days of the king's own death. But it is very uncertain whether we can believe such tales. As for the Darius's wife Stateira, the Greek sources say she was a bewitching beauty and that Alexander did not wish to be tempted even by setting eyes on her – another questionable tale which gulled earlier historians who saw Alexander anachronistically as a model of rectitude and chivalry. Stateira's fate is unknown. Captured in autumn 333, she died eighteen months later, Curtius says of illness and exhaustion; Plutarch and Justin claim in childbirth. Perhaps her treatment at Alexander's hands was not quite what his apologists have suggested.

There is a last image from that scene after Issus. In the corner of the tent were Darius's six-year-old son and the two teenage daughters of Darius and Stateira. Years later, back in Susa, Alexander and Hephaistion would marry the young girls now cowering before them in the flickering lamplight. Nothing would be left to chance. Darius's family had been shipwrecked by history.

Night was coming on over Issus as we prepared to leave for the Syrian border. Looking down from the hills above the Greek right-wing we could see the last glint of daylight catch the waters of the Payas. It made a suitably apocalyptic setting: the noise of the factories booming and howling like wind; smoke hanging in a great pall of pollution over the hills; the sun setting in an indistinct red ball into the thick haze over the sea; along the road were the headlights of long-distance lorries driving between Syria and Anatolia.

Alexander's battlefield casualties had been 302 infantry and 150 cavalry with maybe 4500 wounded. The Persian losses were probably several times more than that. But many more of the survivors must have died on the way home. How did they even find their way back to Babylon or Persia? How did they feed themselves, or keep warm in the cold winter of northern Syria? Most, perhaps, never made it home. Darius's Grand Army had ceased to exist.

Darius would fight again, in two years' time with a new army raised from scratch, but Issus was a shattering blow. The news was received with amazement in Greece and Anatolia. Greeks had defeated Persians before. But the Great King himself at the head of the full army had never experienced such a comprehensive disaster. From this moment Darius was living on borrowed time. As for Alexander, we don't know how far he intended to go when he started the great expedition, whether he already had it in his mind to go to the very ends of the earth. But he must have known now, if he hadn't before, that he really could do it.

# PART TWO

# SON *of* GOD

# SYRIA, LEBANON, ISRAEL AND EGYPT

## SPRING 332 – SPRING 331

*Alexander marches through Phoenicia (modern Syria and Lebanon);
his siege of Tyre and the fate of its people; the Palestinian resistance and
the gruesome death of governor Batis of Gaza; into Egypt: Alexander journeys
across the desert to the Siwa Oasis where the oracle of Zeus declares him
Son of God; the return across the Great Sand Sea and the discovery of a lost
temple to the deified Alexander; Alexander founds Alexandria,
destined to become 'the first city of the world'*

IN THE AFTERMATH OF THE BATTLE OF ISSUS, Alexander sent General Parmenio to Damascus to capture the main Persian baggage train. There, Parmenio took some unexpected prisoners, among them the enigmatic and captivating Barsine. Daughter of a Persian nobleman and a mother of royal blood, she had had a Greek education and had spent time in Macedonia. (Perhaps she had met Alexander before?) First married to the Rhodian mercenary captain Mentor, after his death she married his brother, Alexander's great adversary Memnon. Before the siege of Halicarnassus she was sent with her children to Darius whom she had accompanied as far as Damascus. Barsine is a mysterious character in the tale. Plutarch tells a story that she was the first women with whom Alexander had a sexual relationship; she had a son by him, called Heracles, who survived Alexander's death, and who was even put forward by some as a possible successor. But nothing else is certain. Once again, we have a key moment in the king's inner biography about which we can only speculate. What would we give for Barsine's diary!

Meanwhile the main army had moved on down the coast of Phoenicia (modern Syria and Lebanon). They crossed the Dog river gorge (Nahr al Kalb) near the limestone caverns of Jeita which the Greeks associated with their legends of the underworld. Here you pass the cliff where foreign conquerors have left a score of inscriptions commemorating invasions of Lebanon from the Egyptian New Kingdom to World War II. Here are Pharaoh Ramses II, Assyrian, Babylonian and Roman emperors, Allenby in 1918 and the Allies in 1942. Alexander may have added his own self advertisement, but the two Greek inscriptions on the cliff are too weathered to decipher.

From Dog river the Greek army marched on along the Lebanese coast. Several Phoenician communities were happy to acknowledge Alexander as the successor to Darius – Arad and Sidon among them. The most powerful, Tyre, was ambivalent. A great commercial city and naval power, one of the strongest in the Mediterranean on their offshore island, the Tyrians gave Alexander a gold crown and provisions, but asked the Macedonians to stay out of the city (perhaps, as some said, to help Darius to buy time, but, more likely, to preserve their neutrality, as Arrian states). Alexander accepted their gifts, but insisted that he must offer sacrifice to Hercules of Tyre. The Tyrians said he should indeed, but at the ancient temple of Old Tyre on the coast. Alexander then demanded the city's

---

Previous pages, left: 'Alexander's Arch' at Tyre, perhaps marking
the place where the king's siege causeway started. Right: Alexander
as Helios Kosmokrator, a divine world ruler, with his head-dress
of stars. Despite the fantasy, the artist has still caught the king's
heavy-jawed face.

Aerial view of Tyre. Now a peninsula, Tyre was once an island,
until it was joined to the mainland by Alexander's siege causeway.

surrender (Persian supremacy at sea would be badly hit by the loss of such a base). But, confident in their walls and weaponry, the Tyrians decided to resist. The siege began – the longest and most terrible of all Alexander's sieges.

Tyre stood on an island 800 metres offshore; Alexander and his siege expert, Diades of Thessaly, later known as 'the man who took Tyre', drafted labour in from the country-side, deporting the 'entire population of all the neighbouring towns', or demolishing their towns to provide stone and wood. Meanwhile his carpenters and engineers were hard at work building mobile siege-towers. The plan was to build a causeway across the sea to the

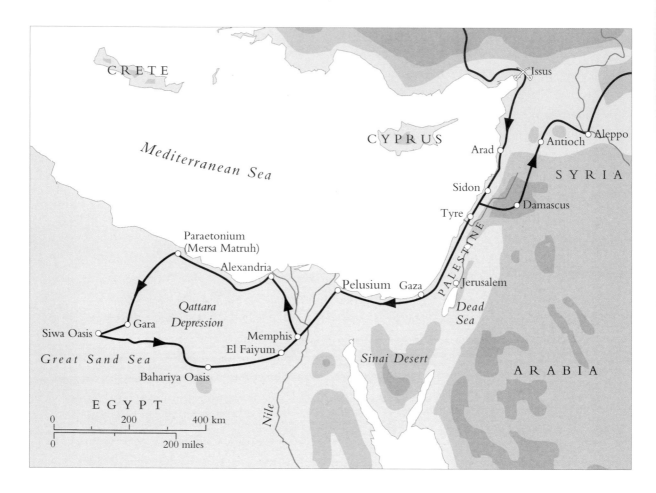

island of Tyre. The water was shallow and muddy for much of the way, but near the island dropped to 5 or 6 metres. Stakes were driven into the bed, braced with stone, to support a 60-metre-wide road out into the sea. At first the islanders mocked the king's efforts, sailing close up 'asking if he thought he could get the better of Poseidon', but as the causeway got nearer they became alarmed and took measures to evacuate the women and children. (They were too late: the siege started with almost everyone still inside.) The Tyrians mounted artillery on the walls to rain down on the construction workers on the mole. In the harbour they had about eighty three-banked galleys, which they armed with catapults, archers and slingers, and these they rowed round the mole to attack the work gangs. Alexander responded by erecting protective screens to hide his workmen. The Tyrians then hit back with surprise commando attacks on the coast to disrupt the supply columns bringing in materials. At this point Alexander himself took a force into the Lebanese mountains to procure timbers for the construction.

As the mole got nearer, Alexander had two wheeled siege towers assembled, each about 17 metres high, operated by an internal capstan, the floors reached by ladders protected by hides, with mechanical catapults mounted on the top floor. Now he was able to hit the defenders, and the causeway construction gangs were able to work more quickly. The Tyrians by now were in desperate need of a counterstroke. At that time of year there are strong south-west winds, and they devised a bold plan. A wide-bodied transport ship was fitted with two masts sticking out beyond the bows. Lashed to these were doubled yard arms hung with containers of bitumen and sulphur. They filled the ship with dry wood, and heavily ballasted the stern with rocks so the bows were lifted out of the water. Waiting for a day when a strong south-westerly was blowing, they towed the fireship round the island to the south and into the gale, then lit it and abandoned ship. The ship crashed into the end of the mole, the projecting masts broke dropping the cauldrons of bitumen over the mole, and the siege towers were engulfed in fire. Then, as Alexander's troops tried to contain the flames, the Tyrian ships landed assault parties along the mole to destroy the palisades and wreck the wooden raft supporting the construction. Curtius says that when Alexander returned the mole was effectively ruined.

The situation was now becoming serious. Alexander had already spent months, with heavy losses of equipment and declining morale, now he faced the possibility of a 'shocking disaster'. In his war council there were evidently recriminations. He may even have contemplated breaking off the siege and leaving a holding force, but he could not afford to leave the Tyrians and their fleet untouched. According to Curtius, the king now decided to build a second mole, to the north of the first, coming down at an angle to the island. Efforts were redoubled, and huge amounts of rock, bounded by whole trees, were used to create a solid ground. Meanwhile, events in the Eastern Mediterranean were going Alexander's way: Phoenician ships came over to him in Sidon, with the Rhodian fleet and then 120 ships of the king of Cyprus. The fate of the Tyrians was sealed. They could now be blockaded in their own harbour.

The second mole was pushed quickly out through the shallows — then only when they reached deep water did the Greeks come within javelin range of the walls. The defenders now resorted to desperate measures employing divers to cut the Greeks' anchor ropes, and attaching lines to pull the mole beams apart. They placed cranes on their walls to drop missiles on to Alexander's ships and used bronze vessels to pour boiling sand on the besiegers. To protect their own walls from missiles, they covered the face of the walls with skins stuffed with seaweed and chaff. They also built a new wall behind the damaged section facing the mole, filling the gap between the two with stones and earth. Wooden extensions were erected on top of their ramparts and towers to get help above the

attackers. The Macedonians countered by lashing ships together and mounting their catapults on platforms, but the choppy sea broke them up. The Tyrians then launched a bold
sally from the harbour, using thirteen warships with élite troops to sink or drive aground
thirty of Alexander's ships.

But it was all hopeless. Finally the mole reached the walls of Tyre. As Alexander had
promised he had made the city part of the mainland. A roadway was laid on top of the
mole and the Macedonians were able to haul their siege-towers right up to the walls and
drop their bridges on the battlements. Even then the Tyrians came back with every con-
ceivable ingenuity: their forges had been working overtime producing huge barbed

tridents, hooked weapons, 'crows and iron hands' and grappling hooks to pull the attack-ers off walls. They had manufactured large nets to pull the Macedonians off the walls and towers, and made long poles with cutting edges to cut the ropes holding the Greeks' battering rams. The pages of Arrian and Diodorus conjure up images of desperate heroism,

---

'Ask me for an image of civilization,' said the Roman Seneca,
'and I'll show you the sack of a great city.' Between Greece and India,
Alexander sacked scores of them and killed tens, maybe hundreds,
of thousands of people. From the Nereid Monument, Xanthos, c. 400.

scenes of 'extreme terror' in which, at times, the fury of the defenders' resistance became almost irresistible. But the Greek high command knew that they could take the city. In council some argued for a negotiated surrender. Alexander demanded unconditional submission and gave them two days to consider. On the morning of day three the last assault began, from the sea and from the mole. The wall was weakest near the naval harbour (on the south). Here, Alexander led the attack from a siege-tower lashed to ships and jumped from the bridge on to the walls, 'a feat of daring hardly believable even to those who saw it' says Arrian. Using triremes lashed together supporting a siege-tower and battering ram, a hole 30 metres wide was smashed in the wall between the mole and the harbour on the south. Meanwhile, there were simultaneous attacks to stretch the defence to the limit. The Egyptian fleet broke into the south harbour; the Cyprian fleet into the northern harbour. With that the defence finally collapsed. The Tyrians' last stand took place in the centre of town, somewhere near the lovely medieval cathedral, with fierce hand-to-hand fighting in the streets. The women and children took sanctuary in the temples which the Greeks had vowed not to harm. The Sidonian fleet may have helped some civilians to escape. One account suggests as many as 15,000 refugees got away through their auspices; but, according to Curtius, these were actually sold into slavery.

Almost no other narrative from the ancient world conveys better the sheer terror of the siege and the sack of a city – the desperate heroism of defenders despite the hopelessness of their situation. Somewhere between 6000 and 8000 were killed and 13,000 taken prisoner. The king of Tyre and his council, and some envoys from Carthage, took refuge in the temple of Hercules and were pardoned, according to Arrian. But Curtius, with more probability, says only the foreign ambassadors were spared. The Tyrian leaders were executed along with the 2000 survivors of the fighting men who were crucified along the coast. The battering ram which made the first breach was dedicated in the temple of Hercules. 'So Tyre had undergone the siege bravely rather than wisely and come into such misfortunes, after a resistance of seven months'.

In July, or early August – high summer in Palestine – Alexander pushed on, supplied by sea. The key Persian fortress on the route from Palestine into the Egyptian delta was at Gaza, defended by governor Batis (or Betis), the local commandant of the Persian empire, with a strong force of Arab mercenaries. Given that the fate of Tyre must have been reported around the Levant by now, they were especially brave to resist. The siege, between September and November 332 BC, was difficult and bitterly fought, with mines and counter mines being dug in the sandy coastal soil. In one sally, Alexander was severely wounded by a catapult bolt and incapacitated for two or three weeks.

It was November before the king was fit to fight. By then the mines had been dug right under the city walls, and the final assault could begin. The mines were fired and the walls partially collapsed. Three frontal assaults then failed, but the fourth, led by Alexander himself, broke down the damaged wall and forced a way in. A ferocious struggle took place in the streets, in which Alexander was again wounded, this time in the leg, and had to leave the field. The city, though, fell and Alexander's revenge was savage. Curtius says 10,000 were killed; the women and children were sold into slavery. Batis himself was captured alive, badly wounded. Brought before Alexander, he was told he would have a most uncomfortable captivity, but he refused even to speak to Alexander and simply looked at him 'with an insulting expression on his face'. Already on edge because of the ferocity of the resistance and his own wounds, Alexander went into a fury and ordered Batis's ankles to be pierced and thongs attached, so that he could be dragged around the walls of Gaza behind his chariot until he was dead. A grim echo of Achilles's treatment of Hector's body in the *Iliad*, but decidedly unheroic.

## INTO EGYPT

In late 332 BC, Alexander moved from Gaza along the coast into Egypt. There was no opposition, no attempt to hold the border fortress and defence wall at Pelusium – in fact, the Greeks claimed huge crowds turned out to greet Alexander as a liberator. This should perhaps be taken with a pinch of salt, though possibly a pro-Greek faction organized a demonstration. There is no reason to assume that the Egyptians would have welcomed him any more than the Persians. But he met no resistance, visiting the sun temple at Heliopolis before sailing up the eastern arm of the delta to reach the Nile. He then camped at Memphis, 'White Walls', the old capital since the two lands were united 3000 years before his time. This was a truly ancient land – 'compared with us', the Egyptian temple priests had told the Greek Solon, 'you Greeks are just children'. The Greeks had time to do a little tourism, and their graffiti show us they were impressed: 'I have gazed on these awesome monuments and am thunderstruck'.

For later Greek historians Alexander's visit to Egypt was dominated by one issue – his visit to the Siwa oracle where, it was said, he was proclaimed Son of God. It is almost impossible now to untangle his real motives. 'He conceived a violent desire, a *pothos*,' says Arrian, a word which crops up again and again in his story, portraying a man propelled by destiny, but perhaps also subject to manically intense drives and sudden swings of mood. That Alexander passionately wanted to visit the oracle at Siwa fits Arrian's idealized portrait of a divinely-inspired hero. Strabo also says he was driven by 'love of glory' to emulate his ancestors Heracles (Hercules) and Perseus. Curtius and Diodorus talk of certain key questions, some perhaps unspoken. Scholars have speculated that, perhaps, Alexander was not yet confident of the outcome of his crusade? Or of his own support? Perhaps he was already in the grip of delusions of divinity? Others point to more stark political concerns, such as continuing nagging fears over his implication in his father's murder (see page 32) and a need to quash the rumours once and for all. Most of these possible motivations are probably later inventions. Seen in an Egyptian context, a different picture emerges.

The key political question right then for Alexander was how to be acknowledged ruler of Egypt. He had made all the right noises, anxious from the start to ingratiate himself with those of the ruling class and the traditional priesthood who were favourably disposed to Greek rule. He visited the bull shrine, the Serapeum outside Memphis, with its eerie subterranean caverns holding the immense sarcophagi of the sacred animals. Unlike the Persian kings he had no qualms about paying respect to mummified bulls. Like most Greeks of his day he was open-minded about other religions, and found it easy to assimilate their symbols and gods into his own beliefs (genuinely, no doubt; till his dying day, he never failed to 'do his daily religious duties', as Arrian put it). The problem, though, was that traditionally it was impossible to accept foreigners as true Pharaohs. Egypt was a huge and rich country, densely populated with four or five million people. If Alexander was going to press on into Asia he needed Egypt not to rock the boat and to keep his army supplied with grain. Sure enough, a solution presented itself. During his stay in Memphis, he must have asked the priesthood there what to do. Seen from the Egyptian perspective, the answer would have been that he could only succeed with divine intervention. Perhaps indeed it was the priests who advised him that he should go to the oracle of Zeus–Ammon at Siwa in the Western Desert to get himself declared Pharaoh. Added to this, though, there may also have been a powerful psychological motive. According to Arrian, Alexander also went to Siwa 'with the purpose of seeking to trace some part of his genesis, his birth, to Ammon'. In the myths, Perseus and Heracles (Hercules), sons of Zeus, were his ancestors. Alexander was a descendant in the male line from Heracles and Perseus and, through his mother, Achilles. His world did not distinguish between myth and history, and such claims were probably believed. For Alexander, Heracles, Perseus and Achilles were real persons and his actual ancestors. Hence, on his journeys, he would try to rival Heracles and Perseus

---

'Beloved of Ra, son of Ammon, Alksndrs' – Alexander, as Pharaoh
of Egypt, worships the phallic god Min in his chapel inside the great
temple of Amenophis III at Luxor.

at Siwa (and, later, Heracles at Aornos, and Dionysus in the North-West Frontier). After quitting this life Heracles had become a god instead of a mortal — a favour owed to his extraordinary virtue, and his noble and brave acts. We can only speculate that such ideas lodged easily in Alexander's boyhood mind, and that he actually believed that if he excelled or equalled Heracles then he could expect a similar reward!

But, first and foremost, the visit to Siwa was good politics. As Napoleon said when he came to Egypt in Alexander's footsteps: 'What I admire most is his political sense. It was an astute move to go to Siwa. Why, I would have gone on pilgrimage to Mecca at the drop of a hat if it would have helped me conquer the east'. Alexander would have agreed.

So Alexander took at least a month off in the middle of this crucial stage of the campaign to go out into the desert to ask questions of a strange god in a darkened room. Whatever his motives (and maybe even he could not have fully articulated them), it turned out to be a key moment of his life.

## THE JOURNEY TO SIWA

The journey to Siwa was later written up in extravagant terms by the expedition historian Callisthenes with romantic embellishments, omens and signs, all of which would suggest to the reader divine intervention. We know the outward journey took Alexander along the coast from the western delta across the later battlefield of Alamein to Mersa Matruh. Then, with a small party, Alexander turned inland.

Following in his track we crossed a dreary scrubby waste still within the Mediterranean coastal rain-belt, then, after 70 kilometres, went up on to the plateau where we reached the real desert. The ancient road, though, did not follow the route of the modern tarmac road. It cut almost due south from Mersa, east of the modern road, along the edge of the Qattara Depression across a low range known as Qarat Iskander. This is the route we now took via the little oasis of Gara with its ancient deserted mud-brick citadel, a fly-blown desolation quivering with heat.

The locals reckon the 250 kilometres to Siwa was an eight-day march for camels on the old route; it was a day's journey by four-wheel drive. Along the way we saw nothing but barren desert. As Arrian said, 'there are no marks along the route, no mountain anywhere, no tree, no solid hillocks by which wayfarers might judge their proper course as sailors do by the stars'. As befits a work of propaganda Callisthenes's account stressed providential happenings, though actually this was a well-beaten caravan route, and there was no reason for Alexander to have run into trouble. The party lost their way, however, and, after four days, they ran out of water which they were carrying in skins (it is true that there is virtually no water on the route). They were saved by a sudden winter rainstorm. Arrian pictures the travellers running about gulping it in, as it fell out of the skies. A good omen, said the army seer, and, it was said, there were other auspicious signs *en route*. When they were lost, two crows were said to have appeared and shown them the path to the oasis (not impossible this – crows are still common at Siwa). After four more days, according to the most circumstantial account, they reached 'the bitter lake' – Birket el Ma'sir salt lakes on the route of Gara to Siwa. Then, in another 15 kilometres, they came to 'the cities of Ammon' (whose remains have been discovered recently along the Birket Zeitun lake); a day later they approached the sanctuary.

Also coming in from Gara, we crested the last dunes to see an amazing sight: a wide green oasis, over 100 kilometres long, between 30 and 8 kilometres wide. We entered a magical world: dense palm groves shading the gardens even in the heat of day, olives, sweet lemons, figs, pomegranates and lemons. Above the vivid green of the oasis is the ancient brown hill of Aghurmi, almost like a fairytale castle, where the oracle temple and the old town stand, a mud-brick warren of walls, jagged pinnacles, conical mosques like bee hives. It is an amazing sight surrounded by absolute desolation. Towards the sunrise are the dunes of the Western Desert, crossed by the old caravan routes to Sudan and Nubia, where the slave trade was active till eighty years ago. To the south, lunar ridges, gravel beds and the burning salt wastes of the Great Sand Sea stretching towards the Sahara, with scarcely a fixed habitation between there and Timbuktu. At our feet, shaded by a quarter of a million date palms, was boundless fertility. No wonder it was a sacred place for so long, a place where the divine was believed to speak directly to humankind. This is what had drawn Alexander here.

The oracle lay on the hill of Aghurmi in the centre of the oasis, inside a mud-brick fortress on a stone outcrop standing above the palm groves. Alexander went straight to the temple of the oracle. One account says that the priests met him at the gate at the foot of the rock; and the high priest greeted him, probably in Greek, as 'son of Zeus-Ammon, master of all lands, unconquered until he is united with the gods'. Any living Pharaoh might be addressed in this way, but Alexander took this as a very special greeting. Plutarch added a circumstantial detail, claiming the high priest intended to say *O Paidion* (my son) but, because he was not fluent in Greek, called him *Pai Dios,* Son of God, Son of Zeus-Ammon. Alexander was delighted with this and, from this simple slip, the report was circulated across the Greek world that the oracle had pronounced him Son of Zeus. The tale is possibly a literary embellishment, but it has a strangely circumstantial ring. On such insignificant happenstances, empires can rise or fall.

## SON OF GOD

Alexander and his small entourage walked up the path from the gate to the temple. Through the temple door they approached the threshold of the inner chamber, which still stands to roof height. Here the image of Ammon in the shape of an omphalos decorated with emerald stones was kept by the priests in a wooden ritual boat (rather like the palanquins you see today used to carry portable images around Hindu temples), and on public festivals this was then paraded around the courtyard to the singing and dancing of priests and dancing girls, all 'in a quite peculiar fashion', the bearers going wherever the god directed their path. A great crowd of women followed them, singing hymns of praise. The palanquin swayed up and down, or back and forward, to give simple yes or no replies to questions until the high priest announced that the heart of the God was satisfied. But it was not enough for Alexander. He came as prospective Pharaoh. He had not come all this way for a bit of tourist show. As befitted a Pharaoh, he requested a written reply and a personal audience with the god in the inner sanctum where only kings were allowed. Alone.

The inner room, only 3 metres by 6, was covered with a false roof which concealed a chamber where one of the priests listened to questions posed to the oracle. It is one of only two or three rooms in existence where we know for certain that Alexander stood. Although it was usual to change clothes or strip off to a loin cloth before the deity, Alexander perhaps went in alone in his customary clothes, still travel-stained from the journey. The door was closed, and his companions waited.

Alexander stood at the entrance to the room, surveyed the image of the god in its golden boat, and there asked his questions overheard by the priest in the false roof. Then he was conducted to an ante-room next to the sanctum where he waited. The oldest of the priests now came in and greeted Alexander as Son of Ammon and King, as he would greet any living Pharaoh. This greeting, translated into Greek, was what was relayed to Greek historians such as Plutarch. The old man came bearing a written reply – not in Greek but Egyptian, the holy language in the sacred script, hieroglyphic (though it is very doubtful that the priesthood could write accurate texts by then; the wall inscriptions at Siwa are in abysmal Egyptian). The answer was then read out. The key point was his kinship with Ammon–Zeus, and, although his motives may have been chiefly political, it is quite possible Alexander believed that he was in some sense 'Son of God'.

We will never know the full truth of what happened at Siwa that day. The precise words given by the oracle were never recorded. Our sources all have slightly different accounts of what the king heard. We cannot now see through the Macedonian

Siwa Oasis. Surrounded by the Libyan desert, it is easy to see why
the Greeks thought this an abode of the gods.

propaganda. It was one of those closed events where, as we would say today, the press was completely controlled. Arrian simply says Alexander heard what his heart desired. Later historians, though, believed there were other questions: first, had his father's murder been punished? The priest answered that he would not speak as Alexander's father was not mortal. Alexander then rephrased the question: Had all the murderers of Philip been punished? The answer was that the death had been sufficiently avenged. On a second question there is some agreement: Would it be given to Alexander to be ruler of the whole world? Zeus-Ammon said yes.

Politics or not, something took place at Siwa which deeply impressed Alexander. (Indeed, the story may be true that a short time before he died Alexander gave orders to Aridaeus, an intimate friend, to bury him near his father 'Ammon' at Siwa. It never took place. He was eventually buried at his new foundation of Alexandria.) As for the exact words of the oracle that winter day in the Western Desert, we must conclude that Alexander took them with him to his grave.

Enough had been said though. The event had been under Alexander's control, and his propagandists, seers and spin-doctors made the most of it: 'He heard all he wanted to know; his heart was gladdened'. In the hands of the expedition historian, the visit could be turned into the final proof of divine approval for the expedition. From then on, Callisthenes would portray him as Son of Zeus, no less. The omens had been consistently optimistic. From the first words of the prophetess at Delphi, through Didyma, Xanthos and Gordion, now this. Destiny was on Alexander's side.

## ACROSS THE GREAT SAND SEA

Which route did he take for the return journey? Most assume he went back the way he came, but Arrian says that, according to Ptolemy (who must have been with the king on the Siwa trip), he came back another way. Where could this have been? In the summer of 1942, on the eve of the battle at El Alamein, the German Field Marshal Rommel asked the same question. He had made his own pilgrimage to Siwa to see if there was a way across the desert from Siwa to the Nile valley which would outflank the British defence of Egypt and the Middle Eastern oilfields. He visited the oracle temple (with a secret question, perhaps, for his own destiny?) then surveyed the desert to the south of Siwa, concluding it was impossible for his armour to get through. Alexander, however, may have thought differently – especially as he must have known a legend about Siwa told by Herodotus. Two hundred years before, so the story went, Cambyses, king of Persia, son of Cyrus the Great, had sent a great army to Siwa 'to attack the Ammonians, reduce them to slavery and burn the oracle of Zeus'. They reached the Kharga Oasis from the Nile valley, then disappeared, swallowed up by a sandstorm half way to Siwa. No trace of it was ever seen again. On the face of it, the tale is not implausible. A famous incident in 1805 when a 2000-person camel caravan was lost without trace in a fierce sandstorm is still recounted in the oases of the Western Desert. Anyway, the story of the disaster to Cambyses may have fired Alexander to cross the same desert the other way, as if to prove his invincibility.

Though the area appears blank in many maps, in fact there are two desert routes eastwards from Siwa to the Nile, and both were still used by camel caravans in the nineteenth century, though they are now virtually abandoned. One went along the Qattara Depression to Memphis without touching the coast, a two-week caravan journey in the old days; the other goes due east to the Bahariya Oasis, then north-east to El Faiyum and on to Memphis. On a hunch that Alexander returned this way, we decided to go straight back to the Nile valley through Bahariya. We set out before dawn from Siwa with two four-wheel drive jeeps, spares and water, heading slightly south of east into the rising sun. These days it is a barely visible vehicle track, easy to lose when the wind is blowing, but it was a recognizable caravan route to El Faiyum in the old days. That life of the desert is now no more: the camels have gone and so have most of the tiny stopping places. The oases themselves are still there, green patches in a wide burning desolation, but not as centres of habitation for not a soul lives in any of them any more. But the very existence of these little staging posts was clear evidence that the route had been here in the distant past.

For the first few hours the dirt-track travels eastwards from Siwa across the harshest terrain imaginable. Over brittle eroded clay flats, gravel beds, and shifting dunes, we passed tall weirdly-shaped sandstone stumps, 30 metres or so high, their bases eroded as if by a sea tide. Here under the overhanging rock we could find a little shade to eat some dates and drink some almost boiling water from our flasks (after the last tiny oasis at 150 kilometres, we found no more water). We passed through a wide belt of dunes, where sandstorms can obliterate the path, and then entered a desiccated wilderness on which, for a period, razor-sharp shards of crystal threatened to rip our tyres to pieces. In the heat of the afternoon we came down to a blistering salt-encrusted plain where the glare was so fierce that sky and sand seemed to merge in one white haze.

The passage to Bahariya took twelve hours. For that entire day we passed no other vehicle. As our sense of isolation grew, so did our realization that this was a risky business. Not surprisingly, a two-hour breakdown caused us great consternation. Finally, in the late afternoon, as the shadows lengthened and the heat mercifully abated, the road came down, after 450 kilometres, into the oasis of Bahariya. Here, in 1939, the Egyptian archaeologist Ahmed Fakhry made a remarkable discovery. Fakhry was a Faiyum man who knew the western oases better than anyone, and who had spoken to old people including former black slaves who had worked on the ancient camel routes. On the outskirts of Bahariya, at the very point where the Siwa track comes in to the oasis, he discovered a hitherto unknown temple filled almost to the roof with sand, weathered in its upper parts by the fierce sandstorms which sweep in from the great desert. Unable to investigate then, he returned the next year and attempted to clear the main chamber. As he dug the drifted sand away from the end wall, a figure emerged, a king worshipping Horus and Isis. Fakhry ran his fingers over the cartouche containing the royal name and, to his surprise, read the name Alexander as Pharaoh. He had found the first known temple of Alexander the Great.

Why was the Bahariya temple built in such an isolated spot? Recently another similar structure – a small chapel to the cult of Alexander and also hitherto unknown – has been discovered by Italian archaeologists at the end of the old caravan road which heads on from Bahariya to the Nile valley and Memphis: a place called Madinet el Ma'adi on the south-west fringe of El Faiyum. Was this the route Alexander took back from Siwa? And did his friends, perhaps general Ptolemy who later ruled Egypt, mark the route with these temples to commemorate the momentous journey? Perhaps even Alexander himself

ordered their construction to thank the gods for deliverance after the hazardous journey to and from Siwa, the key moment in the story when the young Macedonian became the son of Zeus-Ammon?

Sandblasted and sunburned from our crossing from Siwa, we stood there in the half silted remains of the Bahariya temple as the sun set over the Western Desert and the hot wind blew in from Africa. Not for the first time in our journey, we felt an intimation that, to follow in Alexander's footsteps, was to do more than merely trace his path; that, if we looked hard enough, and read the ancient sources carefully enough, Alexander's expedition was in some sense still recoverable; that, if we only knew where to look the signs were still there even after so long. And that sense grew stronger as our pursuit of Alexander took us eastwards through Iran, across the high passes of the Hindu Kush, as far as the mountains of Tajikistan on the very verge of China, and on to the perils of the Makran Desert.

## THE FOUNDING OF ALEXANDRIA

The events at Siwa and the return took place over midwinter and the first weeks of January. By then, Macedonian power in Egypt was safely consolidated. When he left to go east, Alexander would only need to leave 4000 front-line troops as a garrison at Memphis. The takeover of the country had been expertly stage-managed. There may, of course, have been rumblings of opposition. We can see now from oracular and apocalyptic papyri, there were those in Egypt who saw the Greeks as thieves and upstarts, and judged them to be people 'addicted to violence'. In a prophecy of the Greek period, one author saw his countrymen looking forward to the day when the 'foreign civilisation planted among us will fade away, and when the foreigners who occupy Egypt will disappear like autumn leaves'. But, in the first flush of success, Alexander seems to have gone out of his way to mollify and conciliate; and we have no evidence of actual resistance. Indeed, before he left, it is just possible he was crowned as Pharaoh by the priesthood of Memphis, but this is not told in any reputable source, only in the later Alexander Romance where fact is impossible to disentangle from fiction. Likewise, he may have made a trip into the interior of Egypt. It was not a long journey up to Thebes, and today in the great temple at Luxor, one may see the young king portrayed in typical Egyptian style as Pharaoh on the walls of the inner sanctum, wearing the ancient crown of the two lands. Although the Egyptians may

---

Previous pages: The Western Desert, near Gara Oasis. Alexander came
this way in the winter of 332–331 BC, camping out under the stars.

not have known it at the time, Alexander's accession signalled the end of the native dynasties who had ruled the Two Kingdoms for three millennia.

The Egyptian priests had told Solon in the *Timaeus* that the Greeks are mere children compared with the Egyptians, and it was true. But the Greeks were now masters of their world; theirs was the future. Rather like the Chinese or the MesoAmericans before their clashes with the Europeans, Egypt was an inward-looking civilization. For all their great practical achievements, their intellectual life had remained static, resistant to outside ideas. (As Herodotus had noted, 'they keep the ancestral laws and resolutely avoid all foreign customs'.) Theirs was a society that looked inwards, to the valley, that long green strip hemmed in by peach-coloured cliffs and surrounded by the vast deserts which make up most of Egypt. Confident in the regularity of the Nile's life-giving flood, they had no need of the outside world. The Greeks in comparison were mobile, aggressive, intelligent. As Aristotle wrote to his pupil Alexander, 'and for that reason they have the strength, means, and capacity to rule the world'.

For Alexander, Egypt would be the cornerstone of the Hellenistic world empire and must be encouraged to look outward. So it was with acute political acumen and geographical insight, on his return from Siwa, that he chose to formally mark out the foundations of a great city on the Mediterranean coast of Egypt – Alexandria. This was the first of over thirty cities that would bear his name, dotted between Central Asia, the Indus valley and North Africa. The traditional date was 25 Tybi, probably 20 January 331 BC.

The founding of Alexandria would bring about a shift in the centre of gravity of Egypt's intellectual and economic life. For the next 1000 years, until the coming of Islam, it would look to the Mediterranean and a wider world. Alexandria's full title was 'Alexandria by Egypt' – *not* 'in Egypt'. It was founded as an entrepôt through which the wealth of Egypt would flow; and, within two centuries, it would become 'the crossroads of the entire world': the El Dorado of the Hellenistic Age. 'If you want to get on in life, my boy,' it was said, 'lace up your boots and get out to Egypt'. Today, only fragments remain of that wonderful age – tombs, theatres, mosaics in Alexandria; the works of the Greek philosophers, artists and geographers who lived there and, from a later period, the dazzling artefacts produced by the dynamic interplay of cultures for which Alexandria was a catalyst; treasures found as far away as Afghanistan and India. In the first century AD Alexandrian merchants sailed to South India on the monsoon winds, linking up with the trade to the Ganges, Vietnam, and China; part of the explosion of ideas and contacts initiated by the age of Alexander. In this way the age-old life of Egypt would be transformed by the 'greatest city in the civilized world'.

All this began, symbolically, that new year of 331 BC.

# PART THREE

# LORD *of the* WORLD

## IRAQ AND IRAN
### SPRING – WINTER 331 BC

*Alexander marches on; Darius tries to buy Alexander off with a
king's ransom; Darius is crushed in the battle of Arbela (Gaugamela);
south into Iraq; rest and recreation in Babylon; the invasion of Iran and a
strange tale from the Bible; the battle at the Persian Gates; Persepolis: 'most hated
city in the world'; the burning of Persepolis; Alexander the Accursed; the death
of Darius; 'no turning back'; on the shores of the Great Ocean; the legend
of the Amazon Queen; the wounded soul of Iran*

THE DECISIVE BATTLE WAS NOW AT HAND. After his defeat at Issus, Darius had retired to lick his wounds and raise another army – a grand army drawn from every corner of the empire. He knew Alexander would not call a halt on the shores of the Mediterranean. The Persian foreign office engaged in a last desperate exchange of letters tried to buy Alexander off. There had already been an approach, not adjusted to the new reality of world politics, but proposing a treaty and asking to ransom Darius's family. This had been refused outright. The Persians then offered to cede the empire as far as the river Halys in Central Anatolia, with a huge ransom for the family. Finally, they offered all the lands of the Persian empire as far as the Euphrates, and a fabulous ransom of 30,000 talents together with the offer of Persian royal wife, one of Darius's daughters, for Alexander. 'I'd accept if I were Alexander,' said old General Parmenio; 'So would I if I were Parmenio,' said Alexander. By now the young conquistador had the scent of blood. His letter told Darius the situation as he saw it: 'Call me Great King now: live as my viceroy or stand and fight, but be assured that I will pursue you wherever you go'. Darius's blood must have chilled.

That spring, early April, rested and reinforced, the Macedonian army held games and sacrifices and then left Memphis, crossed to Gaza and moved back up the coast of Palestine to Tyre. Here their intelligence picked up news of Darius's troop concentrations around Babylon, and they turned inland to Damascus. From there, via Aleppo, they crossed the Euphrates near Jerablus and marched, via Nisibis, into Assyria (now northern Iraq).

The Persian army of Darius was now drawn from every corner of the empire east-wards, with troops from Central Asia and the Indus valley beyond the Hindu Kush. The Greeks claimed it was a million strong, but this is clearly impossible. A more realistic guess might put it at twice the size of Alexander's army. With his heavy infantry forces mauled in previous battles, Darius now put his faith in cavalry, in which he out-numbered the Macedonians over five to one. Other innovations he tried were specialist units, and longer spears forged to combat the phalanx. This, again, gives the lie to the Greek picture of him as a leader incompetent in war and paralysed by misfortune. The problem was that changing tactics and equipment in mid-campaign was very risky. To weld such a disparate force together takes more than just time – and time Darius did not have.

The Persian army had assembled near Babylon, expecting Alexander to advance along the Euphrates from northern Syria. But again Alexander took an indirect and

----

Previous pages, left: Pity and Fear. A Persian infantryman on the
Alexander Sarcophagus. Right: Young Alexander idealized as the
androgynous dreamer of the Hellenistic Age.

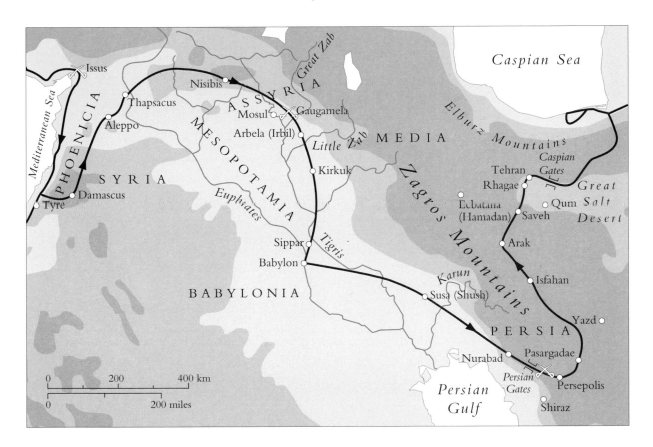

unexpected route, marching the long way round through northern Iraq, where it was easier to supply his forces. Then, for reasons we do not fully understand, Darius, instead of electing to bide his time and wait for the Greeks north of Babylon, now moved 320 kilometres to the north and camped near the ancient city of Arbela waiting to see which route Alexander might take across the river Tigris. Alexander's scouts were now able to fix Darius's position, and Alexander moved up on the northern route and forded the Tigris north-west of Mosul around 18 September (the front line of the war zone between Saddam Hussein and the free Kurdish forces after the Gulf War of 1991). Across the countryside beyond the Tigris, Darius now operated a scorched-earth policy to deny the Greeks supplies. The smoke of burning fires and villages rose as far as the eye could see, so that 'daytime was dimmed by a dark blanket of smoke'.

Darius had again given the initiative to Alexander, and knowing he would have to fight soon, did his best to fight on ground of his own choosing. He spent the next few days levelling a battleground to give his chariots maximum chance against the Macedonian phalanx. The place he chose was near the small town of Gaugamela (Tell Gomel) north of

87

the Jebel Maqlub Hills which rise over 1000 metres straight out of the plain, near the Gomel river, about 120 kilometres north-west of Arbela (Irbil). On 20-21 September a near total lunar eclipse took place, which was received with consternation in the Macedonian ranks, but which the army seers were quick to interpret as a sign of victory. Propitiatory sacrifices were made the next day and then Alexander pushed on. On 25 September he made contact with the enemy, seizing the heights overlooking the battle-field. He then reconnoitred and rested the army for four days, presumably also to reorganize and drill the special units as he worked out his plan. On 30 September he closed on Darius and camped opposite for the final showdown. Alexander had 40,000 infantry and about 7000 front-line cavalry; Darius had 34,000 cavalry and infantry forces, variously estimated by the Greeks between 200,000 and a million men. The smaller figure, although no doubt exaggerated, is likely to be nearer the truth.

On 1 October 331 BC, the late summer heat would have been dying in the Arbela plain after the ferocious temperatures at the end of August, when it reaches 50 degrees. But it would have been still hot and very dusty – dust storms frequently roll across the bare eroded hills of Kurdistan. Our sources, even though they had access to detailed account of Alexander's unit lists and battle plans along with the full written dispositions of the Persian army which fell into Alexander's hands after the battle, are all confused over the events that followed. What appears on paper, though, is a far cry from the messy confused reality of a battle. This was fought on a front of 4 kilometres amid swirling clouds of dust, and large parts of the action were concealed from the gaze of the leaders, so none of the surviving accounts tells the whole story.

Alexander knew the Persian line would outflank him by a long way. Indeed he encouraged them to do so by deliberately staggering back his formation at a 45-degree angle. His intention was to lure the Persians into a premature assault which would open up gaps in their line. As it happened though, in the early part of the battle it was the Greek line which became disjointed. Bessus, the commander of the élite Bactrian cavalry from north Afghanistan, launched a heavy attack on Alexander's right, and a gap then opened in the advancing Macedonian phalanx. This allowed other Persian cavalry units to break through to attack the Greek baggage park. On the other side, the Persian right-wing cavalry were also able to sweep round the Greek line. At this moment the Persians had a chance of victory, but perhaps already thinking the battle was won the Persian cavalry charged on to raid the Macedonian camp some kilometres to the rear. This indiscipline was fatal to Darius's hopes.

While Parmenio held off the main Persian attacks on the Greek left, Alexander formed a kind of moving castle with his main phalanx battalions and specialist troops, from

'If you dispute the kingship of Asia with me, stand and fight, but wherever you flee I will pursue you.' The recurring Persian nightmare: Alexander on the heels of the fleeing Darius. After the battle of Arbela, the Persian war effort collapsed and Alexander could declare himself Lord of Asia. From a Greek amphora.

which he launched an attack by a massed wedge of cavalry and royal guards into the gap which had opened up in the Persian front. Amid clouds of dust, Darius suddenly found himself once again exposed, his royal guards, cavalry and Greek mercenaries rocked by a hammer blow. The scene must have been one of total confusion, with Darius unable to keep communications with his widespread and unwieldy forces. At this point, seeing the centre give, and the royal squadrons recoil, Bessus with the cavalry on the Persian left sounded the retreat. The battle was lost, and with it the destiny of the Persian monarchy which had been founded two centuries before by Cyrus; the greatest empire which had yet existed in history.

Targeted by Alexander and his guard, Darius fled, as he had at Issus, only just escaping the Greek attack. The battle was effectively over, though the fighting on the field lasted longer. The right-wing of the Persian cavalry attacked the baggage train and then returned to clash bloodily with Alexander. The day ended with Darius charging off on his chariot bound hell-for-leather for Arbela, pursued by Alexander. There was a fierce chase across the plain which was called off at dusk while the Greeks rested for a few hours, took food and drink and then resumed at midnight. Alexander rode into Arbela at dawn, coming in from the Gomel river. The ancient city stood on a great mound, visible from far across the plain as it still is today. Darius had gone. The Greeks later learned that he had gathered a nucleus of survivors and headed eastwards through the Armenian mountains for Ecbatana (Hamadan) in Media. He had effectively abandoned not only Babylon and Mesopotamia to the Greeks, but also Susa, the winter capital down by the Gulf.

The battle of Arbela (or Gaugamela) is often called one of the most decisive in history. The most realistic ancient estimate of the Persian losses was 56,000 killed, although their entire army may not have been much more than that. The true figure most likely was never known. Greek losses are given by Arrian and Curtius as a few hundred. More realistic, a papyrus fragment found in Egypt gives 1000 foot and 200 horse, including 60 Companions killed in the cavalry battle after Darius had fled. Arrian also says that 1000 horses were killed. They were heavy losses, but a small price to pay to become Lord of Asia.

Our only non-Greek narrative of the battle is a couple of lines long, but it is of great interest. It comes from a recently identified clay tablet written in cuneiform, part of a contemporary diary written in Babylon, so it is our earliest source for these events, and offers us a tiny glimpse into the view of Alexander from the other side. As was customary in such texts, the scribe first notes the month's prices ('Oil 1 pi, wool 5 shekels') and the astrological conjunction ('At that time Jupiter was in Scorpio'), then he continues: 'On day eleven of that month there was panic in the military camp … Before the king (the Greek army appeared) then they pitched camp in front of the king (Darius). On day 24 in the morning its king set up the standard. They fought one another and the Greeks inflicted a defeat. Important officers (were killed?) He (Darius) abandoned his army …(they fled?) to their cities … He disappeared into the land of Guti (Western Iran)'. Laconic, it may be, in the extreme, but it gives us a dramatic sense of news as it was being made, not as filtered by Greek propaganda.

The omens had proved to be true. Alexander now knew the way was open to his becoming Lord of Asia, as the oracles at Gordion, Didyma, Xanthos, Siwa had all intimated. (For a time then, it was said, he stopped consulting soothsayers altogether – stop when you are winning!). Ahead Mesopotamia lay open, a rich, populous and ancient country, the heartland of civilization. Although ruled by the Persians for two centuries, the land had still not accommodated to their rule. It was claimed that King Xerxes had demolished the holiest temple in Babylon, so the Persians had incurred enmity from the Aramaic-speaking ruling class in their grand mud-brick estates in the Diyala plain; from the old families who had run the huge temples for generations, with their vast landholdings in the south (rather like the later mosques); and from the old priestly classes with their archaic cuneiform learning. And, especially perhaps, from the mixed-race commercial classes: Jews, Aramaeans, Arabs, bankers and traders in the cities which traded with Persian Gulf, Bahrain and the Indian coast. These people, such as the Murashu family, financiers and dealers in dates and grain, had connections as far away as Anatolia and Egypt. Did they though have any reason to favour the Greeks? Perhaps not. There were, however, many city councils in the south – Uruk, for example, or Larsa – who may have welcomed a liberator. Alexander knew this and swiftly pushed an advance mission to Babylon, both to sort out arrangements for the billeting and provisioning of his army and to smooth the way to a negotiated surrender, while the city councils of the south waited with bated breath to see with what sort of a king they were to be saddled.

## REST AND RECREATION IN BABYLON

In October the weather is pleasant in northern and central Iraq. Alexander moved south quickly from the city of Arbela (Irbil), through the rolling wheatfields of Assyria. The battle of Arbela we now know was on 1 October. After only a day or two to cremate his dead and patch up the wounded, he then took the Kirkuk road along the foothills of the Kurdish mountains. This is a land which has been fought over since the beginning of history. (I can remember travelling that road early in 1989, after the Kurdish Anfal, in grey sleeting rain, stuck behind trucks of blind-folded prisoners as we passed devastated villages and the sinister blockhouses of the occupying forces – rather like the fortified police posts, built by the Greeks, which have been uncovered by modern archaeology: history in these parts has an uncanny way of repeating itself.) The Greeks stopped at a place called Mennis, evidently near the Kirkuk oilfield. Here, Alexander was shown a pool of bitumen and a well of naphtha (crude petroleum). That night, the natives sprinkled it down both sides of the street leading to Alexander's headquarters, and then torched it: 'so that in a flash the road became one continuous line of fire', an apt metaphor for the king's terrifying advance.

They pushed on southwards via Tikrit and Samarra. For Alexander it was an easy journey. New information on this march again comes from the Babylonian astronomical diary. Negotiations were conducted as he marched and messengers had already gone to the citizens of Babylon. The diary seems to mention the demand of the surrender of temple treasures. He stopped 60 kilometres north of Babylon, on 20 October, at the ancient city of the Sun God, Sippar. An old warren of mud-brick streets, with a decaying brick ziggurat, Sippar stood inside the so-called 'Medean wall', a great brick defence work between the Euphrates and the Tigris, but Alexander met no resistance. The diary records a series of evidently bullying messages from Alexander. 'An order from Alexander came, it says [evidently telling the people] you shall not go into your buildings'. (Perhaps these were the temples, where the treasures and valuables were kept, and this was an edict against looting?) Two days later he reached the outskirts where, according to the Greeks, the city elders met him with gifts of horses, cattle, livestock, and also lions, leopards and assorted exotica which sound rather like the hastily gathered contents of a Babylon zoo. Exchanges followed: some were deprived (of office? or life?); then sacrifices were made. It is easy to imagine the scene: the king's minders and bodyguards warily scanning the crowd; interpreters trying to sort out the arrangements made by the city council; a chanting group of Babylonian priests fanning incense and waving fronds; and the Persian household cavalry turned out in parade uniform, under satrap Mazaeus, leader of the right wing at Arbela, who now submitted to the Greeks and was confirmed in his position.

Then, says the diary, on 24 or 25 October, 'Alexander its king entered Babylon with horses and the accoutrements of war to be received by the citizens of Babylon and the people'. According to the Greeks he mounted a chariot and made a ceremonial entrance, probably down the great processional way to the Ishtar Gate, the dazzling north portal of the city which was faced with glazed blue tiles, picked out with heraldic animals. Behind him were the élite forces, the Companions, cutting a dash with their rakish Boeotian cavalry helmets and billowing neck scarves. The city elders had hastily organized a welcome, and the street was strewn with flowers and garlands; altars burned incense and oil on the sidewalks and wafted pleasant smells as the citizens showered Alexander with rose petals. Soon, while the army quartermasters were sorting out provisions for supplies

---

Aerial view of Babylon, the 'metropolis of the world'.
Looking north over the heart of the city, at centre left are the
dug-out foundations of the Etemenanki, the 'Tower of Babel';
the Euphrates is at top left. Alexander came down the processional
way and entered through the Ishtar Gate, top right.

and rest and recreation, Alexander could kick off his boots in the palace of Nebuchadnezzar, lord of all he surveyed.

Babylon was one of the most ancient and famous of cities. For three millennia Iraq had been the centre of the civilized world, and in recent times Babylon had been its greatest city. The core of the place was a huge mud-brick rectangle divided by the Euphrates, largely as it stood the work of biblical Nebuchadnezzar two and a half centuries ago. The towering burned brick ramparts, though now old and crumbling, still 'gleamed like burnished bronze' in the autumn sunlight; there were great temples and pyramids, huge inner defence works, the main walls wide enough to drive four-horse teams along the top wall walks, the outer lines studded with massive bastions, berms and glacis of baked brick, surrounded by the Euphrates and a network of canals. In the northern sector, on the bank, there was a huge raised platform with immense moat walls reaching under the river to stop erosion. Here stood Nebuchadnezzar's palace, with four huge courtyards, their magnificent upper walls decorated with bands of blue enamelled bricks; their cedar-wood doors encased in bronze and inlaid with gold, silver and ivory – rather like the style employed later in great Iraqi mosques with their cedar-columned porticoes and geometric patterns of coloured stone, copper and mother of pearl. The apartments were roofed with cedar beams from the Lebanon, some gilded. Here was the private residence of the king with its audience hall, plunge bath, and sleeping accommodation which overlooked the river and the quay wall on one side and the royal gardens on the other. Outside his window was a lovely view. Northwards, in a curve of the river, he could look across terraces of a great garden planted with trees and dotted with pavilions or 'summer houses' – the famous Hanging Gardens. There were fruits, vines, date palms, oaks, tamarisks, fruit trees and pomegranates all fed by canal waters which came gushing down on to the gardens from above. Here, at the centre of the world, Alexander could take stock of things and plan the next phase of the war. (And, although there was, as yet, no cloud on his horizon, it would be in this same palace that he would die eight years later after his return from India.)

The tour guides no doubt did a roaring trade – fragments of one guide book to the city survive. *The city has ten quarters, each with its own gate, twenty-four great boulevards, forty-three temples of the great gods, 900 chapels of lesser gods and hundreds more neighbourhood shrines.* Along the river was a line of quays and docks, with stairs coming up into the streets, where traders landed their wares from the Gulf and India. Some landmarks were crumbling after the Persian occupation: the great temple Etemenanki (where the Amran shrine stands today in a walled garden) was decrepit and in need of renovation. Babylon had seen better days, but it was still probably the biggest and most glamorous city in the world. The Greeks had been there before, of course, as merchants, mercenaries and travellers. The city had been the subject of a famous set-piece by Herodotus in his *History* written a century before. This had contained descriptions of the ziggurat, the stepped pyramid sometimes identified with the Biblical Tower of Babel, and the Hanging Gardens; Herodotus had also included racy accounts of Babylonian social life, including ritual sex on the top of the ziggurat and prostitution with crocodiles(!) – a great forerunner of modern sensationalist anthropological travel literature.

Alexander, as usual, was solicitous of the local cults. Most pointedly, like a Babylonian king, he promised to rebuild the Esagila, the great shrine of the god Marduk, which Greek propaganda falsely claimed had been levelled by the Persian Xerxes the previous century. The Macedonian leaders had time to inspect the great tourist sites. For the army there was the usual round of games, festivals, athletic contests, and organized home-comforts. There was one month's leave, with many officers billeted in private homes; vast amounts of pay were spent on wine, women and song. Apart from professional prostitutes, the Greeks claimed that many other women were willing to entertain the troops and separate them from their hard-earned bonuses. The scenes described, in Curtius, of striptease at drunken banquets were perhaps isolated sensational cases, but sexual morality had not been a major element in Babylonian religion, especially in the big cities. For many in such a cosmopolitan place there may have been a mood of enjoyment and license.

Others spent this brief period in more intellectual pursuits. Callisthenes, the expedition historian, who was now riding on the crest of a wave, asked to inspect the astronomical records of the Babylonian priests which, through interpreters, they claimed went back over 30,000 years. (These were still written in cuneiform, which would only die out at the beginning of the Christian era.) No doubt Callisthenes's hosts spun him a few tall stories to impress him with the antiquity and greatness of their culture, although, of course, he was no slouch at hyperbole himself and was certainly not averse to embellishing a good story in the retelling. Those weeks in the great city must have been an eye-opening experience for the Macedonians. Still, though, along with the rest and recuperation, there was drill and training. Hard fighting lay ahead.

Was there any resistance in Babylonia? It seems not, but that is not to say the Greeks were welcomed by everyone, or even the majority. Until recently, the story has only been told from the Greek side. Now, however, with the discovery of the hitherto unknown Babylonian texts, including the astronomical diary, we can get a new slant on the native view of the Greek conquest of Babylonia. A recently translated Dynastic prophecy, for example, shows signs of overt hostility to Alexander and Macedonian rule expressed, to our knowledge, for the first time:

*A foreign prince will arise and seize the throne*
*For five years he will exercise sovereignty*
*The army of the Greeks will attack –*
*The Greeks will bring about the defeat of Darius's army*
*They will plunder and rob him.*
*But afterwards the king will refit*
*His army and raise his weapons again*
*Enlil Shamsh and Marduk*
*Will go at the side of his army and*
*He will bring about the overthrow of the Greek army*
*… The people who had gone through misfortune*
*will enjoy well being … the land will again be happy …*

This literary reversal of Darius's defeat echoes the last Shah of Iran who, till his dying day, refused to recognize or discuss the Macedonian conquest of Iran. But the prophecy was a pious hope. Alexander was now gathering intelligence on Darius prior to his next move. The advance was preceded by a major shake-up of army units, breaking down the old territorial divisions in the cavalry units (a possible hint that not all were keen to go any further, thinking the job done?). Alexander, though, was determined to capture Darius, and had already sent messengers ahead to negotiate the surrender of the enormous treasury of the Persian king at Susa, the winter capital of the Persian empire, over 600 kilometres to the south-east, near the head of the Persian Gulf. This was his next goal.

## INVASION OF IRAN

He left Babylon on 25 November to march on Susa. The full army was now with him, reinforced to 70,000 strong, and there have been few more expert and ruthless fighting machines in history. The route led him first over the Tigris, and through the well-ordered world of the Iraqi plain, criss-crossed by a tracery of rivers and irrigation canals, dotted with ancient cities of burnished mud-brick on their high mounds above the emerald-green flood plain.

Susa lies east of the Tigris in the hot plain of what is now Iranian Khuzestan, the Arabic-speaking corner of Persia. It lies in the lee of the Zagros Mountains, the great chain which extends from Armenia to the Persian Gulf. This is the dividing line between Iran and Iraq, between the alluvial plain of Mesopotamia and the high plateau which extends

Susa from the air, looking south. On the right is the acropolis by the
Shaoor river; at bottom right are the footings of the audience hall of
the Persian kings where Alexander sat on the throne of Xerxes.

from Iran all the way to the heart of Asia. It has been a war zone since the dawn of history, battled over by the kings of Ur and Elam, and by the Sasanian and Roman emperors, whose empire, at its most extended, reached the boiling south of Mesopotamia and the Gulf. In the 1980s it was a battleground again when Saddam Hussein attacked Iran and launched one of the most terrible of modern wars. In this border zone of Iran, trenches and ruined tanks are still seen by the roadside, and even in the streets.

That summer, we entered Iran during the month of Muharram, the time of mourning for Shiite Muslims, when great processions pass through the streets, and the hot nights echo to the sound of ancient laments: the tales of the great defeats. The greatest defeats of Persian culture were by Alexander, and then by the Arabs who came bearing the message of Islam. Both were assimilated, and, as we shall see, both Hellenism and Islam transformed the ancient Iranian civilization. There are many traditions here of Alexander, some of them radically opposed to each other. The folk memory of Iran is divided over Alexander. Here he is both The Accursed and the Shah of Shahs. He is a hero in Firdowsi's tenth-century epic, the *Shahnama*, which is still recited in coffee houses despite the convulsions of the last decades. For Firdowsi, Alexander is the rightful Shah, bequeathed the kingdom by Darius with his dying breath. On the other hand, Alexander appears in religious folk plays stalking the stage in a pith helmet and dark glasses along with the other villains of history, the wicked Caliph Yazid and the great Satan himself – Uncle Sam. Then again, to the Zoroastrians, the surviving followers of the ancient religion of Iran, he is the hated invader who destroyed their sacred books and killed their priests. As we had already seen on our journey, Alexander's is a tale which can be (and is) interpreted in many conflicting ways.

In Egypt and Babylon, Alexander had been greeted as a liberator with little or no opposition. From Iran on, though, he was on hostile territory. From here to India there would be resistance, often ferocious. He entered Iran in the winter of 331 BC, heading for the Zagros Mountains and the heartland of Darius's empire.

Near the Iraqi border we rejoined his route, the old Persian Royal Road coming from Babylon to Susa. This was still marked on maps which I carried with me, which were drawn up by British army intelligence for the invasion here in 1917. North-west of Susa we crossed the Karkheh river – where Alexander did – on a pontoon bridge built by the Iranian army. There, passports and identities were checked: this is a military zone and bridges are military installations. We were detained for a while by a zealous but charming captain. Alexander, however, met no opposition there. At this point in December 331, the governor of Susa met him at the river with a delegation bearing rich gifts – racing camels and a dozen Indian elephants. With that, the city was delivered to him without a fight.

Alexander arrived at the ancient city of Xerxes and Darius on 15 December. Modern Susa (Shush) is a dusty town in a wide fertile plain on the Karkeh river, an affluent of the Karun; it was the great emporium of Khuzestan up to Islamic times, though replaced now as the chief port by Ahwaz. Here, the first rains come mid-November – hence the timing of Alexander's march. He had clearly delayed to let the boiling heat of the Susa plain die down. The Greek geographer Strabo has a graphic description of it being so hot there in the summer that lizards and snakes could fry in the sun before they crossed the road. (We came in late summer, through a white haze of heat and dust, and I can vouch for Strabo on that. The streets were almost unwalkable in the middle of the day.)

Above the ugly concrete sprawl of the modern streets, what is left is a vast brown city mound burrowed by treasure seekers; mud-brick ruins; stovey heat; pearly white sky; and harsh glare off the beaten ground. Nothing remains of the dazzling colours which banded the walls and buildings. Fragments of the beautiful polychrome wall decorations, found in the palace, are now in the Louvre and Tehran. Recently discovered royal halls below the site, though, still have all the column bases in situ. On the top of the main mound is the French 'chateau' built in the nineteenth century and shell-damaged from the war with Iraq (the front line was only 6 kilometres off). The old city stood on a huge acropolis over the river, surrounded by a channelled arm of the river. Further great buildings lay outside, huge reception halls built by Artaxerxes, grand new building projects, not long before Alexander, which give the lie to the idea that the Persian empire was moribund by his time, and exhausted of its creativity.

The Macedonian officer corps strode into the great halls with their forest of cedar-wood columns glinting with gold leaf and pearl inlay (recalling newsreel images of the Nazi High Command inspecting Les Invalides or the Athens' Acropolis). Alexander sat on Xerxes's throne, but his feet did not touch the floor. Someone rushed a table under his feet. Applause. Then there was the sound of choked crying: an old Persian retainer, one of the palace staff, could not hold back his tears. Through interpreters, Alexander asked why he was weeping: 'His Majesty King Darius used to take his food from that table: it breaks my heart to see an uncivilised conqueror treading on it.' This was a sacrilege to Persian sensibility. Then a Macedonian spoke up: 'Your enemy's table has become your footstool: take that as an omen of your coming victory.'

The Biblical Book of Esther gives a hint of the riches Alexander would have found there. The storerooms were stacked with centuries of heirlooms and treasures. To their amazement the Greeks saw the loot taken by the Persians from the sack of Greece 150 years before: the famous statues of the regicides lifted from the Athenian acropolis, bales of beautiful purple-dyed cloths from the town of Hermione in the Peloponnese. A huge standing statue of Darius the Great, as an Egyptian Pharaoh, with inscriptions in cuneiform and hieroglyphic, was found headless in the debris by a French archaeologist in 1975. Of the wonderful Persian goldwork the Greeks saw, only a handful of exquisite pieces survived, the best in Tehran. Most of it must have been looted and melted down. Alexander also found bullion: 50,000 talents, another nine of minted coin (£22 million in

The glory of Susa: glazed brick wall decorations from the palace of
Darius the Great, c. 500 BC. Above: Griffons under the winged disc of Ahura
Mazda, the god of Wisdom. Right: The frieze of archers of the Persian royal
guard, the Immortals. A splendid archaic world swept away by Alexander.

1913 gold value – equivalent to the national income of the fifth-century Athenian empire for 150 years). There would be far more to come. At that moment, however, as the Persian palace officials busied themselves fearfully around Alexander, he must have realized he could now finance any war he wished – as far as the ends of the earth.

Out of the windows of the chateau, in the evening light, just as Alexander must have seen from the palace terrace, we glimpsed the far-off wall of the Zagros Mountains, the gateway to Persia and, beyond, the high plateau of Asia.

Towards sunset, the heat eases off a little and the little town comes to life after the long siesta: people go for a stroll round the bazaar streets and visit the mosque below the mound. This is the shrine of the prophet Daniel and is widely venerated by the Arabs of Iranian Khuzestan, and by Iranian Muslims, Jews and Christians from farther afield. A little courtyard, with a cloister and a pool for ablutions, leads into the carpeted tomb chamber, all cut-glass, prisms, and mirrored squinches which reflect the devotees who hang around offering their prayers before the silver cage. Inside, under a green cloth, is the tomb of the prophet. The custodian took an interest in our story. 'Christians and Jews, as well as Muslims, come here,' he said, 'all the people of the book.' He reminded us of the Book of Daniel and pulled out a copy of the Old Testament. Here in the Book of Daniel, Alexander appears in a weird prophecy which may preserve something of the cyclonic force of his arrival in Persia – as if he had some terrifying supernatural power – 'made by wrath', as if, in fact, he was the devil incarnate. In the Book of Daniel is the vision of the monster from the sea; The Third Beast:

> *It will be a time such as has never been seen … the people will fall by sword and flame, suffer captivity and devastation … a wicked man his mind set against the covenant.*

## FALL OF THE PERSIAN GATES

Past the winter solstice, towards New Year's Eve on the modern calendar, Alexander broke camp on the outskirts of Susa. The first part of our story is nearing its climax. Ahead lay the final thrust on Pars, the heartland of Persia. The old Ahwaz road leads along the flat southern plain past gas burn-offs and eroded sills of rock, on into the Uxian Mountains. Dramatic cliffs are clothed in small gnarled oak trees. Here, the natives demanded and received tolls from the Great King just as the Afghan hill-tribes did from the British Raj. Alexander was not the sort to stand for that and ruthlessly overpowered them in a brief campaign. He then pushed on eastwards. With him for his march into the interior was an army of 80,000. His goal was Persepolis, 'Parsa' – the huge Persian palace with the nearby royal tombs and shrines and sacred fires – the very heart of the empire.

When you travel today from Ahwaz towards the rugged mountainscape of Fars, the great mass of the Zagros Mountains gradually rises up on the left-hand side, and the old road soon runs right under their foothills as you near Nurabad. For Alexander, it was now mid-January, and the 5000-metre Zagros were covered with snow, the high routes impassable. Alexander stopped at what Diodorus Siculus calls the 'Susian Rocks' – perhaps the gigantic table mountain now called the White Castle, a legendary citadel in the tenth-century epic *Shahnama*, and besieged, among others, by Tamerlane. Here, where the Fahliun river flows out into a green plain, Alexander split the army. Parmenio took the main column round the waggon road on the long southerly loop to Persepolis via Shiraz. Parmenio was a safe pair of hands, but Alexander was often glad to split up. Parmenio was old guard, old school, his father's right-hand man. Alexander's apologists always portray the old man as conservative and cautious, a drag on Alexander's impetuous vision. Whatever the truth of that, he and Alexander did not always see eye-to-eye, and the king now seems to have preferred to get him out of his hair. Alexander took an élite force of nearly 20,000 through a short cut, a narrow defile through which the plain of Persepolis was entered. He wanted to get to Persepolis before Darius's men escaped with the treasury and was prepared to risk a little used route, an ancient military and trade route through the Zagros, a pass the Greeks knew as the Persian Gates.

The road he took leads up the valley of the Fahliun river: a bumpy uneven track which twice fords the river and zigzags over steep hills. Impossible, without local knowledge, to have travelled this way, I would guess. I had been up there before on reconnaissance trips and was forewarned. This time, we took our crew up on a local farm pick up which doubles as a taxi, and slept at the driver Bandar's house, ready for a dawn start. The road is so bad that it is scarcely believable this was once a famous route – let alone that an army could get through – but this was the ancient 'key to Anshan', a route thousands of years old, and it is still used by today's travellers on foot. In the suspicious world of today's Iran, it is guarded by a new police station on the east where the path comes out into the Fars plain. Before cars came to these parts twenty-five years ago, it was still the main short-cut from Nurabad plain into Fars.

Around us on the horizon, were the higher peaks of the Zagros. It is an isolated austere world out here, especially in winter. There is no electricity, for example, and in the uplands you cross paths with Bakhtiari nomads whose temporary villages are only open for the summer pastures. We passed ruined caravanserais, intact ancient bridges and the remains of a big Sasanian viaduct. Finally we stopped at the mouth of a deep-cut pass,

where a few wood and reed houses and a collapsed caravanserai stood under a great stand of poplars, all autumnal gold. This is the entrance to the Persian Gates. It was the scene of one of the most dramatic, and perhaps the most crucial, events in the whole of Alexander's invasion of Asia.

Today you have to walk in, as he did. At first, for Alexander, it was a gentle ascent alongside waterfalls and streams, oak and plane trees. (Ironically, later Arab and Persian geographers thought this one of the four earthly paradises.) Then disaster struck. The official version, in Arrian, only admitted to local difficulties. The alternative tradition of Diodorus and Curtius shows that the Greeks went deep into the pass before they realized the Persians had led them into a trap. At the narrowest and most difficult point, where the cliffs come right in, the path was blocked by a wall. Suddenly stones, javelins and artillery rained down upon them. There were heavy losses. Leaving his dead where they fell, Alexander retreated to the open area below the modern hamlet of Mulla Susan. There the Greeks made camp, lit fires and tried to come up with an alternative plan. At that moment the success of the invasion of Persia was in the balance.

That first night, we were forced to make our way down the Pass and back to our campsite in pitch darkness under a moonless sky, stumbling across steep broken ground under the jagged spurs at the mouth of the gorge. It gave us a graphic insight into conditions the Greek troops must have experienced. We had a local guide (Zavore is a teacher in Nurabad whose summer home is up here), but we could hardly see the person in front, and getting down a thickly wooded ravine and across a stream in total darkness, aided by only a box of matches, was nerve shredding. After a couple of hours we struggled into Mulla Susan. Desperately weary we put up our tents on the terrace of Zavore's house, which he had opened up for us. It was late November, but uncommonly sunny. Below us was the entrance to the Persian Gates and the open space where Alexander must have camped after his reverse in the Pass.

With the Gates blocked, Alexander interrogated his prisoners for another way round. It was the usual thing: good information lavishly rewarded; false or incorrect information rewarded with death – simple, but effective. A local shepherd came to Alexander. He was from Lycia, a former captive, and spoke Greek. He had grazed his flocks in these hills for years. He said there was a way – a rocky and difficult route round to the back of the Pass; nearly 20 kilometres on donkey paths. But is it possible for an army? Alexander asked.

---

At the Persian Gates. The white cliff at the narrows of the pass where
Alexander was surprised by the Persian defenders and forced to retreat.
The exact location had never been discovered until our expedition.

Absolutely not, said the shepherd. None the less, Alexander decided to go. He probably had no choice now. But where was the secret path? No one has ever found it.

Round our campfire, Zavore and his brother argued over which path Alexander might have taken; the older brother was adamant that the way straight up behind us was out of the question because of the thick snow which falls there in January. (We know for sure that the Greeks encountered snow.) Zavore would have none of this. With the fire burning low, they continued to disagree as we bedded down for the night. They had, however, agreed to take us next day with donkeys carrying our gear – perhaps the first time anybody had attempted this in modern times.

At dawn, we loaded the donkeys, dampened the camp fires and began the circling move up the long valley from Mulla Susan, a two- or three-hour ascent at a brisk walk with mules. But imagine 15,000 men making this journey at night. The sheer daring of it all became all too apparent as we pursued him. Then, suddenly, we came out on to a wide tableland fringed by mountains. In the summer the black tents are everywhere here with their herds. (If the story of the shepherd is true, this is where he grazed his flocks.) At a lunch stop in a chill wind, we brewed black tea over a wood fire sheltered from the gale by piled stones. Zavore cooked handfuls of bitter woody acorns and we ate them with thin Iranian bread, goats cheese and olives. (I imagined something like this for Alexander's men too.)

On top, all became clear, not least the incredible bravado of Alexander's plan if, as Arrian says, it was really all done in one night. Here the Greeks said the forces split and made a turn to the right. They would have stopped up here before midnight. The troops would have filed up, making a brief halt to take some food and wine. (Each man carried basic rations for three days.) As the wind scoured the bleak hills, I imagined Alexander in urgent conference with his commanders; the head of engineers, in case they needed bridges building; the surveyor Baethon, working out marching speeds and timings and all the while interrogating their local guides: 'How far is the Kur river? How far to Persepolis? What are the obstacles? Are the rivers fordable?' There would have been ruthless interrogation of prisoners: 'How many troops has Ariobarzanes got in the pass? How many men does he have in the plain behind? Is Parsa defended?' Then came the division of the forces, each led by closely guarded local guides. Three phalanx brigades led by Amyntas, Philotas and Coenus, with some light units (about 7000 men) were to go straight on to bridge the Kur river ready for the lightning attack on Persepolis. Alexander himself took the Longshields, Perdiccas' phalanx brigade, the archers, 1000 Agrianians (light armed mountain specialists), the Royal Squadron of the Companions, plus one double squadron of cavalry. These men, about 5000 strong, were to make the turning movement on to the back of the pass. After midnight they set off again, gritting their teeth in the icy wind. And still the Persians had no inkling of their approach.

Following in their footsteps, there was almost a thrill of fear as we set off; one could only be awestruck at the sheer daring of it all. Only people inured to warfare (and hardened to living in mountains) could have even thought of attempting it, let alone pulling it off. But the Macedonian army was a tight-knit military machine; its men so confident in their charismatic young leader and in their own collective ability that they were prepared to undergo any hardship; so disciplined that they lacked fear. In the early hours, Alexander closed in on the back of the Pass. Meanwhile, according to Arrian (who had Ptolemy's memoirs on his desk), Ptolemy was left with 3000 specialist infantry to come down on to the middle of the enemy position by a secret route. This has never been explained because no one has ever traced the route on the ground, but we found the key clue.

From the edge of the high plateau where the Greek army split up, we could overlook the middle of the Pass and the heart of the Persian defences; and, just here, is a deep ravine which brings you down off the heights right on to the middle of the Persian position. This must be where Ptolemy came. As dusk came on, we descended it with donkeys, stumbling down a narrow deep-cut gorge into growing darkness. Eventually we were forced to light torches made of the bark of the gum tree (an old shepherds' trick), each of which will burn for fifteen minutes. According to Curtius, at some point on the night journey, there was a frighteningly deep ravine blocking the route and only at first light did the way down this become clear. If he got this detail from Ptolemy's memoirs, then this must have been the ravine we struggled down that night, with the sound of wolves howling up on the plateau, trying to eke out our precious supply of bark torches. It was a nerve-wracking couple of hours till we made camp. What it had been like for the Greeks that January night, we could only imagine.

Soon, as first light came, the way down was clear, and Ptolemy moved his forces down out of sight of the defenders, close to the inner defences ready for the attack. Meanwhile, at daybreak, Alexander had reached the back of the Pass. The trap was sprung. Alexander's trumpets sounded behind the Persians, and were answered by Craterus who had moved from the original camp back to the wall where the Greeks were first repulsed. The Persians were caught. Both ends of the Pass were blocked and Ptolemy was waiting at the middle. At first light, Alexander fell on the Persians from behind; Craterus attacked the wall; Ptolemy hit the heart of their defences. Despite their desperate position, the Persians fought with great bravery. In a savage battle the Persians were overwhelmed, although Ariobarzanes broke through and escaped with a few cavalry and 5000 infantry. The victory was decisive and has been called 'one of the most hazardous, audacious, and certainly the most profitable of mountain campaigns in the annals of history'.

## PERSEPOLIS – 'MOST HATED CITY IN THE WORLD'

The way to Persepolis was clear for Alexander. The Persians were now in total disarray and virtually paralysed with fear. Ariobarzanes – the one Persian hero in the sorry story – fell back on Persepolis, only to die fighting in a desperate last-ditch stand in front of the walls, shut out by his own side. Up in the windswept hills around Mulla Susan, though, among the Luri shepherds he is still a local hero – the one man 'who beat the great Iskander'.

Alexander reached Persepolis – the ritual and symbolic centre of the empire – on 30 January 330 BC. It is an atmospheric spot: a wide plain fringed by mountains, wheat fields, goatbells tinkling at sunset. It is resonant with echoes of Persian history. Behind a screen of fir trees are the tents of the abandoned encampment built by the last Shah for his great celebration here in 1970 to celebrate two and a half millennia of Persian monarchy. As a symbol the palace is hard to beat and has remained so, not only to the last Shah. Indeed, after the Shah's fall in 1979, one of the more extreme clerics, aware of the power of the place as a symbol of the monarchy, called for Persepolis to be demolished. Thankfully, it survived.

Anxious to stay as close to the palace ruins as possible, we persuaded the old hotel by the ruins to open up. An Art Deco place, built in the time of the last Shah's father, it has seen better days but deserves resurrection. The gardens are overgrown, palms hang sadly, the stagnant pool is full of croaking frogs, but, from its terrace, one may glimpse through the trees the ghostly shape of the palace on its natural rock platform, reminiscent of the Athenian acropolis, huge columns like white fingers in the misty night. Beyond the palace ruins was a dark shadow against the sky, the Mount of Mercy, site of the royal tombs of the last Persian kings. A sacred place in the Persian story.

The palace is open to the sky, only a dozen of its immense columns still standing. It once stood in splendid isolation, surrounded by three huge walls, with bronze gates flanked by great flagstaffs, as described by the later Greek historian Diodorus of Sicily from a unique eye-witness account which must come from someone on Alexander's expedition. Also scattered about the royal terrace were royal treasuries and the residences of the kings and members of the royal family, as well as quarters for the great nobles, the leaders of the royal army, all luxuriously appointed. The main town was 3 kilometres away at Istakhr where there were grand houses of the Persian aristocracy and lesser members of the royal family. Here, too, was kept the main sacred fire of the empire, the holiest religious symbol for the ancient Persians, which will play a part later on in our story.

Alexander ascended the citadel terrace and took possession of the palace of the Great King. His first sight of the palace – perhaps the most magnificent building in his world – must have been awe inspiring. Built by successive generations, it was still being added to in the years before Alexander. The palace was a great theatre where the rituals of the empire – hidden from the eyes of the masses – were acted out rather like the durbars of the British in India. The great audience halls and royal apartments were excavated in the 1930s and, under a great layer of debris, the carved friezes were found intact. They showed ambassadors from Ethiopia, India, Central Asia and from Greek Ionia, lining up to ascend the grand staircase to the hall of audiences, holding gifts from half the world. Images of the king are everywhere: receiving homage, slaying demons, attended by the bearers of fly whisk, towel and unguent pot; the face impassive and featureless under a starched, curled wig, marcelled beard and make-up. To the Greeks such things were the essence of despotic oriental kingship. The Greek sources make much of Darius's effeminacy and cowardice, in portraits larded with all the clichés of oriental tyranny; indeed some of the Greek descriptions of the Persians and their kings take their place among the early manifestations of European 'orientalism'. As we have seen, the story from Darius's point of view has yet to be told.

Also still here in the vaults – due to the speed and surprise of Alexander's march – was the main treasure of the Persian king: 120,000 talents of gold and another 8000 in treasure (£44 million in 1913 gold-standard equivalent; the national income of the Athenian empire for 300 years by fifth-century BC purchasing power). It would take 7000 pack animals to carry it off. Into Alexander's hands had fallen the greatest treasure in history. He was now able to wage war across the entire land mass of Asia.

The army was ordered not to touch the palace, but Alexander had to reward his troops for their victory – he had after all long ago promised them the loot of the 'most hated city on earth'. The city, which the Greeks also call Persepolis, cannot have abutted the palace. Most likely it was the nearby city of Istakhr, a site of one of the three great sacred fires of pre-Islamic Persia. Now, only a few broken columns and lotus capitals remain amid a heap of debris on the road to Pasargadae to show where it stood. The city was given over to the Macedonian troops for plunder and a horrific sack took place, with looting and rape on an horrendous scale (recalling to us modern atrocities like the Soviet sack of Berlin in May 1945). The description of the sack is probably authentic, even though it comes from a source hostile to Alexander. The following quote from Diodorus, in its use of the word *hubris* (overwhelming arrogance such as invites disaster) conveys the sense of a great wrong done, an offence against natural order and justice: a mark over-stepped and punishable by the gods.

> *Alexander described the city to the Macedonians as the most hateful city in Asia and gave it over to his soldiers to plunder, all but the royal palaces. It was the richest city under the sun and over the years the private houses had been furnished with every sort of wealth. The Macedonians raced into it killing all the men and looting the residences; many of the houses belonged to the ordinary people and were abundantly supplied with furniture and clothes of every kind. Here much silver was carried off and no little gold, and many rich dresses gay with sea purple or with gold embroidery were seized by the victors. The grand mansions of the royal family, famed throughout the whole civilised world fell victim to hubris and utter destruction. The Macedonians gave themselves up to this orgy of plunder for a whole day and still could not satisfy their boundless greed for more. In fact such was their overpowering lust for loot that they ended up fighting each other for it and killed many of their companions who had got more of it for themselves. The richest finds some hacked apart with their swords so each could have his share. In arguments over some pieces, grasping hands were actually cut off, so their frenzy drove them mad. And the women they dragged off, clothes and all, turning captives into slaves. And so, as Persepolis had exceeded all other cities in prosperity, so in the same measure it now exceeded all in misery.*
>
> DIODORUS SICULUS *Library of History* Book XVII 70

During his stay at Persepolis, Alexander rode out to the Persian royal tombs at Naksh-i-Rustam. There, perhaps, he mused in front of these imposing memorials of the emperors who had made the empire: Darius I whose invasion of Greece had ended at Marathon; Xerxes who had scourged and bridged the Hellespont, and defeated the Spartans at Thermopylae, only to suffer disaster at Salamis. Sombre and magnificent, each bearing the winged symbol of Ahura Mazda, the Zoroastrian creator God, these tombs were testimony to the long vistas of Iranian history. What were the thoughts of the young Greek conqueror at that moment? Not only the present wealth of the Persians, but even the graves of the ancestors were in his power.

Alexander also visited Pasargadae to confiscate the treasure held in the palace there. Its broken columns still stand in a wide plain ringed with mountains, blown by icy winds in winter, scorched in summer. These fields are an old nomadic gathering ground, the heartland of ancient Persian kingship. Here, on a little stone plinth with seven high steps, was the tomb of Cyrus the Great, the founder of the empire. Alexander entered. Inside, was a gilt coffin on a table, ancient swords, a shield and bow. Like the inner sanctum at Siwa, this is one of the few rooms still standing in which we know he stood. It is said that the inscription over the door read 'Know traveller that I was Cyrus, who founded the empire of the Persians. Grudge me not therefore this small piece of earth which covers my body'. Chastened, Alexander respected the remains. It is an atmospheric spot which emphasizes the origin of the Persian monarchy in itinerant cattle-herding warrior bands whose vigorous early chiefs created settled kingship only in the 530s BC, and whose descendants rose to world empire in two generations. The local tribespeople call the tomb the Mother of Solomon. Until recently, the Luri nomads on their annual migrations from the plains to the high pastures in the Zagros would circle it singing and leave mares' milk and honey smeared on its steps; one of the strange survivals of the archaic Iranian universe upon which the traveller continually stumbles on his journey through today's Iran.

Alexander now waited at Persepolis until late May or early June. But why? At Persepolis, the Persian kings held their great annual New Year festival. Was Alexander expecting to be crowned by the Persians, accepted as easily as he had been in Egypt? No such luck. No procession took place that year, no New Year Festival proclaimed Alexander as Ahura Mazda's representative on earth. At Luxor, in Egypt, the king is depicted on the walls in full pharaonic garb, and in recent years archaeologists have found statues of the deified Alexander from Anatolia to Tajikistan. At Persepolis, however, there is no picture of Alexander with Persian beard attended by the major domos of fly whisk and sunshade, and the bearers of the unguent pot and towel. Indeed, nowhere in Iran is he portrayed as a Persian king.

So there may have been negotiations with Darius, or with opposition elements in the Persian high command. Other reasons for the long delay may be as persuasive. The passes over the Zagros are often thick with snow in winter and sometimes do not open till April. (Modern British military intelligence surveys and travellers' reports from the nineteenth century often remark on the impassability of the Zagros in the winter.) On the other hand, sometimes the road north is open as early as January — so perhaps we have to seek another explanation for the king's delay.

In late May or early June, an unexpected and extraordinary twist comes in the tale. The story is told in substantially the same way by Plutarch, Curtius and Diodorus, although barely mentioned by Arrian who perhaps thought it a blot on the king's reputation; but there may have been some doubt on the part of the ancient authorities as to the

Parsa. The magnificent palace of Persian kings which the Greeks called Persepolis. The picture on the right shows the apadana, the reception hall where the Persian kings held their annual durbars to receive tribute from half the world.

truth of the tale. This, at any rate, was the most widely told, and sensational version. The king had held games at Persepolis in honour of his victories, and performed costly sacrifices. On the fateful night a great banquet was held at which women were present (which was not customary in traditional Macedonian drinking parties). Among them was a famous Athenian courtesan called Thais. This is how Diodorus tells it:

> *While they were feasting and the drinking was far advanced, as they began to be intoxicated, a madness* [lussa – has a connotation of possession] *took possession of the minds of the intoxicated guests. At this point one of the women present an Athenian called Thais, said that it would be the crowning achievement in Asia if Alexander would join them in a triumphal procession* [kommos – a ritual dance] *to set fire to the palaces and let women's hands extinguish the glories of the Persians. This was said to young men giddy with wine, as would be expected someone shouted form the line and light the torches, take vengeance for the destruction of the Greek temples* [i.e., by Xerxes 150 years previously]. *Others joined in saying this was a deed worthy of Alexander alone. The king caught fire at their words and all leaped from their couches and passed the word to form a victory procession in honour of Dionysus* [the God of possession, ecstasy]. *Quickly many torches were brought. There were flute girls present so the king led them all out to singing and the sound of flutes and pipes, Thais the prostitute* [tes etairas] *leading. She was the first, after the king, to hurl her blazing torch into the palace. As the others did the same, the entire palace area was immediately engulfed in fire, so great was the conflagration. It was most remarkable that the impious act of Xerxes King of the Persians, should have been repaid in kind after so many years, by one woman, a citizen of the land which had suffered it – and all in sport.*
>
> <div align="center">DIODORUS SICULUS <i>Library of History</i> Book XVII 72</div>

To us it is a crucial psychological moment in Alexander's story. What was he up to? Was it an accident? Or deliberate vandalism? Can the story about Thais be true? There is general agreement today that the palace was deliberately destroyed, but a new examination of the archaelogical evidence for the fire has suggested a systematic firing of Xerxes's rooms rather than the haphazard work of drunken revellers. What does that tell us? Maybe Alexander was letting the Greeks at home know he had not forgotten his mission of pan-Hellenic vengeance (especially at a time when his Spartan enemy King Agis was mounting armed resistance against him in Southern Greece).

Perhaps, too, though Alexander was saying to the Persians, this is the end of your time: my time has begun now. Perhaps he was drawing a line under the past which led back to the Persian burning of the Acropolis 150 years before. By destroying the psycho-spiritual centre of their empire he was announcing the cutting off of their ancient past and the dawn of a new age.

## ALEXANDER THE ACCURSED

How did the Persians feel about him at this moment? As always with Alexander's tale we are stuck with a story only told by the victors. But not entirely. In fact, strange oracle texts have survived which speak of the long-haired man of violence who came from the west wreaking havoc, respecting neither god nor man:

> *One day there shall come into the rich lands of Asia an unbelieving man,*
> *Wearing on his shoulders a purple cloak,*
> *Savage, fiery, a stranger to justice. For a thunderbolt raised him up,*
> *Though he is but a man. All Asia shall suffer a yoke of evil,*
> *And its soaked earth shall drink much blood.*
> *But even so Hades shall attend him even though he knows it not:*
> *And in the end those whom he wished to destroy,*
> *By them will he and his race be destroyed.*

This tradition of Alexander has never died out in Persia, and it is still maintained by the keepers of the old religion in Persia – the Zoroastrians. These are the survivors of the ancient Persians, direct descendants of the people conquered by Alexander. They still light their lamps, tend their sacred trees and perform their ancient rituals to Ahura Mazda. Only a few thousand are left now in Iran. But theirs is the religion of Darius and Xerxes, and it shaped all that came after. Theirs are the symbols found on the walls of Persepolis, Naksh-i-Rustam, Pasargadae. They follow Zoroaster, first of the great monotheistic prophets. He lived around 1500 BC near the Aral Sea in what is now Uzbekistan. He preached a robust and moral way of life in words which have been passed down orally for thousands of years. The Zoroastrians have maintained his ideals despite the blows of history (the biggest of which were Alexander, and the Arab Muslim conquest), and they give us a living contact with the world of Darius.

To meet them, we made a detour from Persepolis out eastwards beyond the Zagros to Yazd in the Great Salt Desert. A magnificent mud-brick city, which was admired by Marco Polo, it gives the best idea of the Persian cities which were seen by the Greeks.

Massive mud-brick defences, storied houses, covered lanes, domed shrines, tanks, and cisterns, all in mud-brick. Here, too, you can see the peculiar architecture evolved here for living with the desert: underground tunnels which carry water from the mountains to the city; ice-houses, and the towering wind-catchers which are designed to trap the slightest breeze and conduct it down into the inner chambers to cool perspiring harems in the furnace heat of the Yazd summer.

Local legend says Alexander used Yazd as his prison, a place for political exiles. This is not impossible. It is an isolated world, protected by the desert and sustained by its own artificial eco-system. Here the last of the ancient Persians have survived, preserving their ancient language, their sacred books, and the rituals of their forefathers, among them the archaic death-rites at the so-called Towers of Silence. No faith, perhaps, has shown such incredible tenacity in the face of long persecution: theirs has been a victory of memory over forgetting. They have not forgotten Alexander either. As one member of the Yazd congregation told me:

> *He may be the Great to the Greeks, and to you Europeans, but we call him a devil. This is because he burned down our temples, killed our priests; he forcibly made our children marry Greeks to make them lose their identity; he destroyed our most precious holy book, our Bible, the* Avesta, *which was written on 12,000 calf skins in letters of gold. So, why should we call him the Great? To us he is a devil. For this reason we call him Iskander Gujaste. Alexander the Accursed.*

The Zoroastrians have not forgotten: they have kept the flame burning. Literally. For, amazingly, the sacred flame of the Persian kings, which was worshipped at Persepolis, has never been snuffed out. During the Middle Ages the priests carried it from place to place, often in secret, to avoid destruction. Sometimes they were even forced to divide the embers. Eventually it came to rest in the Yazd plain, and finally early this century to a little village north of Yazd – where it still burns today. It is kept in the village fire temple in a locked room with no windows. No one may enter except consecrated priests. Only a purified Zoroastrian may even look on it. Here each morning, the hereditary custodians, the Belivani family, still tend the fire – chanting the ancient hymns which Darius and Xerxes knew.

---

The old religion of Iran. Zoroastrian pilgrims, at the shrine of Pir-i-Sabz, near Yazd, reciting the *Avesta*, a text already old in Alexander's day.

I waited outside the room, the smoke hanging in a beam of light, surrounded by pictures of the prophet and photos of Zoroastrian boys who had died fighting in the war with Iraq. Through the door Belivani's son recited the *Avesta*, amid choking smoke from the fire. It was one of the most amazing moments on our journey: the knowledge that, through the revolutions of history, something as insubstantial as fire could survive: a fire which has burned since the days of Alexander, the fire before which Darius worshipped.

## THE HUNTING OF DARIUS

Back at Persepolis, Alexander had now been waiting since mid-January. It was now early June – harvest time in the Zagros. The passes were open, food supply dumps for the army had been set up in each of the little plains along the route through the Zagros. Alexander had to decide what to do next. Persepolis was destroyed. Darius was still at large, still it seems hoping to mount further resistance. Perhaps Alexander's intelligence had discovered by now that Darius was in Ecbatana, 600 kilometres to the north. With him were his élite cavalry, his Greek mercenaries (who remained loyal to him) and some of his nobles, including Bessus, satrap of Bactria, a royal kinsman, and cavalry leader at Arbela. Their backs were against the wall now. Darius may, as one source suggests, have contemplated fighting at Ecbatana, but he seems to have rapidly given up the idea. For what happened next we have not only the Greek story, but also information from the Persian side incorporated into later Greek and Latin writings. Clearly, after these events someone took the trouble to interview Persian participants about the events during the last grim month of Darius's life. In these passages, the Persian king does not appear as the cowardly effeminate portrayed by the Greeks, the man who, as Arrian says, was almost 'irrationally incompetent in matters of war'. They afford us a privileged glimpse into the tent of the doomed Persian king as he and his officers desperately tried to stave off disaster, along with the loyal Greek mercenaries, who had no reason to love Alexander and every reason to fear his triumph and who stuck by Darius until the end. In these accounts, Darius emerges as a brave man in an impossible position, still trying to organize resistance, condemned to act out the roles of the cosmic king and army leader despite the fact that all around him was collapsing.

Alexander headed north. His journey led us on, via Pasargadae, to Isfahan. Here, the modern road often runs close to the old through an empty countryside. *En route*, between bleak uplands, we passed oases dotted with mounds and the ruins of caravanserais, tombs and forts. We saw the mud-brick fortified farms at Surmaq which must have looked no different from those of Alexander's day. (There, the road splits to Abarqu and the most ancient sacred tree in Iran, which was already old when the Greeks came through.) In the middle of the day we went through the mud-brick village of Izadhvast teetering with its balconied houses over a steep gorge. Towards dusk, the weird rock outcrops of Sahreza loomed ahead. Alexander was advancing with a relatively small mobile force – largely because none of these oases before Isfahan could support the full army. This explains the historical importance of Isfahan, whose name means 'the army camp': the ancient Persian city of Gabae. What you see today is pre-eminently the imperial city of the seventeenth century with its gorgeous mosques and bridges and the grand central piazza, where horse and traps trot to and fro, while the townsfolk sit in the cafés taking faloudeh and ice-cream under domes of gold and kingfisher.

We spent the night in the old city behind the great mosque in a narrow overhanging street. There, in a wrestlers café, we saw a tale-teller from Luristan in a tight-waisted Luri coat and white felt hat. On request, he was prepared to perform a tale of Iskander, although they are not done now by the reciters of the *Shahnama:* 'The public like to hear the old favourites, Rustam and Sorabh, but I can do it for you,' he said. He was nearly seventy, and worked as a butcher in a state shop for army personnel in a drab suburb. In the café a fountain bubbled while waiters rushed trays of tea in little bulbous glasses to a clientele of market-workers smoking hookahs. Above them the TV showed a Koranic quiz-show as the Luri strode up and down swinging his wooden staff, telling the story of Alexander's Persian mother, and his fabulous journey to China.

Later, I wandered the streets round the old bazaar and found myself in a delightful college courtyard with a pool and rose garden. There, a pleasant young Shiite scholar in a long black robe engaged me in conversation:

'Alexander's in the Holy Koran you know.'

'Really?' 'Yes, he is Dhul Qarnain, which means the Two Horned one.' (A title which curiously recalls the famous image of Alexander on his coins with the rams' horns as son of Zeus-Ammon.) 'It's a strange passage and, of course, Muslim scholars have argued over it for centuries, but many say it's him. Iranians never accepted Greek rule, but Greek thought was always important to Islam – especially for us Shiites. We still teach the Greek philosophers and doctors in our university courses. For us Plato is still divine.'

He smiled as we parted: 'Iskander. Ah, yes, when we were children my mother used to frighten us. "If you don't do your homework, go to bed early, Iskander will get you!"'

Outside, night had fallen over the Great Mosque, one of the handful of most wonderful buildings of the world. Sodium lights in the streets spilled on to its great terracotta-coloured dome. I strolled on into a little courtyard, with a late-night tea stall, piles of grain and the bustle of business. Upstairs, the light was still burning where the comptroller sat in

'The world-lord held Sikander's hand and wept'. A traditional
Iranian tale-teller performs the story of Darius's death as told by the
medieval Persian poet Firdowsi. On the painted backdrop Alexander
cradles the dying Darius in his arms. This story, which goes back to
the Greek Alexander Romance, was written in Alexandria in
Hellenistic times.

his little blue-curtained accounting room above a rickety wooden arcade. Alexander can
only have stayed here long enough to replenish his own supplies. Time was now of the
essence.

Now came the climax of this part of the tale, when Alexander finally caught up with
Darius after a series of almost superhuman forced marches. It was July and very hot

indeed. Alexander heard that Darius had left Ecbatana and had cut across eastwards towards Afghanistan. Alexander set off in pursuit. His journey took us across the corner of the Great Salt Desert, one of the most inhospitable places in the world. Today, you go via the Shiite holy city of Qum, and out to the east you see a white 'sea' of salt like a mirage. Alexander's journey took eleven days to Ray (old Tehran), a march which had the army on its knees with heat, thirst and fatigue.

Alexander's route took him on eastwards in hot pursuit of Darius. The Great King was now a hunted man and did not have long to live. He passed through the Caspian Gates: a sinister dark defile whose crags are capped with a Sasanian fortress. Liquid salt streams down the cliff face. According to the Persian source, there was some discussion as to whether they should fight Alexander there, but again they rejected the idea when a bold offensive might just have pulled off a miracle. Often Alexander's impetuosity left him personally exposed and put him at risk. A courageous commando attack to try to kill him might have saved Darius. But by now Darius lacked the will, resource or cunning to pull it off.

Alexander's marches continued on through the night until noon, then he stopped for food and water, and rested till dusk – the best way to travel in this climate. The route marches and overnight stops are the same as those undertaken by medieval geographers and travellers. The oases have not changed over the centuries, and are still there on the old road at the end of each day's journey, by-passed by the heavy lorries now roaring east to Mashad on the new highway. Alexander must have camped at the oasis of Deh Namak. This is now a sprawl of mud-brick houses, crumbling caravanserais, derelict cisterns and ice-houses. Beyond these is the railway track to Mashad and, through the white glare, the distant shore of the Great Salt Desert. The route eastwards, the old Khorasan Road, is the Silk Route here, following the narrow fertile strip of oases between the Elburz Mountains and the Salt Desert. Alexander was not the first (nor the last) world-conqueror to come through. In the middle of Deh Namak is a towering old mud-brick fort, built long ago to protect the village in time of troubles. Over a cup of chai under its walls, the villagers explained:

> *This fort was thrown up when the Mongols came through, somewhere for the people to take shelter. Things have not been the same for us since Genghis Khan came through.*

They could have been talking of recent history. But then history in a lot of these places stopped for centuries after Genghis Khan.

'What about *Iskander e Rumi; Iskander dhul carnain*?' I asked. 'Any stories about him?'

An old villager shook his head, a twinkle in his eye: 'Yes. He came through, too. I didn't see him myself, though! He was bad for Iran. He killed so many people. We old folks still have a saying about a greedy person. We say he's just like Iskander, he wants the whole world!'

## DEATH OF DARIUS

Alexander reached a place called Thara (perhaps the modern Semnan) and there learned that, only the previous night, Darius had been overthrown by his own commanders, led by Bessus. Our source from the Persian side (summarized by the Roman historian Curtius) says there was a heated exchange in the Persian council. Everyone could see the situation was desperate; Darius declared that he wanted to continue the fight. Nabarzanes, the second in rank in the empire after Darius, pointed out that adverse gods and bad fortune had plagued the Persians: 'There is need of a new initiative and new omens'. He proposed that 'the auspices and the rule' be temporarily entrusted to a substitute king, Darius's kinsman Bessus, the satrap of Bactria. Then, after the victory, they would return the sovereignty to its rightful owner. (Note they still respect the numinous power of the office of Great King.) This proposal, however, Darius vehemently refused. Only then, with the king apparently deeply depressed, was Darius taken prisoner and ceremonially bound in 'fetters of gold'. At this moment, says Curtius, there was heard a loud wailing and weeping by the king's eunuchs. Perhaps this was a lament to the gods for the kingship in supreme crisis; perhaps a foreshadowing of his fate? To hide the king from the gaze of the rank-and-file, they put him in a covered wagon and then pressed on.

Alexander knew the Persians were within reach. This prompted the last urgent night-dash. He needed to overtake Darius, but the long chaotic train of refugees, and fleeing troops, blocked the road ahead. Alexander questioned the locals about an alternative route.

On the eastern horizon, as the sun sets, is the great massif of the Ahuran hills. The main caravan road follows these hills up to the Ahuran Pass. It is a slow narrow road that winds and climbs up to the top of the Pass where there are two magnificent serais, one early Islamic, one Safavid. (This is an old stopping place on the road to Afghanistan.) This was the route taken by the retreating Persians, but Alexander could never have over-taken them by following them this way, as the road was jammed with fugitives. He asked the locals for an out-flanking route, and they gave him one: 80 kilometres with no water round the hills to the south through the fringe of the Salt Desert. He immediately saddled up, dismounting some of his weary cavalry and putting 500 of his toughest infantry on the cavalry horses. There was no time to lose.

The out-flanking route was longer as the crow flies, but, looking at it on a map, it makes sense. The railway engineers – practical men – took the same route. When you pick up the Mashad slow train at Semnan, you follow it, an easy gradient circling south of the Ahuran hills. We got off at Gerd Ab, and slept in the station waiting-room surrounded by a deserted cluster of mud-brick houses, a grove of trees and a long wind-swept platform. Walking down below the village, we soon picked up the route Alexander had taken, a wide dried-up wadi snaking 30 kilometres through the weirdly coloured ridges of the Salt Desert. It is good riding country – a five-hour trot on a warm summer night; quicker still at a jog. Just before dusk I walked out and climbed a great eroded ridge above the wadi, from where wide vistas opened up in both directions. As darkness fell it was easy to imagine Alexander coming through, harnesses jangling, muffled whispers in Greek. For the last 25 kilometres you head up a long rise towards the main caravan road at the back of the pass. Starting in the night, it would have been simple for Alexander to overtake much of the retreating Persian column and get behind the Pass before dawn.

In the first light, somewhere on the old Tehran-Mashad road beyond the Ahuran Pass, Alexander caught up with the Persian leaders. At the first sight of the Macedonians, Bessus and his fellow conspirators told Darius to get on a horse and go with them. They would ride east to Bactria. Still dignified in this extremity, Darius refused. Exasperated, they stabbed him and left him dying in his covered waggon. Bessus and the conspirators then rode off just as Alexander closed in with a mere 150 troops. If the Persians had kept their wits about them, they might even have killed Alexander there and then – but all order was gone and they were just desperate to save themselves. Dust-streaked and wild-haired, Alexander and his men rode up and down the pile-up of vehicles, searching frantically for the Great King.

By the time they found him, the light was up. Imagine a patch of vivid green cultivation in a brown desert. A few hundred metres off the road there was a spring in a little valley, perhaps with a few cypress trees. According to the Greek historians, the cart bearing the King of the World had stopped at the pool, the animals stuck with spears. There, a Greek soldier found Darius still alive, stabbed by his captors. The soldier brought him some water in a helmet, and exchanged a few words (Darius spoke some Greek). He conveyed to Alexander his thanks for his honourable treatment of his mother and family (a very Persian thing to say, this). It was also said, by the Greeks, that before his death Darius bequeathed his empire to Alexander. But this is, surely, just the crowning example of Greek propaganda – they would say that, wouldn't they? Darius was dead by the time Alexander came up. He covered the body with his cloak, and was said to have been visibly shocked by the squalid end of the King of the World.

The place has never been found but, if my hunch is right, there is only one place this can have happened. There is only one source of water between the Ahuran Pass and Quse where Alexander subsequently stopped. Just 800 metres from the now-abandoned old Khorasan road, a little way downhill from the junction with the desert path which must have been taken by Alexander, there is a lovely village by a spring-fed pond. It is a country place of mud-brick with walled gardens and cypresses. Its name is Ab Khore: 'the place where there is water' – an important stop on the road east precisely because you can find water. 'I don't know about Iskander,' said a man hoeing his pomegranate orchard, 'but my grandfather said Nadir Shah watered his horses here on his way to invade India 300 years ago.' Landscapes change, of course, and one can be led a little too far by the eye of faith. But, perhaps, this is where Darius died. Fortune had never been on his side.

Later stories said the two kings spoke in person. In his great Iranian national epic, the tenth-century poet Firdowsi turned the moment into an eternal tableau like the heroes Rustam and Sorabh. By then, Alexander had become a great Iranian national hero, a real son of Iran, a Muslim hero, too. (His story has been conserved better in the Muslim world than in the West.) In the old days, it was told by the tale-tellers who wandered the by-ways of Iran, travelling one-man shows with their painted canvas backdrops, and by the amateur religious folk players. At Quse village, close to the spot where Alexander found Darius, a tale-teller told the story for us and the villagers in an open space in the village. He used a covered farmcart as a prop, and, as he spoke, he lifted up the corner of the cloth, as if something – a body? – was under it:

> *Then the world-lord held Sikander's hand and wept, and he said: 'Let God be thy refuge: I resign my kingdom to you and give my soul to God'. Then he died and the people began to cry for him. Sikander tore his clothes and threw dust on his head ... they laid Dara on a bier of gold, draped in brocade of Rum, with jewelled pattern and ground of gold ... Sikander walked before it. And when the nobles of Iran saw how much Sikander mourned for their Shah, they all began to praise his worth, and they hailed him as ruler of the earth.*
>
> FIRDOWSI *Shahnama*

Alexander comforts the Persian king Darius in a version of the Alexander story painted in Bukhara, Central Asia, in 1533. A favourite theme of medieval miniaturists, the fictitious story that the two kings actually spoke before Darius died, goes back to the Hellenistic Romance.

That, of course, is the legend. Alexander becomes the lawful Shah, the true successor. In fact, the Persians never accommodated to Greek rule and, when the next great Persian empire arose in the third century AD, the Sasanian kings saw themselves as true successors to Darius and his ancestors, after the interregnum of the Hellenistic Greeks and the Parthians. They were deeply indebted to Hellenistic culture but, like the modern Shah, they never recognized the Greek occupiers. At Naksh-i-Rustam, the royal tombs near Persepolis, they emphasized this continuity by adding their own reliefs to the grand facades of the royal tombs of Darius the Great and Xerxes.

Darius's body was sent back to Persepolis for burial. His family were all in Alexander's hands. All the children would have been removed or married to Greeks, so that no future resistance could centre on the royal blood-line. As for Bessus and the regicides, they had escaped to the eastern provinces where Bessus would soon declare himself king. They would now be hunted down. No pretenders to the throne would be countenanced. This was the brutal reality of the power-politics of the fourth century. In the meantime, Alexander's fast advance had left most of his own army behind. He now waited for them all to come up at the nearest city on the Khorasan road, about 30 kilometres from the spot where Darius had died.

At Hecatompylos, the City of a Hundred Gates, Alexander's army re-grouped. In one sense the crusade, which had been launched at Amphipolis, was over. Alexander had arrived at another key psychological moment. The Persian monarchy had been over-thrown. The Great King was dead. So what next? Long live the Great King? What would Alexander do now? Become the Great King himself.

## 'NO TURNING BACK'

Qummis ruins lie just off the Mashad road between Semnan and Damqan. The turn-off is the tea shop at the way station of Quse – a kind of Iranian Paris, Texas. Long-distance trucks and buses thunder through without slowing. In the village are some mud-brick houses with walled compounds and wooden verandas; a lovely brick courtyard communal house, and a small but well-preserved caravanserai. Beyond are wheatfields, a long line of poplars and, further out, undulating hills of melted mud-brick. Recent excavations have identified this immense almost featureless ruin field as the lost city of Hecatompylos, the capital of ancient Parthia. Here, Alexander stopped that faraway summer of 330 BC. It is an exposed weather-beaten place, sun-scorched in summer under a vast blue sky, fringed

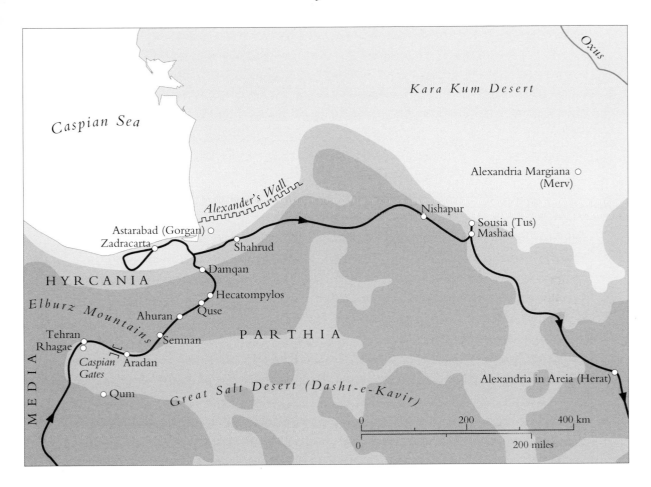

by the distant ranges of the Elburz Mountains. Across the site, all that remains are huge mud-brick stumps of the central buildings and a brown sea of pulverized pottery.

Here, not far east of the spot where Darius was found, Alexander stopped. The troops were jubilant. With the death of Darius, the Persians were finished. The objective of the invasion, which had landed them on the Trojan shore three years ago, had now been achieved, or so they thought. Now they could go home. When this rumour got back to Alexander, he had the officers and the key units assemble, and addressed them. His speech, like most of the reported speeches in our sources, is a later concoction, but it may enshrine some truth. We can picture Alexander's address to his men – cajoling, flattering, a stocky little man, with his harsh voice. Soldiers' language is never reported by a stylist like Arrian, but we can imagine it as coarse, demotic, barrack-room speech: 'If we stop now we will lose everything. We are not turning back. We are going on to conquer all the lands which were under the Persian king. Bessus and the killers are still loose. If we go back they will raise another army and soon the whole pack of cards will collapse behind our backs'. Then the calculated lie: 'It's only a few days more.' (He would say the same in India at the Beas river.) How much more he said we do not know. Did he tell them they were going to India? (And, who knows, maybe further? Did he even yet know himself the limit of his ambition? Maybe already he was dreaming of the farthest Ocean and the ends of the earth?)

## TOUCHING THE GREAT OCEAN

The expedition, then, was to go on eastwards. Alexander now announced that the troops were free to take wives from captive women and bring them along on the campaign. Previously newly-weds had been given leave to go home for periods, but women had not accompanied the army (except perhaps among the higher ranks). This move was as good as saying they would not see home again for the foreseeable future. Slowly, inexorably, ties with Macedonia were being cut.

First, though, he had to secure the northern fringe of Iran. So his journey now led him into the region known as Hyrcania, the 'land of wolves' on the shores of the Caspian Sea. The Greeks imagined the Caspian was part of the Great Ocean which encircled the whole of the earth.

The army was split into three groups, and crossed the Elburz by the main passes northwards (the most dramatic of which was negotiated by British railway engineers in the 1940s, with an astonishing series of switch-backs. Twenty years ago you would have seen huge articulated locomotives, built in Manchester, rumbling through these hills). Here you enter a different world, almost northern European in climate. It is green and damp, with thickly forested mountains which are still frequented by wolves and wild boar. You come down to the shore of the Caspian Sea near Bandar Turkoman, along a desultory shore of clapboard houses and straggling palms, with big wooden fishing boats drawn up on the beach. We tasted the water, as they did. It was, as the Greeks reported, only slightly salty. This should have alerted them, but it did not change them in their belief that the Caspian was part of the Great Ocean. From here they thought they could navigate westwards to Britain, and east to India. The Greeks, for the first time, had come to the limit of their geographical knowledge.

Moving eastwards you enter the green plain of Gorgan, which has been inhabited since pre-history. This is Turkoman country. They were late immigrants (comparatively) into Persia but, till the 1930s, they still lived the same nomadic herding life as their

Parthian predecessors. Then they were deprived of their wide grazing lands by Reza Shah, the last Shah's father, and now live as a dispossessed minority, but they are still great horsemen.

We camped near Kalaleh (where our host had lost three horses to wolves that summer). One night we rode across the plain to reach the Wall of Alexander – the 200-kilometre frontier which snakes from the Caspian to the foothills of Afghanistan. Standing on the wall we looked north across the great rolling plains of Turkmenistan. Also known as Shapur's Wall or the Red Snake, it marks as neatly as any monument can the boundary of the world of settled civilization and the world of the nomads, one of the key divides in history.

The tenth-century poet Firdowsi preserves the legend that Alexander built the great wall. Archaeology now dates it to a couple of centuries after his day (though could there have been a more limited Achaemenian or Hellenistic predecessor?). It is yet another testimony to the enduring power of Alexander's legend in Iran. Recent speculation is that the wall may have been inspired by the third-century BC Han mud-brick predecessor of the Great Wall of China which was pushed out into Central Asia soon after Alexander's day, when Far East and West first made contact.

We pulled up our horses on the crest of the wall, by a huge square fort, with great defensive ditches in front. There we watched the sun set over the Central Asian steppe. On the horizon on the Gorgan road, long-distance lorries were heading towards Turkmenistan. With the end of Soviet Union these connections, which have driven Central Asian history, are opening up again. Turkic peoples live from Bosphorus to Gobi, while the Iranian culture zone goes from Persian Gulf to Afghanistan and the Tajik lands which touch Chinese Xinjiang. Across these immense expanses, the Alexander story is still told. It was hard for us at this moment to resist the impulse to go straight on across the plain to the legendary Silk Route oases of Merv and Bukhara. But we – and Alexander – had other priorities.

## TALE OF THE AMAZON QUEEN

Alexander spent two weeks here in Hyrcania, in the capital Zadracarta. This place is still unidentified, but was clearly one of the dozens of great mounds or tepes which rise silently above the lush green plain of Gorgan. At one point Bucephalus was stolen by the local tribespeople, and Alexander threatened murderous reprisals unless he was returned unharmed, which he duly was. The other stories told here are less believable. One is the famous tale of the Amazon queen who came to Alexander wanting to have a child by him. According to Curtius she stayed for thirteen days, but 'her appetite for sex was greater than his'. (There is also a Turkoman legend, still current in these parts, which tells of a fairy tribe of Amazon women who capture unwary men for use as studs and then kill them!) Regretfully, delightful as she is, we must reject the Amazon queen as fantasy.

We stayed for four days out on the edge of the steppe by Alexander's Wall, sleeping in a felt yurt round a brick hearth with a circular opening in the roof to let in the light and let out the smoke. One night, around the fire, we heard from the village tale-teller the Turkoman legend of the demonic Alexander, the two-horned monster eventually consumed by his own ambitions, who, having conquered all of the earth, was tempted to go to heaven on a flying machine pulled by griffons, winged monsters, only for God to throw him down for his arrogance. This story is told all the way across Asia, and appears sculpted on European cathedrals from Otranto to Wells. The following is my favourite, which is found all the way from Turkey to Kazakhstan:

> *Iskander was actually a devil and he had horns. But his hair was long and wavy and the horns were never seen. Only his barbers knew. But he feared they could not keep the secret. So, he killed them when they discovered. His last barber pretended not to notice and kept the secret. Eventually though he could bear it no longer and, as he could tell no one, he ran to a well and called down the well: 'Iskander has horns!' But in the bottom of the well were whispering reeds* [used in flutes] *and they echoed the story until it went round the whole world.*

## THE SOUL OF IRAN

The centre of gravity of the tale now shifts eastwards. Alexander's world view had already left Greece behind (he would never see it again). If Babylon was now the centre of his world, Iran had become the source of his power; the axis of the empire he had overcome. Now, in one sense, it would triumph over him. The intuition of the Iranian tale-tellers was right. He had become the Shah.

Alexander's route led back over Elburz to Shahrud and eastwards along the old Khorasan road, past ancient caravan cities, Omar Khayam's Nishapur and Firdowsi's Tus. We pushed on in his footsteps to Mashad. After the destruction or closure of the great shrine cities in Iraq, Mashad has become the greatest shrine of the Shiite world. We found lodgings overlooking the sacred precinct – a vast glittering circle of light, golden domes and turquoise gateways. My hotel room was complete with the prayer-mat and turbah, the clay tablet, which Shias touch in prayer. Outside the window were crowds along the sacred way, the sounds of Ashura – lamentation, singing – pilgrims from all over Iran and further afield: Afghanistan, India, Pakistan, Central Asia.

That night, looking down on the streets of Mashad, I found myself puzzling over the Hellenistic legacy in Iran. In the long run, what was the effect of the Greek irruption into Persia? Under the fundamentalist regime of the Ayatollahs you might have thought that the Greek legacy is long gone. But travel through today's Iran and you can still see Alexander in Shiite folk-plays wearing a pith helmet and jodhpurs; he still struts on the floats at Ashura in dark glasses, sipping whisky with other earthly tyrants like the last Shah, the Wicked Caliphs and the Great Satan, Uncle Sam himself. His tale is still taught in Muslim primary schools; Zoroastrians still remember him as the accursed. Learned Ayatollahs still write editorials about him in the newspapers. He still appears in Firdowsi as a great Iranian king, the true successor to the great shahs and heroes of the past. Mothers still scold their children at bedtime with the threat that, if they are not good, Alexander will get them.

In a deeper way, the legacy lives on, too. In fact, the Greeks made a profound impact on the Persians for 2000 years. Their great medieval civilization was essentially made from three roots: the ancient Persian and Zoroastrian legacy; Arab Islam; and the Hellenistic. Indeed, few nations cultivated the Greek legacy more obsessively through the Middle Ages, as you will still discover if you wander into a teaching school of a traditional Shiite university where the scholars wear the long black gowns they bequeathed later to the dons of Oxford and Harvard. And, in the battle now being fought for the soul of Iran – not just of Iranian Islam – the spirit of Hellenism may yet have a part to play.

Beyond the jagged mountains outside the city of Mashad, darkness was falling over the vast steppe stretching away from Alexander's Wall into Central Asia. Where next for Alexander? Just outside Mashad there is a road-junction called Toroq (the name means crossroads). Here the roads go west to the Mediterranean, south to the Arabian Sea and the Indian Ocean; north via Mashad to Central Asia; south-east to Herat, Kandahar and Kabul in Afghanistan. It is a real crossroads of history. They all came this way: Genghis Khan, Tamerlane, Marco Polo and Alexander.

Alexander's intelligence officers had already debriefed the Persian military experts and planned out his track; his surveyors could already tell him the precise distances between the way-stations for the next 3000 kilometres on the Persian royal roads. He would head east into Afghanistan, and then on to India – and the end of the earth.

# PART FOUR

# The ROAD to SAMARKAND

## AFGHANISTAN, UZBEKISTAN AND TAJIKISTAN

### 329 - 327 BC

*Into Afghanistan; through the Desert of Death;
Kabul under siege; journey to the Hindu Kush; the crossing of the
Khawak Pass; into Bactria; the 'Mother of Cities'; the road to Oxiana;
the massacre of the Branchidae; Samarkand the Golden; at Alexandria the
Farthermost; fire and sword in Central Asia; Alexander murders Black Cleitus;
Alexander marries Roxanne, 'the most beautiful girl in Asia';
the death of Callisthenes; Alexander 'murderous and melancholy mad'*

BEAUTIFUL AUTUMN MORNING IN HERAT. From the teahouse on Takht-i-Safar, the Traveller's Throne, by a garden of tall trees, there is a wonderful view of the city. North of the old walls the famous cluster of tall minarets stands over green gardens; in the distance are the jagged remains of the great mud-brick citadel where Alexander built his new town, Alexandria in Areia. Of that city there are few signs now, though the huge rectangle of the medieval Herat may mark the spot. It has always been a key junction on the road to India, which runs southwards over the wonderful 1000-year-old bridge, the Pul-i-Madan, and on through wheatfields lined with pollarded willows and dotted with crumbling pigeon towers and the strange stepped Herat windmills.

Alexander's next task was to conquer the eastern provinces of the Persian Empire, reducing all the places which had acknowledged its hegemony. He was now the king of Persia and all who had given allegiance to Darius would give it to him. His prime goal by now was probably India, but he could not leave the Central Asian provinces (former Soviet Central Asia) behind him, especially as this was where Bessus had fled. First, Alexander had to hunt down Darius's murderers. Bessus had now donned the upright tiara and royal robes and taken the name Artaxerxes IV. Announcing himself to be Darius's successor, and declaring himself pillar of resistance against the conquerors of Persia, was a direct challenge to Alexander. Alexander could have forgiven him the murder of Darius, but not this — especially, as governor of Bactria, Bessus had access to the fine cavalry of North Afghanistan. Alexander had to corner him for both military and political reasons.

This explains his long journey through southern Afghanistan. Alexander had, perhaps, originally intended to strike eastwards straight to Kabul from Herat. Instead, he marched south in a huge loop to Fara, then up along the Helmand river to Kandahar and Ghazni: it was an immense journey of some 1600 kilometres, but in those days the landscape was much more fertile than it is now. Today, going south from Fara, you enter a dreadful wilderness known as the Desert of Death. It is a trackless sea of sand which stretches across the forgotten corner of the world where Pakistan, Iran and Afghanistan meet, ignoring modern borders which have no relevance to the ancient landscape, nor indeed to the caravans of drug-smugglers who ply their trade between Pakistan and Iran in great armed columns protected by machine guns.

---

Previous pages, left: The turquoise domes of Samarkand – Alexander's base during the two years of campaigning in Central Asia.
Right: This life-size head of Alexander was made soon after his death for a monument which showed him with his favourite Hephaistion and the goddess of fortune, Tyche.

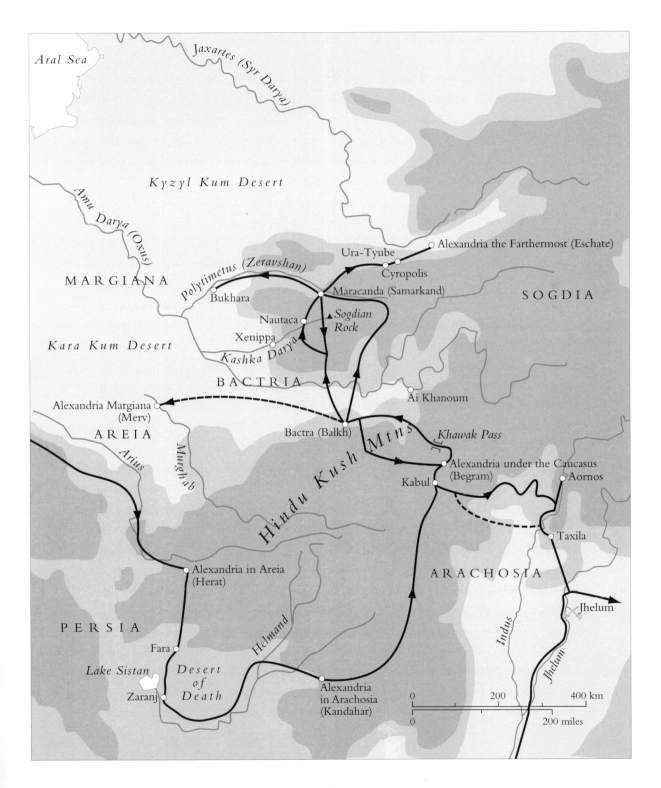

## INTO THE DESERT OF DEATH

All along the Helmand river you pass the remains of ancient cities: jagged-toothed mud-brick reefs silted with immense moving tides of sand. The biggest town is Fara, which is surrounded by high medieval walls, and is now under the rule of the fundamentalist Muslim Taliban. Turbaned gun-slingers patrol the streets; the women covered from head to toe. Here, the most sensational event of Alexander's reign took place – an alleged plot which led to a terrifying purge, show-trials, torture and execution of some of the king's most intimate companions.

A disaffected royal attendant was reported to Philotas, leader of the Companions, and son of Alexander's general Parmenio, who had been left behind in Hamadan (Ecbatana). For some reason Philotas kept this information to himself rather than divulge it to Alexander. Perhaps, as he claimed, he thought it too trivial to mention; maybe he secretly sympathized. When the story came out, Philotas was arrested, tried in a very loaded atmosphere, and horribly tortured by Hephaistion and others of the inner circle. Eventually a confession was extorted, then Philotas was killed.

Although in agreement that there was some kind of plot, the ancients were divided over whether Philotas was implicated. Conceivably he had been happy to keep silent and wait to see if it might succeed. Alexander, however, took the opportunity to dispose of Parmenio, for so long his loyal number two. After Philotas had been executed, Alexander sent racing camels, with agents in Arab dress, across the Great Salt Desert. Unaware of his son's death, Parmenio was stabbed to death in a walled garden in Hamadan. No one was safe now.

Alexander moved on swiftly to Kandahar, where he founded another town, Alexandria in Arachosia (the part of Baluchistan which lies behind the Quetta Hills). Again, this has been a strategic site throughout Afghan history, and Kandahar has been occupied from then till now. In the old citadel, a temple to the deified Alexander has been discovered, along with an inscription in Greek and Aramaic by the Indian emperor Ashoka who lived a few decades after Alexander. (This is a place where the Indian and West Asian culture zones have always overlapped.) In the bazaar in the old town, the hakims (traditional doctors) claim descent from the doctors who went with Alexander – descendants of the physicians Philip and Critobulos. They still practise the Yunnani (Greek) herbal medicine which can be found right across Pakistan and North India. Then, as winter came on, Alexander pushed on up the long road to Kabul – the crossroads of Afghanistan; and for us, following in his footsteps, for the first time in our journey, this meant entering a war zone.

## CHANCE MEETINGS IN KABUL

From the encircling hills at dusk, we saw tracer-fire and the occasional car headlight, but there were no city lights as darkness came on. Across the valley, the great warren of tenements in the old city was dotted with oil lamps. Kabul had been without electricity and running-water for two years. The city had been devastated by war, by the Russian invasion and, worse, by the civil war which followed. Kabul's modern fate echoes its history: it has been a strategic site since ancient times, the key crossroads between Iran, Central Asia and India. The reason is simple: the centre of Afghanistan is a high circle of rugged mountains, rising well over 6000 metres and forming a great barrier between the Iranian plateau and the plains of India. The main ancient land-route to India has passed through the Kabul valley since prehistory.

Alexander made his base near Begram, north of Kabul at the foot of the Hindu Kush. It is a strategic site, which was used by the Russians as their main base during their war here. The remains of the Hellenistic and later city were found in 1939 and, in its storerooms, was an amazing treasure – one of the greatest archaeological finds of the century. There was Alexandrian glass, Chinese lacquer, Hindu ivory sculptures – all witness to the contacts opened up by Alexander's world. It is all gone now, looted by the factions who have torn Afghanistan to pieces in the last few years. Now, in the gutted and ransacked museum, are severed heads of Buddha wearing Greek togas, inscriptions in Greek and Sanskrit, all part of the intermixing of Indian and Hellenic culture which had taken place here. For centuries Greek was spoken here and in the North-West Frontier. In the flickering light of our oil-lamps we picked over the ruins of Afghan history. I held a fragment of relief, a precious testimony to the Greek legacy preserved in the face of the ravages of war. The museum-keeper surveyed the wreckage: 'The whole history of our country is here … The morning we came in and found this it felt as if our father and mother had died'.

Later I had tea with an old Afghan scholar, in his wood-panelled house, his precious collection of ancient manuscripts protected by sandbags. There were illuminated Korans, Aristotle in Arabic, Firdowsi, and Nizami's tale of Alexander – a testimony to the humanistic learning which united the educated élites of Muslim Asia for 1000 years or more from Cairo to Delhi.

'We dread every attack,' he said. 'Not for ourselves, but for the books.' He spread his hands, 'Afghans will fight over a handful of dust. There's a famous Afghan story that Alexander sent his mother four Afghans and a heap of dust to prove the point when she wrote asking why it had taken him so long in Bactria!'

## JOURNEY TO THE HINDU KUSH

By early spring Alexander was ready to go. He had to cross the Hindu Kush, the great rampart of mountains which rises north of Kabul – the 'killer of Hindus' as it was called by the Muslim conquerors who came this way in the Middle Ages. This was the great route used by all invaders of the subcontinent. There are about sixteen passes, some up to 5 or 6000 metres in height, but only three have really counted in history. The main one today is the Salang Pass, now a modern road and tunnel used by the Russian convoys on their way up from Termez. The second route is westwards to Bamian, one of the most extraordinary sites in Asia – the Valley of the Great Buddhas. This hauntingly beautiful place, with its gigantic statues carved into the cliffs, was visited by Marco Polo and by the Chinese explorers who came overland to bring back the Buddhist sacred texts from India. But this, and the Salang, were probably barred to Alexander because Bessus had devastated the countryside beyond them all the way to Balkh, the capital of Bactria. Alexander's intelligence would have informed him that supplying his army was out of the question on those routes. That left him one obvious alternative – the Khawak Pass. This is the eastern route rising up on a gentle gradient. It was used by Tamerlane, Genghis Khan and other invaders of India. This was the route we decided to take.

We prepared for our expedition by renovating the old BBC Landrover and getting hold of a back-up Jeep, with spare axles and tyres (no mean feat in Kabul these days). Then, as the storm-clouds of war gathered over Kabul, with Taliban attacks growing in intensity, we headed north towards Charikar and the Panjshir valley to follow once more in Alexander's footsteps.

At Begram, near Charikar, he founded Alexandria under the Caucasus, with several thousand retired veterans, invalids and press-ganged locals. It is a wide and pleasant plain, 2000 metres up, but sheltered in the lee of the great spurs of the mountains. Fertile and well-watered, the vine and the olive will grow here, some compensation, perhaps, for the men Alexander forced to stay behind. He then continued up the Panjshir valley and into the mountains. The Greeks called these ranges the Caucasus, believing them to be close to the end of the earth. Here, the army entered mythical space and time: marching under mountains where, so it was said, the Titan Prometheus had been tortured for aeons by Zeus for revealing to humankind the secret of fire and the arts of civilization. Here, as elsewhere with the tales of Hercules and Dionysus, real and mythical history merged in the impressionable mind of the young Alexander.

It took us two days on a very rough road to negotiate the 80 kilometres of the Panjshir valley, driving slowly under great brown ridges which keep the sun off the valley bottoms for the first two hours of the morning. All along the road we passed ruined Russian gear (this had been one of the main routes by which the Mujahaddin resistance kept up pressure on the invaders). It is a harsh terrain for modern armies, and wrecked APCs (armoured-personnel carriers) lay everywhere. They had met fierce resistance here and, in the end, for all their technological superiority the poor Russian conscripts from Omsk and Tomsk just couldn't take it. The Macedonians though, like Afghans, were a mountain people, hard as nails. The valley was beautiful: the cold blue water of the river, green gardens and fields, neat brown mud-brick houses, with vivid splashes of colour from the maize and apricots drying on their roofs. And above, the great bare-ribbed mountains.

Alexander's army must have moved forward only slowly; an immense column miles long; a logistical headache for the high command and for the quartermasters who had to supply and feed them. Even by Landrover it was slow progress, crossing and recrossing the river. The vehicle broke down, ran out of petrol and, at one point, a landslide blocked the route for a night. Then, towards the end of the valley, the stony track began to rise up into the mountains and we passed single lines of travellers on foot and on horseback. Suddenly, it was easy to imagine the Macedonian army stretched out all the way down the Panjshir.

Finally, on the third day, we reached the village of Ao Khawak. It stands at the junction of two fast-flowing mountain rivers. Ahead the path goes up into the mountains of Nuristan, and to the north a rough dirt-track led off towards the Khawak Pass. From there it is about 80 kilometres down into the Pul i Kumri valley. We crossed the Khawak river by a wooden bridge and entered what looks like a nest of brigands and footpads: a huddle of hovels, stables and warehouses of squat stone, timber roofs weighed with heavy stones. There were clusters of dank hostels and smoke-blackened shanties where meals are cooked round the clock for traders and travellers. In the street, there was a great hubbub of activity for, although much of the goods and the people are brought here by truck, this is the jumping-off place for an older kind of travel, by foot and horseback on one of the ancient routes between India and Asia. From here, to get to north Afghanistan, we would have to walk.

In the middle of all this, surrounded by roaring waters and overlooked by the pyramid peak of Deh Parian, we found an open space for hundreds of horses, thin ribby animals with cloth nosebags, wicker panniers, ropes and harnesses. Their drivers are mostly young (old men would not last such a hard life). Wiry young jockeys, thin and sun-blackened, they charge 60,000 Afghanis (about £12) to take you and your baggage across the mountains. In charge is the redoubtable commander Khalil, a shaggy giant of a man with a long black beard and a gimlet eye. He chose our horses, drivers and arranged for armed

guards to accompany us the following day, to ward off the bandits which he said might attack us on the path. We were five strong, Peter, Tim, David, me, and Hanif Sharzat, an Afghan friend and journalist, who had gamely volunteered to be our translator. Hanif speaks Pashto, Farsi, Uzbek, Urdu and Russian, which he reckoned should be enough to talk our way out of the clutches of the various warlords across our path, and get us through to the Afghan-Uzbek border.

We were travelling now only with what we and three horses could carry. Before we set out I experienced another sharp pang of excitement. Once again, as nearly as we could, we were about to experience what the Greeks had gone through, and the sense of treading right in their footsteps was palpable. We had stripped down to essentials: a warm jacket, rucksack, sleeping bag, some emergency food (apples, nuts, and some stony chunks of dried mulberries) and, as always, Arrian and Curtius. We loaded the camera, stock-box and the other film gear into rope and cloth panniers, and in the early afternoon our drivers led the horses off over the bridge and up the river valley alongside the rushing torrent. Soon we were into the ravines, then up a narrow dirt path on the first precipitous climb above the river. By three in the afternoon the air was unexpectedly chilly, and the valley bottoms were already in deep shadow as we left Nuristan behind us, the Land of Light, and headed north towards the snowy peaks of the Hindu Kush and, beyond, the fabled Oxus.

## CROSSING THE KHAWAK PASS

That first afternoon, to my surprise, all along the route we saw people – on camels, horses and mules, on foot, too. There were traders, smugglers, refugees, and travellers. We even met some newly-weds, a man with his two wives on horseback, covered from head to foot in billowing robes as their horses gingerly crossed rickety plank bridges and sometimes waded chest-deep through the raging torrent. Sometimes we went up narrow earth paths along towering hillsides over the river gorge, across the face of long stony screes, down which any stumble could have been fatal, but the horses knew the path well. So, I reflected, the Khawak – an ancient route used throughout history – was still a great thoroughfare today. It seemed unbelievable, at first, as I took in the terrain, but the ancient armies were so tough and mobile, that for them this was a serviceable route.

---

Previous pages: The Khawak Pass over the Hindu Kush in Afghanistan (3850 metres). Like Alexander, our team had no alternative but to walk, carrying the gear on horses.

That night we stopped at a cluster of stables and mud-brick dormitories which we shared with our fellow travellers. We ate bread and gruel by oil lamp with the local headman. We were, he told us, the first Westerners to come through since the war with the Russians. During the war the conditions here had been terrible. The people of the Pass had lived in caves by day, emerging only at night to cook and bake their bread. It must have been like that in 329 BC, too: killed if you didn't give up your precious winter stores to the invaders, killed perhaps even if you did.

Later, as I stretched out on our hostel floor, I turned over the pages of Arrian in the light of a Tilly lamp and reflected once more on the character of Alexander and his men. The Macedonians were inured to war but, even so, the journey was tough. It took the army sixteen days from front-to-tail to get over the Khawak Pass; it was January, bitterly cold at night. For food, they could plunder the winter stores of the locals, but two weeks of food for an army that size runs into several thousand tonnes – and unless they carried it with them they would starve. Reading Arrian in that spot, it also occurred to me that it is virtually the same Afghanistan now. The long vicious war with the Russians has brought them back almost to the same subsistence level. They have got guns now, but otherwise the equation is the same. The same mountains, same harsh climate, same hard people.

Next day we said goodbye to the commander. The situation was tense, with trouble expected ahead, but Khalil had been as good as his word. The local headman left us with two gunmen to hold off bandits reported to be lying ahead in ambush. The path was higher and colder now, the wind more biting. We can guess from the Greeks' accounts that they, too, found it harder as the land grew more barren. They were into something of a logistical nightmare by now. As we walked on, I found myself trying to make rough calculations: how long does it take an army to march past a single point? Their army could have been spread over 25 kilometres or more. It was for this reason that their crossing of the Khawak had run into a second week; then the supply corps had found it could no longer feed the long line of troops funnelling into the Pass from the Panjshir valley. The army had run out of food.

The quartermasters asked for permission to start killing the pack animals, but there was no wood on the bare hills to make cooking fires, and they were reduced to eating the flesh raw. This they did, but to offset illness, says Arrian, they used the juice of a plant which grew on the mountains, apparently to chew with the meat. Historians have often wondered about this tale. Tall story? Propaganda? Perhaps. But the army doctors would have been trained in the use of herbal medicines – this is still the basis of the Yunnani medicine, practised in Afghanistan by the hakims who, as I have already mentioned, claim descent from the doctors who went with Alexander. In the event, we only had to ask our

143

horse-handlers to find the answer. There, on the Khawak, grew a plant which fitted the bill. Arrian called it sylphion; we know it as asafoetida – a resin obtained from the roots of plants of the genus *Ferula*. It grows in the spring and is widely used as medicine. In the Middle Ages it was produced in bulk and sold in the bazaars of Merv and Bukhara. Even during the Russian occupation, we were told, the guerrillas used it to heal wounds and cure stomach upsets. The Greeks had not been telling fairy tales.

We stopped at midday in rarefied air at a subterranean stone-roofed chai-stop where the horsemen took food and the horses grazed on the thin grass. Smoke curled from a cairn of stones over the roof, recalling the Greek story of Afghan houses so bedded down in rocks that only smoke from chimneys showed where they were. We ate hot coarse bread and drank green tea flavoured with cardamoms; someone brought some grapes washed in the icy blue stream below the path. Inside, under a smoke-blackened brick vault, was an ancient samovar, a rice-steamer and various teapots. Along the wall, there was a crowd of turbaned men with bandoliers and guns. In the air was the sweet resinous smell of fire-wood. On hearing why we were there, an old man told a story that many Greeks had died on Alexander's passage through the Pass, and that a circle of stones with tattered flags on the way to the top marked the graves of his troops.

We pushed on up the long slope, as the wind started to course down between the hills. Sixteen kilometres up from Ao Khawak, at a little under 4000 metres, we reached the summit. In thin air and a chill wind, we were surrounded by snow streaked peaks with creamy white clouds coming over the tops. The last few metres drew us on to see the view the Greeks had seen all those years before. Again, there was that eerie feeling of standing on the very spot where Alexander had stood. He knew at that moment he had got through, that his gamble had paid off. The Pass had been undefended. Below us, the road snaked down, still sunlit towards northern Afghanistan and the Oxus, beyond which lay the great plains of central Asia.

'Nothing put him off,' said Arrian. 'Starvation, the freezing cold, nothing – he just kept coming on and on. And in the end his enemies were struck with fear and amazement.'

Standing shivering on top of the Khawak Pass, it was easy for us to see why. Once again Alexander had shown that left any chance he would take it. As we set off we met a group of Tajiks and Uzbeks coming up from Central Asia. The way was clear, the high-waymen had been chased off. 'Get a move on and you'll be in Anderab by nightfall,' one said.

---

On the summit of the Khawak Pass surrounded by the crags
of the Hindu Kush.

## INTO BACTRIA

For Alexander, the way to Bactria lay open. He could now rest and recuperate in the fertile valleys around Kunduz while the tail of his exhausted and starving army filtered through. These lands are particularly fertile. The great traveller Ibn Battuta, when he crossed the Khawak in 1333, stopped here for forty days, and speaks of their 'fine pastures and herbage'. We rested at Pul i Kumri with the hospitable local warlord, an Ismaeli Shia. It was an unlikely meeting in such a place and time. Jaffar went to school in Harrow and once delivered pizzas in Detroit. He and his clan have protected their valleys from the war around them, and from the passage of armies, while Afghanistan has fallen back into its ancient regional divisions. Such warlords seem to be affectionately regarded by their people, but they inhabit a strange world. Some I have met mix intermittent bursts of warfare with prodigious drinking sessions on Russian vodka and Johnny Walker, enlivened by Tajik girls and the latest CDs from the West. I guessed the Macedonians were no different. In his villa Jaffar showed me antiquities, a great Greek inscription from a nearby site, medieval bronzes from Balkh, Greek coins from lost cities on the Oxus. His, I suspect, was a world not unlike that of 330 BC, a time of shifting allegiances as local hard men try to keep their position like the satraps of old. Back in Alexander's day, however, the difference was that the outside power – Alexander's power – was so overwhelming nobody could resist him.

After a few days of Jaffar's hospitality, we decided to push on. As we set out to head north once more, I experienced a sudden sharp taste of anxiety. Jaffar's tanks were rumbling through the streets belching black oily diesel smoke and the wind was whipping up fierce eddies of dust as they began to move their forces towards the mountain passes we had just crossed. On BBC World Service radio we heard that the Taliban were closing in on Kabul. We were besieged by ever-present thoughts of war; so much of Afghan history has been – and still is – foreign invasion and civil struggle. Once the Russians had been beaten, no one seemed to care any more if the land was torn to pieces. So the cycle of history comes round. Poor Afghanistan.

We had hired a battered Russian pick-up to make the run north to the Oxus. It had no rear windows, which made it pleasantly draughty by day when the sun scorches, but freezing by night. We were also beset by all the usual worries about breaking down as we headed on in Alexander's footsteps.

As soon as Alexander's army had recovered from the crossing of the Khawak, he moved quickly towards the Oxus river, which divides present-day Afghanistan from the former Soviet Central Asia. Following in his track through northern Afghanistan, you go through a string of fertile valleys between barren ranges of hills; then enter huge gorges which lead down to the Oxus plain.

That nightfall we came to Tashkurgan, the Greek Aornos, to find the town shattered by war. The ancient citadel, with its great mud-brick castle which stood over lush orchards, had been pounded to bits in the fighting; the lovely wooden souk, and the bazaar whose ceiling had been delightfully inlaid with blue Chinese porcelain bowls, had been levelled; the old town was a wasteland of devastated mud-brick buildings. This was no time to explore. The town is held by Hisbe Islami who have been known to kidnap Westerners and seize their gear – especially cameras. Suddenly our driver muttered urgently that we should get out of the place. We attempted to, but, unbelievably, we broke down on the outskirts just by an armed post. Providence intervened. At that moment the muezzin sang out the call for Friday prayers and our potential captors melted away, just as a dust-storm whirled down the street and hid us from prying eyes. Five minutes tinkering under the bonnet by torchlight and we were on the road again. After a couple of more hours huddled in cold bumpy darkness, we entered Mazar. We had made it across Afghanistan from Kabul to the north. Given the fact that we were only five people, and unarmed at that, it seemed an achievement. At the UN rest-house, a kindly diplomat gave us half a crate of Turkish beer and we had a quiet celebration.

## THE MOTHER OF CITIES

'You BBC? Come this way,' said the man in combat fatigues, peaked hat, and sharp moustache. By eleven at night, after several hours' wait, we were desperate for a bed, any kind of bed. General Dustom, though, had required us to wait. Then, suddenly, he required us to go. We were back in the strange world of petty fiefdoms and satrapies into which Afghanistan has broken down like the days of old. Dustom is the Uzbek warlord who controls the northern plain of Afghanistan – the modern-day satrap of Bactria whose badly painted portraits look down from lamp-posts and official buildings around the town (Alexander had a better class of official artist). We were told to put our gear into the general's Jeep, and were then driven into the night down darkened desert roads to find ourselves on a sprawling military base, with no means of getting back. I was worried. We were effectively under house-arrest. The general's hospitality, however, was good. We had asked permission to go to the ancient city of Balkh, but were told the road ahead was infested with bandits. The general's aide announced they would drop us off next day by helicopter. Ravaged by Genghis, and restored by Tamerlane, our goal was the great Silk

Above: Standing by one of the towers in the mud-brick walls of the ancient city of Balkh in northern Afghanistan. A great crossroads on the Silk Route, Balkh was once known as the 'Mother of Cities'.

Left: The old town of Tashkurgan, where Alexander stopped after crossing the Hindu Kush, has now been devastated in the Afghan civil war.

Route metropolis known to the Arabs who conquered it in the eighth century simply as 'The Mother of Cities'.

Today, it is a vast ruin field – a huge citadel, with great towered outer walls of sun-dried brick; ruined Buddhist stupas, Zoroastrian fire temples, and Nestorian Christian churches – all religions made their homes here. A medieval Muslim poet describes the city in a lovely image, surrounded by its gardens: 'as delightful as a Mani painting'. The City sits under the north side of the Hindu Kush, where the sun rises over fertile fields, fed by a spread of tributaries fanning out from the Balkh river. It was replaced by Mazar in the last century, and there is not much left of its civic life now, beyond a few winding mud-brick lanes amid the groves and gardens in the centre. Old Balkh is virtually gone, but a few people still live here. At the ancient gates, there are little shrines to ancient holy men, still neatly maintained with offering flags, and swept floors. Right in the centre of the old city, in a circle of palm trees, are the great shrines of the Timurid Age. Still especially popular with the people of the region is the grave of Rabia Balkhi. Even today she is the female protectress of the city, just as the ancient patroness of Balkh, Anahita goddess of the Oxus, was in Alexander's day. Anahita's magnificent gilded statue had been gifted by one of Darius's predecessors, Artaxerxes II. Thousands had come to licentious rites in the precinct of the 'High girdled one clad in a mantle of gold, on her head a golden crown with rays of light and a hundred stars clad in a robe of thirty otter skins of shining fur'.

Here, in Balkh, as we shall see, some fateful events of Alexander's life took place. Here, tradition says, Alexander married Roxanne (a tale told to Marco Polo by the locals in the thirteenth century). But Alexander's initial stay was short. He paid off the Thessalians, still restive after Parmenio's murder; and 900 Macedonians, said to have reached retirement age, were given lavish long-service bonuses. He then procured an agreement from the Macedonians that they would 'serve for the rest of the war', when-ever that would be. Then, with Bessus, the murderer and self-proclaimed successor of Darius, already having gone north of the river, Alexander decided immediately to journey on to the Oxus.

## THE ROAD TO OXIANA

From Balkh, it was only 80 kilometres to the river, a four-day journey for Alexander's main army, but a minor disaster was narrowly averted as they ran into the sand dunes beyond the oasis and suffered very badly from heat and thirst. The time was early summer – very very hot – and what the Greeks experienced, modern travellers still experience.

*The sand burned through one's boots and a breath of wind from the burning hot drift-sand hills struck the face like flames from a fire. Gun barrels were heated to such a degree that they could not be touched, and even the water of the Amu-Darya was heated in July to 28 degrees … The fine dust particles are everywhere, and in connection with the heat and the drought it occasions a terrible thirst which is not easily satisfied.*

OLUFSEN *Emir of Bokhara (1911)*

The old road goes directly north from the Balkh oasis. It is not a long way, but the road is still very dangerous and easy to lose in drifting sands. The UN agent in Mazar recommended us to take chains, shovels, boards, water-containers and two reliable four-wheel drive vehicles. The vehicles proved a problem. We simply could not get hold of good Jeeps, so in the end we had to stick with our old Russian pick-up and travel to one side of Alexander's path, on the new asphalt road to the Friendship Bridge on the Oxus at new Termez. Even so, we got a taste of the conditions he experienced. The desert was still swept by winds which heaped sand-dunes over the road in a matter of hours. At one point, the road was cleared by an old man with a spade, who received his tips in showers of small notes from passing truck drivers.

On the old route, the Macedonians had miscalculated. Desperate for a drink they had breached the wine supplies which only made matters worse; things had degenerated into a shambles by the time they reached the river, and the leading columns broke ranks and ran in to gulp the water. As darkness fell, Alexander lit big fires of camel-thorn to guide the rear units in. In military parlance it had not been a good army day.

To delay Alexander's advance Bessus had commandeered and burned all the river-boats he could lay his hands on, so the Greeks had to cross on improvised rafts made of tents and skins and sewn up stuffed with chaff and dried grass. This took five days, but Alexander did not wait. He just pressed on with his Companions.

The Macedonians had entered Sogdia, the fabled land between Oxus (Amu Darya) and Jaxartes (Syr Darya). This is where the Great Game was played out between the British and Russian empires in the nineteenth century; it then disappeared in twentieth-century history under the Soviet Empire and is only now re-emerging. Formerly on the ancient Silk Route, this has always been a meeting place of civilizations: for example, it was in the Fergana region of Uzbekistan that the Chinese first met Westerners in the second century BC. It was a wide fertile and populous land, with Bukhara and Samarkand among the great cities of Asia. In Alexander's day, all the land as far as the Jaxartes river had been a frontier district of the Persian empire, the province of Sogdia, held down by a system of fortresses and garrisons. Beyond were the Kazakh steppelands, and, in Greek minds, only nomads as far as the shores of the Great Ocean. So, out here, they had believed themselves to be near to the edge.

Today the Oxus and Jaxartes flow through a wide desert into the dying Aral Sea. To the north of the Oxus is the Kyzyl Kum, the Red Desert, to the south, between the Elburz ranges of Iran and the Oxus, is the Kara Kum, the Black Desert. (In ancient times, though, it seems that the Oxus flowed into the Caspian and the Greeks may not have known of the Aral.) The climate here is extreme: cold frosty winters, excessive dry heat in the summers. Winters are short but are sandwiched between unpleasant rainy seasons which turn much of the land into a sea of mud, making army manoeuvres very difficult in the soft light soil of the oases. The best time is after the spring rains, mid-April to mid-May, when the steppes and deserts, even the arid depths of the Kara Kum, bloom with plants, bushes and tamarisk trees.

In the oases there has always been irrigation agriculture, but the key element in the economies before modern times was animal husbandry – herding. So, though Alexander's Greeks could seize barley, millet, wheat from the storehouses of the land, the chief wealth was cattle and sheep, and the foraging expeditions of Greeks now had to gather herds to sustain the army with dairy products and meat. In one sense that made their task easier, and cut down their logistical difficulties. They were able to take their food with them – cattle and sheep could graze almost everywhere, even in the desert. By and large, though, Alexander avoided desert-fighting, for which he was ill-equipped against the local nomadic horsemen. What he could not have anticipated, however, was that he would become bogged down, fighting here for two years against his most difficult adversary. First, though, he had to get Bessus.

## FEAR AND LOATHING IN BACTRIA: THE MASSACRE OF THE BRANCHIDAE

Before Alexander finally caught up with Bessus, however, there took place another strange and sinister story, so strange in fact that many modern historians have refused to believe it. The tale is not mentioned by Arrian, possibly because it was felt to damage the king's reputation. It is told in detail only by the Roman historian Curtius, but must ultimately have come from the expedition historian Callisthenes. According to Curtius, the Macedonians were moving from the Oxus on the road into the interior, when they came to a small walled town. To their great surprise the inhabitants were Greek-speaking people who identified themselves as descendants of Ionian Greeks, the priestly family of the

Branchidae, the guardians of the famous oracle sanctuary of Apollo of Didyma. Theirs was a remarkable tale, on which we have already touched (see page 44).

Over 150 years before, in 494 BC, the Greek cities of Ionia had revolted against the Persian empire, Miletus had been sacked and its temple at Didyma looted. At that time, the temple priests' ancestors had been resettled by the Persian king out on the fringe of his empire in Central Asia. This was done because they had violated the sanctuary of Didyma in handing it over to the Persians to avoid retribution. The story must have been known to Alexander, given his interest in the oracle and its subsequent prophecies of his triumph in Asia. However, a new slant seems to have been given to these events by Alexander's historian Callisthenes, who claimed Didyma was not sacked during the revolt against Darius but in the great war waged against the Greeks by Xerxes. In other words, the betrayal of Apollo's shrine had taken place during Xerxes's sacrilegious assault on the shrines of the Greeks. We now know this simply was not true, but was it actually believed by Alexander and his generals? We cannot see through the 'fog' of propaganda to find the answer, but, according to Curtius, this is what happened next.

'The culture of their ancestors had not yet disappeared, though they were now bilingual (in Greek and Persian – or Sogdian?) and the foreign tongue had greatly eroded their own. They welcomed Alexander warmly and surrendered their city to him,' says Curtius. That night Alexander called a meeting of the Milesians in the army, 'since it was their ancestors who had been betrayed'. Alexander let them decide freely, 'but,' says Curtius ominously, 'when they couldn't make up their minds, he took the decision for them'.

The next day the unsuspecting Branchidae came to meet him and accompanied him to their city. He entered with a unit of lightly-armed soldiers. The phalanx troops, meanwhile, had been ordered to surround the place. When the signal was given, they began to massacre the inhabitants. The Branchidae, who were unarmed, were killed to a man: 'Neither the common language, the olive branches they held out, nor their entreaties put a halt to the savagery'. Afterwards the Macedonians plundered the city, demolished its walls and dug out their foundations 'so as to leave not a single trace of the city'. The woods, too, and the sacred groves were cut down and uprooted. 'It was not fair revenge,' says Curtius, 'but sheer brutality against people who had never even seen Miletus.'

It is an amazing tale: revenge taken on ancestors' descendants 150 years later. But is it true? Circumstantial as the tale is, we have no corroboration for the massacre. But recent excavations by Afghan, Russian and Uzbek archaeologists have at least provided evidence of the cult of Apollo of Didyma in Central Asia at Dilbergin Tepe on the road from Balkh to the Oxus at Kilif. A 15-metre-high mound has revealed a thriving city from the late Persian period which, in its heyday under Greco-Bactrian rule, built temples adorned with Greek motifs, fine wall-paintings and statues of Greek gods, including Hercules. Here amphorae were found stamped with the mark of the Branchidae, the clan of Apollo of Didyma. The city of the Branchidae itself appears to have been north of the river, conceivably at Talashkan Tepe, a tiny site on the old road from Termez; destroyed at just this time Talashkan Tepe was never lived in again, and when the archaeologists began to explore it some years ago, they found a litter of catapult bolts and slingshots in the debris.

It is a grim tale. Today, we would describe the massacre as a war crime. But why did Alexander order it? We can only assume that his propagandist Callisthenes presented the atrocity to the Greeks back home as revenge for the sacrilege of Xerxes; in other words, the story was intended to redound to Alexander's credit, reminding the Greeks of the self-proclaimed ideals of the Crusade. But we know that Xerxes had not been responsible for the sack of Didyma. So was the massacre an act of retribution at all? Or was the ancient tale simply an opportunistic excuse for casual violence of a kind which must have happened far more often than our sources reveal? The sacking of cities, after all, was their way of life, just as it was in the heroic age in the pages of the *Iliad*. To be a sacker of cities was worthy of emulation. In such a world, giving a city or a village over to murder, rape and plunder may have had a cathartic effect in assuaging the troops' blood-lust after the ordeal of the crossing of the desert and the river. The Branchidae themselves were redundant now that Alexander had reconstituted the oracle under a new regime; they were best disposed of, their history erased and rewritten for posterity (as is so often the case with tyrants). Whatever the reason, it is an appalling story and, for some, must have cast a shadow over the events of the summer.

Alexander then pushed on to the Jaxartes (Syr Darya) river, 550 kilometres from the Oxus, in a pursuit so fast that Bessus was abandoned by his own troops and then finally turned in to Alexander. For Bessus, as he must have expected, a grim fate awaited. Naked, in a wooden halter, he was scourged by the side of the road as the whole army passed him; then mutilated in Persian fashion, his nose and ears cut off before he was sent back to Hamadan for trial and gruesome execution. Resistance, however, did not end with the death of Bessus. Both in Bactria and Sogdia the ancient warrior classes were fiercely independent and excellent horsemen who lived in great baronial strongholds, fortified castles and farms. Seven thousand top-notch cavalry could be raised from Bactria alone. The leaders and their local supporters needed only a short look at Alexander to see which way the wind would blow; to understand that Macedonian overlordship could be very much more oppressive than the Persians had been. Suddenly revolts flared up everywhere:

Macedonian garrisons were wiped out; in one skirmish Alexander was hit in the leg by an arrow, suffering a fractured fibula, and, for a while, had to be carried around on a litter. He fell back to Maracanda, the fabled oasis of Samarkand which now enters our story for the first time.

## SAMARKAND

You can see the great domes of Samarkand, the towering portals of the Registan and Bibi Khanum, from miles away across the fields of cotton. Crumbling sun-baked bricks rise over bright green gardens; the kashi tiles of deep blue and turquoise are dazzling. The backdrop now is of Soviet-style concrete modernism, but the medieval town still dominates. Like all the great Central Asian cities, its heyday was the fifteenth century, the Age of Tamerlane, but its origins lie back in the time of the Persian empire. Samarkand lies in an oasis on the edge of the Kyzyl Kum desert, set between two mountain ranges and watered by the Zeravshan river. Such a favourable spot has been inhabited since prehistory and, in more recent times, the Silk Route made it rich. In 982 a Persian geographer called it 'huge populous and very pleasant, the resort of merchants from all over the world'.

When the Greeks arrived in Samarkand, it was the key Persian fortress in Sogdia. The citadel and palace stood on Afrasiab hill over a sheer drop down to the Siab river. From there, today, there is a fine view of the medieval city. It was, even then, a major urban centre, a vast site with a 14-kilometre wall (still standing 13 metres high in places). Destroyed by Genghis Khan in 1220, the town was refounded close by its present site. It recovered: when Ibn Battuta came through in 1333 he described it as 'one of the largest and most perfectly beautiful cities in the world'.

Samarkand/Maracanda would be Alexander's forward base for the next eighteen months. From here he would use a scorched-earth policy against the surrounding region, which only inflamed local opposition. This focused on Spitamenes, one of the chiefs who had turned Bessus in. Summoned by Alexander to join him, Spitamenes refused and began to raise forces against him. Having initially co-operated with Alexander, Spitamenes now decided to risk all by coming out in open revolt. A high-ranking local nobleman of Iranian descent, kinsman of Bessus and therefore distantly of the Achaemenian royal line, Spitamenes was able to mount the fiercest, most protracted and most successful resistance of any of Alexander's opponents. Although his resources were comparatively slender, he realized the best way to fight the Greeks was by hit-and-run raids, mobile warfare and guerrilla groups. (Perhaps he also knew that Alexander would be hampered here by

language. Sogdian was a very difficult language which few could speak; Greek sources single out the role of Pharnuces, a diplomat and interpreter of Iranian origin, who alone could speak Sogdian. In terms of using spies and gathering intelligence, language problems may have made it much harder for Alexander to crack the resistance.)

## ALEXANDRIA THE FARTHERMOST

Alexander now camped on the Syr Darya river, 250 kilometres to the north-east of Samarkand, and the northern frontier of the Persian empire. Here, he had selected a site for a city, but work was postponed by news of the growing rebellion in Sogdia, which was spreading to Bactria, where a 7000 cavalry nucleus had joined Spitamenes. Alexander immediately sent forces to blockade Cyropolis (today's Kurkath is Kurus katha: 'city of Cyrus') a frontier town founded by Cyrus of Persia in 530 BC. Cyropolis was the centre of seven towns and the Greeks sacked these, one by one, mercilessly applying their

Left: Samarkand. On the skyline is the mound of Afrasiab
where the city stood in Alexander's time.

Above: Alexandria the Farthermost today, the Tajik city of Khodzent.

military convention of killing all the men of military age. Cyropolis resisted sharply; so, too, did the fortress of a people known as the Memaceni — probably the ancient citadel of Ura-Tyube, which stands on a high mound 50 kilometres south of the river. 'No other town put up such fierce resistance,' says Curtius. Many of the king's best troops were killed, and Alexander himself sustained a serious wound when he was hit on the neck by a stone and knocked unconscious, losing sight and speech for a while. For a moment, his doctors feared for his life and the revenge was terrible. Using mines, the Macedonian engineers caused a massive breach in the walls, and the whole place was destroyed. It was a grim fore-taste of events further east, the Greeks letting it be known that any town which resisted would have all males of military age killed, the women and children enslaved.

After the fall of Cyropolis, and its neighbouring towns, Alexander returned to the Syr Darya to build his new town, which was now urgently needed as a forward-campaign base, given the worsening military situation. In seventeen days, a wall of sun-dried brick, 6 kilometres long, was thrown up around the camp to form the basis of the city which would have the honour, among over thirty Alexandrias, of being Alexandria Eschate – the Farthermost. It was populated by the usual mix: wounded, invalids, press-ganged mercenaries, retired veterans (some unwilling), but also with freed captives. Curtius claims (although how he knows this is unclear) that in his day (AD 30s) the descendants of these people still retained their identity as a group because of their memory of Alexander. The town was a successful place in the Middle Ages, notable for its 'chivalrous' population, and 'as famous for its pomegranates as Samarkand is for its apples'. It survived and is still a nice spot today, though burning hot in summer. Khodzent, in Tajikistan (having recently reverted to its medieval name after a few decades as Leninabad), is a pleasant modern town with a promenade along the river, and the Mogul Tau mountains rising nearly 1600 metres immediately beyond the town. Here Alexander would build his northernmost altars dedicated to Dionysus, perhaps somewhere near the spot where, today, a gleaming titanium statue of Lenin stands gesturing to the East, a monument to another wave of history which shook the world and then receded. Although the city may not quite have fulfilled Alexander's hopes of being a 'world famous place', Khodzent is still one of his happier legacies.

As Spitamenes's revolt gathered momentum, Alexander's situation took another turn for the worse. He had sent a general Menedemus to blockade Spitamenes at Samarkand with over 2000 infantry and several hundred cavalry, including sixty Companions. But when the Macedonians arrived, the rebels pulled away from the city down the Zeravshan river and drew them into an ambush. All the Macedonian leaders were killed, and most of the force was wiped out. Two thousand infantry and 300 cavalry were lost. It was the first serious military reverse the Macedonians had suffered for over twenty years. Back on the Jaxartes, Alexander interviewed the survivors and gave orders to conceal the disaster from his troops. Witnesses were threatened with death if they divulged what had happened – a graphic insight into his control of information.

Alexander now knew, if he didn't know it before, that he was in a serious war. To make matters worse, north of the river, nomadic Scythians and Sacae, formidable horsemen, were gathering to attack the newly-built Alexandria the Farthermost. Curtius paints a vivid cameo of the king at night in his HQ on the Syr Darya, mulling over his narrowing options, lifting his tent-flap to watch the enemy fires glinting across the river. He had never been more isolated: nomadic tribes massing to the north; Sogdia and Bactria in revolt to the south; his line of retreat threatened and his health still precarious.

*He had still not recovered from his wound; in particular he had difficulty in speaking,*
*a condition stemming from malnutrition and the pain in his neck ... he could not stand*
*in the ranks, ride a horse or give his men instructions or encouragement ... his voice was*
*so quavering and feeble that it was difficult even for those next to him to hear.*

But he had to act. He decided to subdue the Scythians first, and put together a lightning attack using catapults mounted on boats to drive the enemy back from the riverbank; then the phalanx troops crossed the Syr Darya on ox-skins stuffed with chaff. Once the bridgehead had been established, the Greek cavalry came over and engaged the enemy, in conjunction with light-armed and archers to combat the hit-and-run tactics of the Scythians' mounted archers. The Greeks won a decisive victory and pursued the Scythians for 12 kilometres to a place where they came upon burial cairns of the Saca people. (These were identified by the Greeks with the boundary stones left by Dionysus himself on his wanderings – another comforting omen to the increasingly superstitious king.)

Alexander himself was, by now, back at base, unable to fight. His leg wound had not healed, and he still had impaired vision and speech from his head and throat wound. To make matters worse he had drunk bad water and had suffered a violent and incapacitating attack of dysentery. (If deaths in modern armies are anything to go by, wastage in the Greek army from such ailments must have been serious, even if the Greek doctors were expert in local remedies.) The Scythian forces, though, were crushed north of the river. Alexander was now free to turn against the main revolt in Sogdia. He marched south on Samarkand and the rebels fled into the Red Desert. Returning to the site of the defeat of his expeditionary force, he buried his dead under a great mound. (This has not yet been located, but it must lie somewhere on the Zeravshan river outside Samarkand.) With winter rains turning the plain into mud around Samarkand, the army moved into winterquarters at Nautaca (Uzunkir, near Shakhrisyabz). According to one Greek source, 120,000 Sogdians had been killed during the fighting.

## THE CAMPAIGN OF 327:
## FIRE AND SWORD IN CENTRAL ASIA

The fighting through the year 328 must have been a shock to Alexander. As Curtius said: 'He had had to fight a war he had not anticipated'. Losses had been heavy, and the pacified areas had required strong garrisons. Alexander's response to the risings and guerrilla warfare was predictable – total war. Over 20,000 reinforcements had been sent out from

Greece (the journey of 6000 kilometres must have taken them nearly a year) and the king now reorganized his army to make it more flexible. Sogdia was a great horse-breeding region (the region around Karshi was especially noted for its horses even in the nineteenth century, and, until the Russian Revolution, great horse-fairs were a feature of the big bazaars). It was easy, then, for Alexander to replenish and expand his mounted forces. The first year had been a near disaster and most of the countryside remained to be pacified. So, ever resourceful, he devised new tactics, dividing his forces into mobile army groups which would comb the country with fire and sword, rooting out opposition by over-whelming firepower.

In the spring of 327, four unit commanders were left in Bactria while the main army moved back to the Oxus and divided into five army groups. What happened next is the subject of much debate. The year 327 has been described as a missing year in the history of Alexander, because the sources are in disagreement over the order and placing of events. But, in the new campaigning season, Alexander started off by following the Oxus east-wards for eleven days. This would have brought him to a remarkable site at the junction of the Oxus and Kokcha Kunduz rivers. Situated on a plateau at the northern limit of Afghanistan, facing the cliffs of Tajikistan, it is called Ai Khanoum, in Uzbek 'Lady of the Moon'. Here, Alexander probably founded Alexandria-on-the-Oxus, the first Greek city ever to be discovered in Central Asia.

Only identified in 1961, Ai Khanoum has all the hallmarks which we associate with Greek civic architecture: an acropolis and a lower city, with palace, agora, gymnasium, temple, and theatre. Now, sadly pock-marked with holes dug by looters (it was devastated during the civil war which followed the Russian pull out), the site is protected by the rivers on two sides, and a deep moat on the landward side with bastion towers and artillery platforms. Standing on Ai Khanoum, looking east, you see hills leading towards the mountains of Badakshan; straight ahead, across the river, are sheer cliffs; in the gap between the two, the plains of Asia stretch as far as the eye can see. No doubt its original foundation was military: a campaign base, just as the Persians had built fortresses along the Oxus. But, at Ai Khanoum, evidently a city soon followed with all the trappings and civic amenities of Hellenic civilization, the oldest structure is a monument to a man called Kineas who may well have been the founder, or first governor, of the city; its date is, perhaps, soon after Alexander's expedition. Inscribed on the base is a copy of the famous Delphic maxims:

> *As children learn good manners.*
> *As young men learn to control the passions.*
> *In middle age be just*

*In old age give good advice.*
*Then die without regret.*

According to the inscription, this was placed here by someone called Clearchos, who says he had copied these words himself on a visit to Delphi. So Clearchos had brought these pearls of wisdom with him all the way out to Central Asia. We know of a Clearchos who was a pupil of Aristotle, so perhaps he had known Alexander at school. It is a tempting fantasy to think that Clearchos and Kineas came here with Alexander's army as members of the officer corps, and that, when the city was founded, Clearchos placed the Delphic precepts in this monument at the centre of the city, where Kineas was later buried. These maxims give us an insight into the mentality of the colonists who enunciated the ideals of settlers and their native collaborators (rather as the British did in India), and put forward the precepts of their own culture while 6000 kilometres and half-a-world away from their homeland.

Again, the city's population would have been the usual mix of invalids, volunteers, press-ganged veterans, mercenaries, punishment units, and native settlers, sustained here (as later in India) by a pool of under-privileged labour. At Ai Khanoum, the rich hinterland, which had already been developed under the Persians, was now divided by the conquerors into manorial domains owned by Greek nabobs, such as Kineas, and worked by a native under-class. Dozens of such settlements would follow in Central Asia and India, some of them long-lasting. The wealth of these places has been revealed by wonderful archaeological finds, such as the Oxus treasure in the British Museum; and the recent hoard of gold from Bactrian noble graves at Tilya Tepe in north Afghanistan. Bactrian-Greek rule would last for centuries in these parts and their coins are still turned up all over the countryside – a testimony to this extraordinary and long-forgotten colonial enterprise.

That spring, though, Alexander's second year of campaigning in Central Asia, his first priority was to establish fire-bases and root out his enemies. Somewhere by Ai Khanoum, the army split up. Alexander then crossed north through Tajikistan, while the other four army groups fanned up the main river valleys towards Dushanbe and the Anzob Pass. We can imagine scorched earth as far as the Hissar range, the great barrier separating east and west Sogdia. That summer he attacked the famous Sogdian Rock, one of the great strongholds of the Sogdian barons, which he captured with the tactic of 'flying men': 300 volunteers experienced in rock-climbing, who used improvised crampons and ropes to assault the impregnable natural fortress somewhere in these mountains, terrifying the defenders into surrender. The war finally was going Alexander's way.

## THE MURDER OF BLACK CLEITUS

Towards the end of summer, after five months campaigning, the army reconvened at Maracanda. There, a fateful and celebrated episode in the king's story now took place. Alexander had decided to appoint Cleitus, brother of the woman who had nursed him, to be the new satrap of Bactria. Cleitus was a member of the old guard who had fought for Alexander's father Philip, and he had saved Alexander's life at the Granicus. Reading between the lines, knowing that Alexander's relations with the older generation of the Macedonian army were strained, the appointment may have been another case of getting a malcontent out of the way. Whatever the truth of that, on the night in question a banquet was held in the palace at Maracanda.

The party, as usual, had started early. Everyone was drunk. By now heavy drinking seems to have been the order of the day ('he always had the tools for a drinking session with him,' says one fragment). We get the impression that Alexander and his officers increasingly needed to anaesthetize themselves against the constant stress and strain, the hard fighting, the killing. Plutarch, even in defending the king over charges that he was a heavy drinker, admits that the king liked to drink and would often sleep it off till midday, sometimes for the whole of the next day. On such occasions, Alexander was never slow to blow his own trumpet. As Plutarch said: 'though delightful company and incomparably charming at other times, when he was drinking he could become offensively arrogant and descend to the level of the common soldier, then he would give way to boasting and let himself be led on by flatterers'.

That night Alexander was sounding off. There were two main strands in his monologue: decrying the leaders of the ill-fated expedition near Samarkand for incompetence; and belittling the achievements of his father, claiming his own were the greater deeds. At one point Curtius claims Alexander accused his father of bearing ill-will and jealousy towards him, and never giving him credit for his own achievements: food for Freudians! Older members of the party, all of whom had served under Philip, kept quiet until Alexander claimed the credit for his father's victory at Chaeronea over the Athenians and Thebans. Cleitus could hold himself back no longer. Bitter home-truths were spoken, acerbic barbs from Euripides traded, until Cleitus baited the king with a jibe calculated to hit home: 'all your glory is due to your father'. In a raging fury, Alexander had to be restrained as he gave the signal in Macedonian for the guards to sound the alarm. Realizing the king was out of control they refused. From here, the different versions of the tale diverge. According to one, Cleitus was escorted out through the front door and across the citadel moat (which has been identified by the excavators), before he charged back in to aim another riposte at the apoplectic king. Another says Alexander barred the door and, as the guests left, challenged Cleitus ('who was not carrying a lamp') whom he recognized by his voice. At any rate, all agree the king then killed Cleitus with a javelin thrust, which covered himself and the vestibule with blood. In drunken remorse, he then tried to turn the point on himself before collapsing in tears and drink-sodden self-pity. Afterwards, he shut himself in his tent. They spent ten days there says Curtius, 'mainly in trying to restore the king's self respect'. According to Arrian, it took the sceptic philosopher Anaxagoras, one of the royal entourage, to cut through Alexander's agonized self recriminations. The king, he said, was the embodiment of justice; whatever he did was right, simply because he was who he was. (A frightening argument, which has been the tyrant's justification throughout history.) The argument, needless to say, found favour with Alexander.

How far did the murder affect the morale of the inner circle? Cleitus was not an important enough character for his murder to alienate many people, but it must have added to the fear of stepping out of line. There is a mysterious passage in Curtius, in which he quite incidentally mentions 'the suspension of free speech which happened after the murder of Cleitus'. It is hardly believable that this was formally so, but with Alexander one can never tell. If not actually true, it may well have been what those around him tacitly understood. For clues to the mood of the court at this time, we can also look to an extra-ordinary fragment from the lost history of Ephippus, a contemporary pamphleteer unfavourable to Alexander. It conjures up a picture of a court increasingly wary of the tyrant's mood swings:

> *Alexander sprinkled the very floor with precious perfumes and scented wine. In his honour myrrh and other kinds of incense were consumed in smoke; a religious stillness and silence born of fear held fast all who were in his presence. For he was intolerable, and murderous, reputed in fact to be melancholy mad.*

It is a chilling portrait if it reflects a real eye-witness account, and resembles images of tyrants from our own time. Psychologists will instantly recognize the picture: the man portrayed here was surely in our terms a manic depressive.


## ROXANNE: 'THE MOST BEAUTIFUL GIRL IN ASIA'

Cleitus was murdered at the end of summer. Autumn was coming on and extensive prepa-rations were set in hand for gathering supplies for another winter camp in the Uzbek plain. This probably involved massive predatory forays on the local population at harvest time. After further campaigning against the last pockets of rebels out towards Bukhara, Alexander moved back to winter quarters at Nautaca, the former base of Bessus (probably Uzunkir, near Shakhrisyabz on the Kashka Darya). The local ruler, Sisimithres, took to his mountain citadel, up the valley towards the source of the Kashka Darya. As winter came on Alexander attacked them with his siege-engines and forced their surrender.

It was here, according to some versions of the story, that Alexander first set eyes on Roxanne, daughter of the Sogdian baron Oxyartes, a girl 'more beautiful than any woman except the wife of Darius'. She had apparently been among the captives taken at the Sogdian Rock and, perhaps, had been in the entourage for some time before the king noticed her. Then, one night at a feast, 'a banquet of barbaric splendour', she danced with other girls. The king fell in love – or became infatuated, 'in the heat of passion' – despite the disapproval of his companions. That she was beautiful, everyone agreed. Though young she also had a dignity and bearing 'rarely seen among the barbarians', but still no one understood Alexander's infatuation, least of all, no doubt, his male companions who were his true intimates. There had been other crushes: the beautiful eunuch, Bagoas, with whom the king had close relations; the young man, Euxenippos (incredibly handsome – 'as good looking as Hephaistion', it was said by the court gossips with a nudge and a wink, 'though rather effeminate – and nothing like Hephaistion's charm'). But marriage? It was even more astonishing that Alexander had agreed to marry the girl. 'Has he come all the way to the Oxus to marry a non Greek?', it was murmured. 'Are we to be ruled in the future by a king descended from a Bactrian landowner of no great birth?'. But Alexander was adamant, cutting the bread with his sword with his new father-in-law, as was – and still is – the Sogdian custom. The tale of Roxanne became a theme for medieval Romance and is still the subject of rich stories among the country people of Afghanistan, who say Alexander and Roxanne married in Balkh, and that Roxanne was a good Afghan girl who, true to her people's hatred of foreign invaders, secreted a knife under her pillow and attempted to murder the king on his wedding night. From Turkey to the Kazakh steppes, but especially among the Farsi-speaking Tajiks and Afghans, Roxanne is still remembered. Few, though, would have envied Roxanne the destiny which now opened up for her in what remained of her short life (see page 231).

---

'Alexander's Lake' in Tajikistan. Local legend says this is the resting place of Bucephalus, and in the cliffs nearby is the cave of Spitamenes (see page 166).

The fall of the Rock of Sisimithres marked the conclusion of the great rebellion in Sogdia. By mid-winter, Spitamenes had been betrayed – some said by his wife, who was embittered by his sexual betrayals; others state more plausibly that he was killed by his own side who had lost the will to fight on in such a punishing war against overwhelming odds. The spring of 326 saw the end of the two-year war beyond the Oxus – Alexander's hardest war. He left a network of a dozen military bases behind him in Bactria and Sogdia, with a field-force of 13,500 men. His union with Roxanne, and marriages between several of his staff and the daughters of local noblemen, sealed the peace which had been so expensively bought. Meanwhile the army with which Alexander now moved on India, was reinforced by many Bactrian and Sogdian troops, who were deliberately moved from their homeland to fight in foreign wars.

There is an extraordinary tailpiece to the story of the brave resistance of Spitamenes. Take the road from Dushanbe, in Tajikistan, up to the Hissar mountains and the Anzob Pass and you are following Alexander's route in the war of 327. In isolated valleys out here, live the last speakers of the ancient Sogdian language. Out here, the ancient religion of Zoroaster survived until the forced conversions of the late nineteenth century; yet, even now, in these valleys, people still revere the fire in the domestic hearth, still pray to Mazdaian angels, still believe in the presence of the evil one, Ahriman, even though they profess to be Muslims. Close by is Iskander Gul, 'Alexander's Lake'. Here, they say, his faithful horse Bucephalus died, but each full moon the horse still rises from the lake to graze on the shore and ride the night sky with his black rider – Alexander himself. Beyond the lake, scoured by winds from the Pamirs, a winding precipitous path leads up to a hidden cave. Inside the cave, a mummified corpse, decked in offerings, sits to receive gifts and prayers from local Muslims while incense and oil are burned before him. This, they say, is the body of the leader of the great Sogdian revolt, Alexander's toughest enemy, Spitamenes himself.

## DISSENSION GROWS: THE DEATH OF CALLISTHENES

We now come to the greatest crisis of Alexander's reign. Resentful of the king's growing despotism, a group of royal pages tried to assassinate Alexander in his tent having manipulated the rota to get the conspirators on duty on the same shift. However, that night Alexander had embarked on one of his now habitual marathon drinking sessions and never went to bed. The next day, the plot was revealed and the pages – teenagers all – were tortured to death. The king's intimates pointed the finger at the court historian, Callisthenes, as the inspiration behind the plot, although none of the plotters had incriminated him, even under duress. Callisthenes's increasingly critical comments on the king's behaviour, however, had seen him rapidly fall from grace, and he was now evidently a target for the festering hostility of Alexander and his inner circle. Some might have observed that Callisthenes was now paying for his appeasement of a tyrant. After all, this was the man who more than any other, had helped build up the myth of Alexander's divinely favoured deeds. His account of the sea parting in Pamphylia to let the king through; the tale of the sacred spring at Didyma coming back to life; the oracle at Siwa; the massacre of the Branchidae – all these stories had been trumpeted around the Greek world. Now, however, Callisthenes seems to have realized that he had helped to create a monster and willingly became a mouth-piece for growing resentment among the old guard over the orientalization of Alexander's court, his adoption of Persian dress and ceremonial, and his attempt to impose Persian-style prostration on his followers. It all came to a head in Balkh, in another very public argument and another bitter falling out. Again, stripped of the myth, it is likely that the gist of the conversation has come down to us. One detail is gripping: as he walked out on Alexander, Callisthenes threw back, three times, a line from the *Iliad*, Alexander's favourite book: 'A better man than you by far was Patroclus, yet still Death did not spare him'.

Callisthenes had signed his own death warrant. On the pretext of the pages' plot, Alexander had him arrested. Accounts differ as to his fate. Some said he died in prison but, according to Curtius, he was tortured and crucified: 'Of all Alexander's acts this one caused the most resentment because Callisthenes was a man of fine character and wholly inno-cent of the charges made against him, and yet Alexander had him barbarously tortured and without trial'.

So, after two years of ferocious campaigning, with heavy but undisclosed losses, a time of unremitting cruelty and hardness, Alexander had pacified Sogdia and Bactria. He could now turn his attention to what the Greeks probably considered the ultimate prize, India – a land of proverbial riches, beyond which was thought to lie the end of the world, and the Great Ocean.

That spring, Alexander returned to the Hindu Kush, probably crossing via Bamian, and readied himself for the invasion of India. To some extent, the way was prepared. The most powerful ruler in north-west India, the king of Taxila, had already sent ambassadors to Alexander promising him help and co-operation. Alexander returned to the Kabul valley, then moved down the Kabul river towards its confluence with the Indus: this is the ancient route from Bactria to India, which has been used by invaders of India from pre-history right down to the British Raj. The last and most dramatic phase of Alexander's campaign of world-conquest was about to begin.

# PART FIVE

# To the ENDS of the EARTH

## PAKISTAN AND INDIA
### 327 – 326 BC

*The invasion of India; the lost valley of Dionysus;
into the North-West Frontier; the Fortress of Hercules; across the Indus;
battle on the Jhelum river; the death of Bucephalus; into deepest India;
the army will go no further; the lost altars; the fleet prepares;
the conquest of Punjab and Sind; the siege of Multan;
on to the Southern Ocean*

IN THE SPRING OF 327 BC ALEXANDER stood on the slopes of the Hindu Kush, somewhere in the mountainous region between Pakistan and Afghan Nuristan. He was twenty-nine; a tough, stocky, hard-bitten little man, still possessed of demonic will and energy; his iron constitution not yet wrecked by the dozen battle wounds, malaria, dysentery, and his increasingly frequent alcoholic binges. Alexander's tutor Aristotle had conjectured, in line with Greek geography as then understood, that it ought to be possible to see the end of the earth from the top of the Hindu Kush. But, amid the wealth of other scientific information being gathered by his expedition, Alexander could say for sure that his eminent teacher was wrong. The end of the earth was nowhere to be seen. Perhaps, however, he was driven still to see it; driven now as much by the desire to know, as by the need to conquer.

## THE INVASION OF INDIA

First, though, India had to be subdued. The Greeks knew little about it. It was only after Alexander's death that Greek understanding of India opened up, after the Greek ambassador Megasthenes visited Patna and gave a detailed account of the Ganges kingdom and its customs. At this moment their knowledge was limited to the North-West Frontier and the Punjab; and then, largely from Persian sources. Darius and his predecessors had claimed loose suzerainty over the Indus valley. Indians ('people of Hindush') are shown on the walls of Persepolis bringing their characteristic gifts, in particular cotton, the produce of the Indus valley. But of the lands beyond the Indus, the Greeks knew next to nothing.

As usual, the invasion of India was meticulously planned. The main army under Hephaistion was sent down the Kabul river and over the Khyber Pass, a route we followed by steam-train on the old British Khyber railway down to Peshawar, where we picked up Alexander's track by road. Alexander knew the king of Taxila was on his side, but the other important Indian king west of the Indus had not submitted and was besieged by Hephaistion at Charsadda. After a forty-day siege the Greeks sacked the city and killed the king before moving on to begin the bridging of the Indus, a crucial preparation for Alexander's passage to India. Alexander meanwhile moved with light armed units along

---

Previous pages, left: Alexander before a Hindu idol, from a Persian
manuscript of 1494. Later ages were fascinated by the Greek
encounter with India. Right: A silver coin showing Alexander wearing
an elephant skin on his head, symbolizing the conquest of India
(Alexandria 315-300 BC).

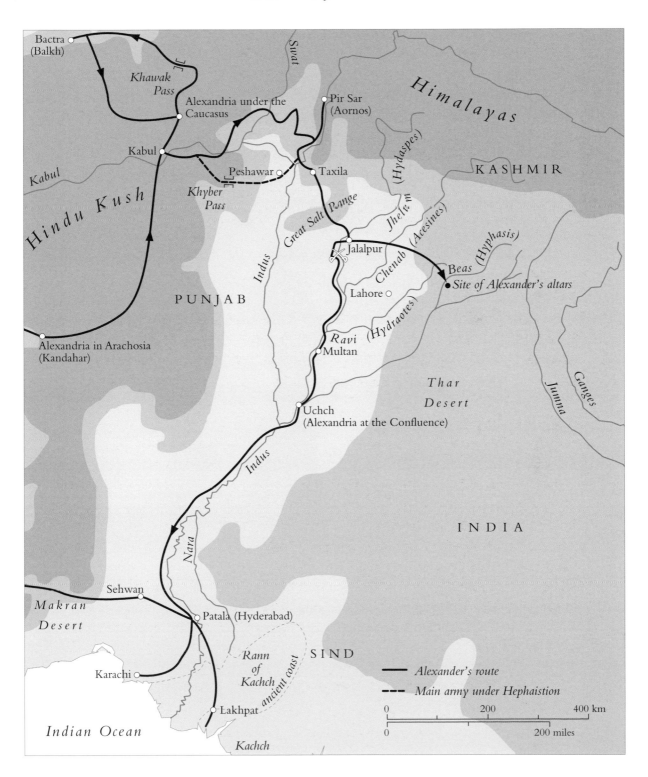

Bactra
(Balkh)

*Khawak
Pass*

Alexandria under the
Caucasus

*Swat*

Pir Sar
(Aornos)

H i m a l a y a s

Kabul

K A S H M I R

*Kabul*

Peshawar

Taxila

(Hydaspes)

*Khyber
Pass*

H i n d u   K u s h

Great Salt Range

Jhelum

(Acesines)

(Hyphasis)

*Indus*

Jalalpur

Chenab

Beas (Hyphasis)

Site of Alexander's altars

Alexandria in Arachosia
(Kandahar)

P U N J A B

Lahore

*Ravi*

(Hydraotes)

Multan

*T h a r
D e s e r t*

*Jumna*

*Ganges*

Uchch
(Alexandria at the Confluence)

I N D I A

*Indus*

*Nara*

Sehwan

*Makran
Desert*

Patala (Hyderabad)

*Rann
of
Kachch*

S I N D

Alexander's route

ancient coast

Main army under Hephaistion

Karachi

0        200        400 km

Lakhpat

0        200 miles

*Indian Ocean*

*Kachch*

the Kunar valley in East Afghanistan, and crossed into the North-West Frontier of Pakistan by the Nawar Pass, leaving a new fortified town at a site that is still known as Iskandero, where a big ancient mound is topped by a decayed British military post.

## AND DID THOSE FEET?
## THE LOST VALLEY OF DIONYSUS

Somewhere in these valleys off the Kunar, on the border between modern Pakistan and Afghanistan, an extraordinary incident took place which allows us another insight into the mentality of Alexander and his high command. The Greeks were about to attack a small town called Nysa when the locals came out to claim protection on the most improbable grounds. They were, they said, descendants of the followers of the Greek god Dionysus who had stayed here on his epic journey which had taken him to Greece back in mythical times. Dionysus was the god of ecstasy and intoxication, provoker of frenzy and possession, a frightening destroyer, an unpredictable man-woman, clad in an animal skin. As with Heracles, Alexander claimed kinship with the dark one, Dionysus. Indeed, so far as we can tell, he was much addicted to Dionysus. Wine was seen as one of the gifts of the god; whether Alexander was actually an alcoholic or not (and there are indications that he was by the end) there can be no doubt that he saw his drinking bouts as inseparable from devotion to the spirit of Dionysus.

The Macedonians, at any rate, were all too ready to believe the tale. On one level frightening in their modernity, on another they were people of their time: credulous, superstitious, possessed by gods and demons. There were legends that Dionysus, and Hercules, had come this way and the Greeks were quite prepared to believe that these wild valleys had seen the footsteps of the god in ancient times. The locals led the Greeks to a glade where they saw ivy for the first time since leaving the Mediterranean Sea, along with bay trees, laurels, and other signs of Dionysus. The Greeks also noted the presence of wine, and of strange wooden funeral monuments hung in the trees. The locals pointed out a mountain whose name the Greeks were quick to equate with Meros, the mountain where Dionysus's nurse Nysa had nursed the divine boy child. (In Hindu myth the *axis mundi* is Mount Meru.) This was enough to arouse Alexander's interest. The Greeks broke off their

---

Dionysiac ecstasy. This ivory, from Vergina, may represent Philip
and the young Alexander (as Pan) with Olympias, 'who would enter
into states of possession with wilder abandon than anyone'.

foray into the North-West Frontier, and Alexander and some senior officers went off to see the mountain. Indeed, according to one account, they went native in a Bacchic frenzy, no doubt fuelled as ever by alcohol, putting laurel wreaths round their foreheads and giving themselves up to mass hysteria, running through forest glades crying the Bacchic cry *Euoi Euoi*.

A former civil servant and retired general, Arrian found such tales all too much to swallow. 'If anyone seriously thinks that distinguished members of the officer corps would stoop to this sort of thing … ' One can almost see his upper lip quivering. But perhaps the story was true. Think, for example, of the weird back-to-nature cults among the Nazi officer corps. In the more remote valleys of the North-West Frontier there are still tribes-people whose culture is distantly cognate with the ancient Greek. In Chitral (and also in neighbouring Afghan Nuristan until they were forcibly converted a century ago) there are still people who worship the ancient Indo-European sky god, make wine, and bury their dead in carved coffins with wooden memorial effigies hung in the trees, just as the Greeks described. Their legends say they are actually descended from the Greeks (see page 8). Most likely, the 'Kafirs' of the Hindu Kush were in these valleys long before the Greeks; and are probably the last survivors of the people Alexander met here that spring.


## INTO THE NORTH-WEST FRONTIER

After the Bacchic revels, Alexander moved towards the Swat valley where he met fierce resistance. The main regional centre was a place called Massaga. It allegedly had a popula-tion of 30,000 and was protected by 8000 mercenaries from the interior (the local ruler was obviously forewarned about the Greeks). The city had a long circuit of walls built in the Swat style with boulders and rubble strengthened with wooden beams, and there was a big natural ditch on the side not protected by the river. The Greeks brought siege-engines across the moat on a massive land-fill and turned the full force of their war-machine on the place. The Indians put up a fierce resistance until the leader of the mercenaries was killed; then they sued for peace. The queen of the place made a personal entreaty to the king which, according to one later story, was helped by her beauty (some said she bore Alexander a child). But the grim denouement is more likely to be historical. The mercenaries were allowed to leave under safe conduct. That night they camped outside the city on raised ground with their baggage, women and children in the belief that they had been permitted to depart altogether. But this was not Alexander's intention. Under cover of darkness he had them surrounded and the next day they were all massacred. Fighting to the death, they continued to protest that Alexander had broken his word. The king's answer, as recorded by one source, has an unpleasant ring of truth about it: 'I said they could leave the city, I did not say that they would be friends of the Macedonians forever'.

The story was the same up the Swat, a wide and beautiful valley walled to the north by the dramatic snow-capped ranges of the Hindu Kush. Alexander attacked two cities here, Ora and Bazira, whose sites were identified by the English explorer Sir Aurel Stein in the 1920s. Bazira (Bir-Kot) stands on a black rock overlooking the river; Ora (Udegram) a site, now being excavated by the Italians, has a fortress with a towered gate on a beetling crag high above the valley.

Along the whole length of Swat, refugees now fled into the mountains around Mount Ilam and beyond to escape the fire and sword of the Greeks, whose mobile columns of mountaineers and crack commando units were mopping up all opposition. The climax of the campaign was one of Alexander's most famous exploits: the siege of the impregnable rock fortress which the Greeks called Aornos (probably from Sanskrit *avarna,* meaning fortress), the place which legend said even the demi-god, Hercules himself, had been unable to take.

## AORNOS: THE FORTRESS OF HERCULES

The refugees from the whole of the North-West Frontier region had gathered on a high natural citadel up the Indus valley, tucked out of the way of the Macedonian advance. Alexander, however, was not prepared to leave any concentration of hostile forces behind him as he pushed on into India. Moreover, he had been told a local legend which said Hercules himself had failed to take this place during his famous wanderings across the earth to accomplish his Twelve Labours (a tale perhaps deriving from a story of the Hindu God Shiva, whose attributes of club and animal skin resemble those of Hercules).

Alexander could not resist such a challenge, once again experiencing a *pothos* (violent longing) to see and take the peak. But where was Aornos? The Greeks give some key facts; its south face was washed by the Indus; the mountain massif was roughly

---

Overleaf: The rugged landscape of the Swat valley in the
North-West Frontier of Pakistan. Alexander pushed up here
in the winter of 327-326 BC, and sacked the cities of
Udegram and Bir-Kot.

circular, 40 kilometres round and a kilometre and a half high above the river; on top there was a flat expanse of cultivatable fields, enough to keep a sizeable population busy. Following these clues, in the freezing April of 1926, the indefatigable explorer Aurel Stein took a donkey-train up these hills to find the lost site. He identified it at an inaccessible height above the Indus valley, a place called Pir Sar ('the Green Man'). Recently Stein's identification has been challenged, but only by scholars sitting in their studies. In the intervening years, few, if any, have gone up there to try to piece the story together on the ground, and no other plausible site has been offered. One reason, of course, is the difficulty of conducting such exploration. On a gusty May day, with the sky presaging storms, the snow mostly gone under 3000 metres, we followed in Alexander's and Stein's footsteps to try to reconstruct the dramatic events of Alexander's epic siege.

Alexander had approached up the Indus from the south, but he soon realized that a frontal assault on the hill was out of the question. The terrain was simply too steep, rocky and overgrown. Once again, he turned to local guides who, no doubt under duress, revealed that there was only one path on to the heights which could be used by a large force. If Stein's identification is right, this can only be the path which runs all the way to Pir Sar from Upal Kandao, and this the route we decided to follow. It approaches from the west along the summit of a pine-forested ridge, 7 kilometres long (as the crow flies – the actual walk is a lot longer, and seems it). The local District Commissioner, responsible for the Shangla Pass, helped to set up our expedition, and, by the time we set off, we were a sizeable group: four donkeys and their handlers (to carry the equipment), four armed frontier police (to keep off wolves and bandits), two archaeologist friends from Swat, and local guides, including the village headman or tahsidar. With them, an amazing story came dramatically to life.

We decided to start from the Upal Kandao saddle to the west of Pir Sar where we thought the Greek outflanking force must have started. In the first 2 kilometres the path rises well over 700 metres along the side of Bane-Sar mountain, which is thickly wooded with towering pine forests, oleander and wild hydrangeas, its grassy slopes dotted with yellow buttercups and pink Alpine flowers. Even our mules found the path hard going. It was a winding rocky track, which sometimes plunged into ravines, so the whole climb had to be repeated all over again. After a three-hour walk, we reached a spring of good water at Acharo-Sar (the Greeks mention a spring on the path). On the north side, through the trees, we could see a circle of snow-capped mountains along the horizon. Below us were steep drops covered with pine trees, with some gulleys still seamed with snow in early May. (Alexander had come through two weeks earlier in the year than us and tried to preserve the snow for drinking water by covering the gulleys with branches.)

Our progress was painfully slow, and we walked the last hour in darkness. Then we came to a deserted summer settlement at about 2700 metres, where we found shelter in the stoutly built mosque – a glorified shepherd's hut with a flat compacted roof held up by thick wooden posts. In the middle of the earth-floor was a hearth where we lit a fire for the night. Our food, however, had already been sent on to Pir Sar by the local governor, so we had to settle for fruit, biscuits and cold water. We spent a cold and uncomfortable night tossing and turning in our smoke-filled den. As I sat by the fire, writing up my notes, I thought of Ptolemy's troops on this path. They had come a little earlier in the year, and must have been colder than we were; however, they were no doubt better prepared, better fed, and a lot tougher of course; they must also have started earlier in the day and reached their goal in daylight.

Next day's dawn revealed a spectacular view all the way down to the Indus valley and the site of Alexander's main camp. At 6.30 we pushed on, cold, bleary and hungry, but, skirting the central peak at a little under 3000 metres, we were soon bathed in sunshine. Sometimes the path, which fell away on either side in spectacular drops, was only wide enough to accommodate two donkeys. Finally, by mid-morning, we came out through the trees on to a sunlit height looking down on to the Pir Sar plateau. Just as the Greeks said, the secret path had led them to a place where they could dominate the citadel. Below us was the Burimar ravine, the only approach on to Pir Sar. Our vantage point must have been where Ptolemy camped and built his fortification blocking off the ridge; indeed, wandering among the trees at this point, I thought I could detect traces of a pronounced earthwork for over 100 metres across the isthmus, which, at one place, was buttressed by a clear line of laid stones.

Once the Greeks had occupied the ridge above the ravine, the Indians were trapped. The only escape was down the precipitous slopes of Pir Sar. Alexander was now able to bring up reinforcements on to the heights. But he still had to get at the defenders, and this meant crossing the ravine, which could not be done in the face of the forces on top of Pir Sar. Alexander's solution was typically daring and uncompromising. He decided to bridge the ravine; to fill a gap of 500 metres to a height of at least 30 metres, maybe more. Each soldier was ordered to cut a hundred stakes to stabilize the earth-fill before bigger logs were laid on top. Over the next few days, an artificial causeway was constructed by the army working in relays day and night. Soon this gigantic siege causeway was pushed out 200 metres towards the plateau. Meanwhile, Alexander had brought up dismantled artillery on donkeys, and his catapults and javelin-throwers were now well within their range of 300 metres and could sweep the defenders off the hill closest to the causeway. Under their covering fire, the Greeks closed in.

Even then, for some reason, the Indians did not attempt to escape. Finally, the Greeks launched a commando-raid to take the knoll at the end of Pir Sar. The Indians were finished now and must have tried to sue for peace. Arrian glosses over what happened next. According to him the Indians tried to escape in the dead of night, the Greeks having deliberately taken the guard off one 'pass' which offered them a line of retreat. However, as at Massaga, this may just have been a ruse by Alexander. When the Indians attempted to evacuate the hill – perhaps believing they had a safe conduct – they were attacked and a wholesale massacre took place. The impregnable rock which had thwarted Hercules had fallen to Alexander.

On top, Alexander built altars to Nike (Victory) and Athena. Fragments of these may still survive, incorporated in the wall round the pond and in the little mosque on top of Pir Sar; a square rubble-built fortress on the northern end, may also be Alexander's work. As for the great causeway, rotted and decayed over the centuries, little sign remains today although the gap is still plainly visible.

The siege of Aornos was perhaps a minor event, amplified into epic proportions by Alexander's propagandists because of the extraordinary circumstances of the assault and the audacious building of the causeway – not to mention the emulation of Hercules. None the less, climbing Pir Sar in Alexander's footsteps, sharing the hardships of his troops, if only for a couple of nights, we could hardly imagine a more graphic illustration of Alexander's daring and irresistible impetus. The story of Aornos illustrates the implacable determination of the Macedonian king to show that resistance was hopeless, that there was nowhere to hide. Not for the first time on our journey I found myself strongly identifying with the hopeless defeated.

On top, we met local chiefs who had come up to see us. They had red henna'd beards, kohl-darkened eyes, bandannas of cartridges and were carrying old Enfields. It is a wild and lawless region up here. None had heard of Alexander's story, although one very old man spoke of an Englishman (clearly Aurel Stein) who came here sixty or seventy years ago: 'Like you he was looking for him. He spoke a lot about Iskander'. They prepared a feast for us, a meal of goat and rice. At the end of our stay, rather than retrace our track, we decided to descend directly from the south end of Pir Sar, using a winding and precipitous donkey path straight down to the river, 1700 metres below. Banks of indigo cloud

---

The march to Aornos: on the path up to the heights of Pir Sar,
looking north towards the Karakorum. Despite freezing conditions,
in April, at nearly 3000 metres, Alexander forced his way up
here with his siege equipment.

came in from the west and tremendous flashes of lightning cracked over Una-Sar and disappeared below us, while a thick veil of rain was loosed over the river to the east. As I began the descent, I turned back for a last view of the heights of Pir Sar just as an enormous flash crashed down into the forest below the crags. At that moment it would not have been a surprise to see the goddess Nike, wings outspread, alighting on the top, or Zeus himself with his thunderbolt, emerging from the swirling dark clouds which spilled over the pinnacles of Aornos.

## ACROSS THE INDUS

For Alexander, all resistance had been overcome west of the Indus, at least for the time being. He could rejoin the main army at Hund on the Indus. Here Hephaistion and the engineering corps had completed a huge bridge of boats, at the place where today Akbar's kiosk overlooks the waters set in a garden of mimosa and acacia trees and ruined Mogul pavilions. This was the crossing place of the Indus on the ancient highway from Central Asia to India. It lost its importance when the Grand Trunk Road shifted south to Attock, but, on this stretch, until twenty years ago you could still see such boat bridges, erected for the dry season, taken down when the Himalayan snows melted and the river began to rise. In only two or three places on the Indus are they still used now. At Mithancot, far to the south, you can see ninety boats moored in a long line with a wooden plank road strewn with earth and straw for the animals, the camels and horses who cross alongside more modern traffic. Here it is easy to imagine the scene the day Alexander crossed. The Army was huge now, with as many as 80,000 troops and 30,000 camp followers, pack animals, siege train, elephants, not forgetting the scientists, botanists, naturalists and the surveyors who were measuring every step from Macedonia to the end of the earth.

Safely across, Alexander's army had marched on Taxila, the kingdom of the friendly king Ambi who had sent his ambassadors to Alexander earlier in the year. The city lies on the Grand Trunk Road west of modern Rawalpindi. Coming from Peshawar and the North-West Frontier, you get off at a dusty busy truck and bus stop with a huge sign straddling the highway: 'Welcome to Taxila'. A kilometre to the north, through a busy but scruffy bazaar, then past deserted Hindu temples, you find the ancient site in open fields. Here is a succession of ancient cities, the most important in this part of the subcontinent and the key meeting place in the exchange of Greek and Indian culture which followed.

The Greeks had arrived expecting a friendly welcome, but there was a momentary panic when they found an army outside the city in full parade dress fronted by an elephant corps caparisoned in war howdahs and body armour. Hastily Alexander deployed the phalanx and funnelled the cavalry out to the wings. Realizing that there had been a misunderstanding, King Ambi then rode forward alone. Alexander did likewise and the two men met. 'They seemed to get on well judging by their expressions', said the Greeks, 'but they didn't know a word of each other's language.' An interpreter was sent and things were cleared up. Ambi agreed to be Alexander's viceroy and to support him in the campaigns ahead; he was also quick to present Alexander with a bill for provisioning Hephaistion's army group during the bridge building. Lavish presents were exchanged, and Alexander went on to spend a few days in the city. The site of his camp may have been the knoll on which the Greek-style temple, Jandial, stands today, with its classical portico, the interior once decorated with pictures of Alexander's victories in India. The site of the Greek camp may have been the large rectangle later taken up by a planned Greek city (the first in the subcontinent) with streets that can still be walked today. It is a huge neat clean rectangle set beside the twisting chaotic streets of the old Indian city, rather as the clean lines of today's capital Islamabad (another artificial creation), were set next to the sprawling hubbub of Pindi: the city of functionaries, bureaucrats and nabobs, serviced by the native town nearby.

Taxila would become one of the centres of Hellenic culture in India, and the great meeting place of East and West in grammar, poetry, art, and philosophy. The Greek language would be spoken here for 500 years. Alexander's arrival is the symbolic beginning of one of the great exchanges of culture between two of the world's most original and creative civilizations. No doubt that is what Alexander would have wished, but, back then, all this was in the future. Alexander's immediate concern was military. On the road ahead his intelligence reports had indicated resistance was massing.

One hundred and twenty kilometres down the Grand Trunk Road is the first great river of the Punjab, the Jhelum. Porus, the rajah of the lands beyond the Jhelum as far as the Chenab, was an enemy of Ambi and news came that he had rejected Alexander's ambassadors and assembled an army in an attempt to block Alexander's crossing. With the spring far advanced, the snow-melt and the monsoon season upon them, the Punjab rivers were rising and would soon be impassable in the face of armed opposition until the autumn. Alexander immediately cut short his stay in Taxila and prepared to move off, which he did after only five days with Ambi. These days must have been frantically active as the engineering corps commandeered hundreds of oxcarts to carry boats in sections for use in bridging, and then lumbered a few kilometres a day across the plains of the North-West. For a time every road must have been jammed.

## BATTLE ON THE JHELUM RIVER

Alexander's route south from Taxila, and the site of his decisive battle with Porus, are still the subject of much scholarly debate. In the early 1930s Aurel Stein came up with a persuasive theory, but his ideas have recently come under fire. However, a new survey of this region by Pakistani archaeologists has effectively settled the matter in his favour. Alexander did not head along the Grand Trunk Road – the medieval Mogul route – but moved directly south from Taxila towards the Great Salt Range. This was the route used throughout prehistory and right up to the Muslim invasions of India in the eleventh century. Until the Great Salt Range the road could not have been easier, for it crosses open undulating farmland. The final stretch into the hills would have been a long haul for the oxcarts, but nothing compared with what the Macedonians had already accomplished.

184

Above: Coin commemorating the battle at the Jhelum river
in the Punjab. Left: Alexander on Bucephalus attacks Porus
on his war elephant. Right: Alexander is crowned by Nike,
the goddess of victory.

Opposite: A modern bridge of boats over the Indus. This was
the technology used by Alexander's engineers to transport the
Macedonian army across the great rivers of the Punjab.

From the top of the hills, at the Nandana Pass, there is a spectacular view of the plain
of the Jhelum river, winding like a silver ribbon through green rice fields, to the distant
wheeze of irrigation pumps and the hoot of a flour mill. Beyond the river the plains of the
Punjab stretch all the way to the Ganges. Here, more than anywhere, feels like the gateway
to India. It must have been an intensely dramatic moment for the Greeks, after all they had
gone through, and the great distances they had travelled, to come down the Nandana Pass,
and see this wonderful vista. Beyond the river, their native guides must have told them, lay
the heartland of India.

They came down into an oval plain between the Salt Range and the river. The main
ford was somewhere near the modern railway bridge at Haranpur. On the other side was
the main army of Rajah Porus, 30,000 men with 2000 cavalry and 300 elephants, nowhere
near enough to defeat the battle-hardened Greeks, but enough to thwart them – provided

Rajah Porus could stop Alexander getting across. The river was rising now with the snow-melt in the Himalayas. If Porus could prevent a Greek crossing until the monsoon, then Alexander would have to wait until September. Could Porus do it?

Alexander camped opposite the Indian army and sent reconnaissance parties up and down the river to assess his chances of forcing his way across. At the north end of the plain, 25 kilometres or so upriver from his camp, there was a very prominent landmark, where the cliffs of the Salt Range come right down to the river plain to form a promontory, an *akra* as the Greeks would have said, rather like the long capes, such as Cnidos or Mykale, which jut into the Aegean Sea.

Opposite the cape was a large wooded island of a kind often formed and remade by the river. (It is likely, incidentally, that the river itself has not shifted its course greatly over the intervening millennia. It cannot have flowed any further west as it is limited by the Salt Range cliffs and the headland; the other way its bed only moves across a 10-kilometre plain in its periodic wanderings – a seventy-two-year cycle according to local lore; so the battlefield must have been shaped something like it is today.) At the end of the promontory on a natural platform above the town is a lovely white marble sufi shrine adorned with blue Multan tiles. Behind this promontory was what the locals call a *nala,* a deep valley cut into the mountains by a seasonal stream. Inside it was a large open ground, completely hidden from the other side, and big enough to hide several thousand troops. Here, Alexander decided to conceal his crossing force. Over some time – and probably under cover of night – he assembled his boats here and then gathered a crack assault force of 5000 cavalry and 4000 infantry. Meanwhile, downriver, his main army engaged in diversionary tactics to keep Porus thinking the attack would come there. Alexander even employed a double – a soldier of his own build and looks, wearing his regalia – so that Indian spies would believe he was preparing his assault at the main ford.

D-Day – the day of the crossing – was around 21 May. Summer storms had begun, the river was rising and, on the night chosen for the crossing, there was a heavy downpour. After nightfall, the turning force ate some rations, drank wine to fortify themselves, then filed out of the gulley to be ferried across the river by boat (or on skin rafts stuffed with chaff, the kind still used during World War II in the Burma campaign). They then marched on only to discover another channel of the river which their advance intelligence had missed. The whole manoeuvre had to be repeated again: most of the units fording the river chest-deep. With dawn coming up, the soaked troops were deployed on the other side. By now the Indians were alerted and Porus's son rushed upriver with 2000 troops and fifty chariots to try to hold Alexander up. But it was too late. The rain-soaked ground immobilized his chariots and he was overwhelmed and killed – all his chariots taken. Porus was trapped. Leaving a force to hold the main crossing against Craterus, he had no alternative but to turn his army to face Alexander and form a battle line.

Porus's only hope had been to stop the Greeks from crossing. But he had never correctly assessed the power and determination of his enemies. An honourable old-fashioned warrior from the epic age Porus had never understood what he was up against. His out-matched troops put up a desperate fight, and, for a while, the elephants caused the Macedonians problems 'wreaking havoc in the phalanx', as Arrian says. But soon, wounded and maddened by the long pikes of the phalanx, the elephants were driven back into their own forces, their mahouts picked off by the Greek archers, leaving the riderless animals to career about, their eyes put out, their trunks hacked by machetes. In the end, they made 'a pitiable sight', says Arrian, 'trumpeting hopelessly', 'standing off like ships backing in water'. The Indian infantry was surrounded and most of them killed. Estimates of the dead vary: Arrian says 20,000, which would be most of the force; Diodorus gives 12,000 killed and 9000 prisoners of war, along with 80 elephants killed, which sounds more likely.

Porus had been out-manoeuvred and out-gunned. And this overwhelming victory against a local petty king would be trumpeted to the Greek world by Alexander's propaganda department as scarcely less than the conquest of India. A magnificent coin, minted in Babylon, showed Alexander on Bucephalus attacking Porus on his elephant; on the reverse, Alexander was portrayed as Zeus with his thunderbolt. In truth, it had been rather different; more as if the heroic warrior aristocracy of the Indian epic, the *Mahabharata,* had come face to face with stormtroopers from another planet. Brilliant tactics they may have been, but the battle at the Jhelum river had been a horrible massacre. From now on, the Macedonians began to appear in their true light: rampaging through an ancient civilization like conquistadors in the Old World.

Porus himself survived the slaughter. Covered with wounds, the Indian king, a giant of a man well over 6 feet tall, eventually surrendered. In one version of the story, his wounded and exhausted elephant knelt down to allow Porus, covered in blood and hardly able to stand, to descend. The exchange between Porus and Alexander has gone down in legend, and it may well contain a grain of truth. Asked through an interpreter how he wished to be treated, Porus replied simply: '*basilikos moi chresai*' ('treat me like a king'). But what else? said Alexander. 'All is contained in that one request,' said Porus. Impressed by the Indian king's noble bearing, Alexander restored his kingdom to him, and added to it from the lands of his enemies. Chivalrous propaganda aside, the message of the massacre was clear to the other rajahs and maharajahs of India. Alexander was much better to have as a friend than an enemy.

Above: Looking eastwards over the battlefield of the Jhelum river. In the foreground the 'cape' of the Salt Range comes down into the plain where Alexander's army made its night crossing. The tomb shrine of Bucephalus may have been where the white marble Sufi shrine stands today.

Opposite: Greek cavalry does battle with Indian war elephants.

## THE DEATH OF BUCEPHALUS

For Alexander the battle brought personal loss. His beloved horse Bucephalus died after the battle of age or wounds. The old horse was aged about twenty. In his honour Alexander founded a city at the site of the night crossing, that is, at the 'cape' on the west side of the river. Here, perhaps, a Greek heroon (monument dedicated to a hero) was erected in a prominent place to commemorate the warhorse. On the other side of the river, nearer to the site of the battle, he founded another town, Nikaea (Victory). These have never been located, but much the likeliest candidate for Nikaea is the ancient town of Mong, a mud-brick warren of streets still standing on a mound over 30 metres deep in pottery-stuffed strata. Here Indo-Greek coins have been found, and the site certainly goes back to the Hellenistic Age.

The site of Bucephala, in that case, would appear to be little Jalalpur, which is visible from the top of Mong at the foot of the long spur of the Salt Range. Here, in later centuries, Chinese Buddhist pilgrims knew of a 'Town of the Famous Horse'. The place was still known to Greek merchants in the first century as Boukephalos Alexandreia. When I first went to Jalalpur, searching for Alexander, I thought it most likely that Bucephalus's tomb had stood on the platform where the modern shrine stands today. But, on the hill above Jalalpur, there is a ruined city known as Garjak, where according to the old British district officer in his gazetteer, one may find Indo-Greek coins of Alexander's successors. Could this be the lost city?

There, high up on the mountain side, an old temple platform commands a magnificent view of the plain, the river and the battlefield. Until Partition this was the site of a Hindu shrine to the goddess of the mountain, Mangla Devi. It is a still visited Muslim holy man's tomb, with sacred tanks and offering trees, and strange burial stones in the shape of a horse. Under the trees are Muslim graves covered with bright green silks picked out with scarlet and golden hems, gently lifting in the evening wind, which stirs the flags and ribbons tied round the branches. Here, a legend of the Hindu shrine was told to us by the Muslim custodian. It was a story of a conflict between the Hindu goddess and the Muslim holy man, when the magical horse ridden by the goddess rose to heaven and then fell to earth to be buried in this place. Perhaps this wonderful spot marks the tomb of Bucephalus.

For the Greeks the battle had been a bruising encounter, and, if a foretaste of what lay ahead, a bad augury. It had been surely a horrible and disturbing experience. If this was what a small rajah could do, what if they met the Great King of India himself, assuming such a king existed? Trying to sift for truth behind the propaganda, the Macedonians may have lost as many as 1200 dead and 1000 wounded in the battle on the Jhelum river; many horses were killed too. These were very heavy casualties. The rank-and-file must have especially dreaded being wounded, despite the skill of the Greek surgeons. Even today wounds are bad things to have in the monsoon heat of the subcontinent; they don't heal quickly or easily, and often get infected. Although tons of medicines had arrived from the west, Greek losses from illness and disease must have been far greater than the minimal battle casualty figures which have come down to us through 'official sources'.

They were now into the monsoon proper. Muggy heat, averaging 30 degrees centigrade, but in the Punjab often reaching the mid-40s, periods of rain, intermittent sunshine, heavy cloud, more rain. It is a time when as the old British guide books cautioned, 'Walking in the heat of the day is better avoided altogether'. Alexander took time to rest and recuperate his troops after the shock of battle. Meanwhile, his engineering corps began the construction of a fleet to sail down the Indus. Evidently Alexander believed he was close enough now to the end of the expedition for this work to start while he took the army on to the eastern ocean. So, Alexander's troops waited for a month by the banks of the Jhelum, amusing themselves with athletics and musical shows to take their mind off the heat and rain. Then, around midsummer Alexander gave the order to push on.

## INTO DEEPEST INDIA

It is not known for certain whether the Greeks thought they had already crossed the extreme limit of the Persian empire. At various times this limit seems to have been marked at the Indus, the Jhelum, and the Beas. Some think Alexander had set his goal at conquering the Persian empire only, and his stopping on the north at the Jaxartes might indicate that. Perhaps, indeed, that had been his plan at an earlier stage of the expedition. But maybe a person of his mind and temper could never think of stopping. The thing was simply to go on. 'A conqueror like a cannon-ball cannot stop,' as the Duke of Wellington said.

In late June, the Greeks broke camp and moved on across the Punjab 'in a generally easterly direction' (according to the Greek geographer Strabo). From Jalalpur the route follows the low range of hills, which run along on the left-hand side as far as the Chenab at Gujarat where the British won the second Sikh War. They probably followed an ancient route from Taxila to the Ganges, but this stage of the journey has never been traced. The clues, however, are there in Strabo:

> *He learned from intelligence gathering that the mountainous and northerly part of India was the most habitable and fruitful, but that the southerly part was in part without water, in part washed by great rivers, and fiercely hot: more suitable for wild beasts than for human beings. So he set out to subdue first the part commended to him, at the same time reckoning that the rivers he would have to cross, since they flow across his line of march, cutting through the lands he wished to traverse, could be more easily crossed nearer their sources.*

By this stage of the journey, the army had been swelled to 120,000, with a vast entourage of camp-followers and hangers-on. The scientists and botanists on the expedition were now having a field day. Masses of their notes are probably contained in later texts, such as the books of Aristotle's pupil, Theophrastus, on natural phenomena. The Greeks were intrigued by flora and fauna they had never seen before: banyan trees ('big enough to give shade to 400 horsemen under their spread!'); cotton ('a white fabric growing on plants which all Indians wear'). The conditions of the monsoon were noted in Theophrastus's treatise on climate, which was long believed lost, but has now been discovered in Persian translation in a North Indian library. As they trudged on sweltering, in gaps between showers, they noted, too, that at midday in the heat of summer in North India 'a man leaves no shadow'.

The rivers were in spate and each crossing was laborious and time-consuming. Each required a bridge of boats to be constructed by Coenus and the engineering corps who had to ferry the segmented boats on oxcarts and build the bridge anew. The Chenab was now nearly 3 kilometres wide, the Ravi the same. It was a wearisome and hazardous job with strong currents sweeping away some sections. By the Chenab, they founded another Alexandria, possibly the old town of Sohadra now east of the river. At some point beyond the Chenab, they turned off to engage with a powerful and numerous enemy at a city called Sangala. A dramatic narrative has come down to us from the memoirs of Alexander's general Ptolemy. It is an horrific story of cordons, night-attacks, massacres, with the glint of fire and sword across the northern Punjab. The city was cut off and attacked across marshes swelled by the summer rains. Arrian says 17,000 Indians died in the assault and 70,000 captives were taken in its territory.

They continued eastwards, probably via Sialkot, 'keeping near to the mountains' – that is, in sight of them – so earlier theories about the army going south, via Lahore, must be discounted. They pushed on, while long lines of bedraggled refugees snaked across the countryside, through sodden fields in stifling heat under laden monsoon skies, away from the columns of smoke. The Greeks skirted the Jammu and Kashmir foothills, crossed the Ravi somewhere near Nainakot (the present border where India was partitioned in 1947), and entered the modern Indian Punjab. There they made their easternmost camp, somewhere on the banks of the Beas river, north of Gurdaspur and south of Pathancot. The great expedition was nearing its climax.

---

Alexander and the Brahmins. Ever an inquiring mind, Alexander is said to have questioned Indian holy men about Hindu philosophy. 'But why have you come here?' asked one. Though the Greeks were remembered in India as 'viciously valiant', Alexander is named in no early Indian source. 'He came and saw,' it has been said, 'but India conquered.'

سمه خورد شان بر میوه دار سکندر رسید از خواب و خورد خردمند نفس ای جهان گیر مرد

ز تخم نیار سته بر کوکاه از آسایش و روز نیک و نبرد سگر از ما نکو یاد نیک و نبرد

از ایران شکیم نخم خبر بود ز خوریس ملک بیننی چه را ید هر زیو سید و ورگ سترد نی

کز خوردن پویش زیو بود ز کر هر خوابی نیست تر با گار هر سمه بی نیاز یم از خورد نی

## 'WE WILL GO NO FURTHER'

Before them was the Beas river, last but one of the great rivers of the Punjab. More than a kilometre wide, with a strong flow. Although the bed of the Beas has moved westwards over the centuries, in historical times it always made a great loop round the Siwalik hills, and the Greeks must have reached it somewhere near the top of this loop. Here, was an ancient town, Dasuya, which is mentioned in the ancient Indian epic, the *Mahabharata*. Somewhere near Dasuya was the traditional crossing place of one of the ancient routes from Taxila to the Ganges. Since medieval times the crossing has been by the Naushera ferry. In winter nowadays there's a pontoon bridge, around which little settlements grow up on either bank with reed-roofed shanties and stalls cooking food. Here you see itiner-ant holy men and travelling shrines moving on the pilgrimage route to Chintpurni in the Siwaliks (an ancient itinerary, older even than Alexander's day). You also see elephants swimming by the bridge and families and travellers always on the move. Although the river may have shifted somewhat, this is still the place where the north Indian travel routes con-verge to cross the Beas.

Somewhere near here, then, Alexander stopped to prepare for the crossing and to gather intelligence on what lay ahead. There has been much debate about Alexander's last plans. Did he intend to go on to conquer all India, let alone all the world? Had he even heard of the Ganges civilization? Likely as this is, our sources allow no certainty. What was in his mind at this moment? Given the uncertain nature of the evidence, we are unlikely ever to know for sure, but it seems impossible that Alexander had not by now heard of the Indian kingdom based at Patna on the Ganges. Indeed, according to Arrian, it was only at this very point, on the banks of the Beas, that clear information was forthcoming: 'Fifteen days beyond the Beas,' Alexander was told, 'you will come to the Ganges, the greatest river in India (and possibly the world) which is all of 5 kilometres across. Beyond the Ganges lies a kingdom with a standing army of 250,000 men with 3000 elephants'.

This land, as we know now from excavation, had many great cities. Kosambi, for example, which was sacked by the Greeks in the second century BC, had a 10-kilometre circuit with huge brick defence systems. The capital city Patna, Alexander might have learned, as Greek ambassadors did after his death, was even greater, with a population of 400,000, a 28-kilometre circuit with 564 towers and 60 gates, protected by the Ganges, the Son, and a massive water-ditch system. It was a city almost to rival Babylon. A vast well-ordered kingdom then, but Alexander was told it was ruled by a king who was of inferior birth, character and reputation, who might be easily overthrown. His informants may also have been able to tell him what would be well known to the Greeks a generation later: that beyond Patna it was 600 kilometres to the sea, and for Alexander the end of the Earth. (China would not enter the consciousness of Western people for two centuries or more, until Far East met West in Fergana on the Silk Route.) To an extent we are reduced to speculation here, but as he listened to this new and tantalizing revelation, Alexander's appetite for conquest, his *pothos,* his desire to see and emulate, can only have been further whetted. Onward to the Eastern Ocean.

The troops, though, had had enough. They had now endured seventy days of monsoon rain and heat. In such conditions, gear rots, weapons rust, and days are spent never getting dry; malaria is a plague; dysentery ever present; snakes are everywhere, driven to higher ground by the flood. Far more troops must have died from sickness and disease than were ever lost in battle. The Greek doctors by now had learned the secret of quinine bark distillation to help bring down the crises of malaria. They had also got snake antidotes from Indians (there had been many deaths from snake-bites when sleeping on the ground, so much so that many took to using hammocks). But, on the banks of the Beas, grumblings rumbled round the camp until the disillusionment finally reached a head. The atmosphere was mutinous. Alexander now held a meeting of the regimental officers. He reminded them of their great deeds, listed their conquests and urged on them one last great effort to crown their achievements: 'For my part I set no limit to exertions for a man of noble spirit … but it is no great distance now for us to the river Ganges and on to the eastern sea … we have gone through all these dangers together, and the prizes will be shared between everyone … when we have overrun the whole of Asia I will make you rich beyond your wildest dreams!'

His speech was greeted with silence. Eyes turned to the floor. No one dared to come out with it. (Not surprising, perhaps, given Alexander's record with dissenting voices. To take up a tyrant's invitation to criticize freely is usually fatal.) Finally, Coenus, one of his senior officers, stood up. Coenus was one of the most dependable and loyal phalanx commanders who had been with him through thick and thin. He had led phalanx brigades at Arbela and the Persian Gates, and commanded the bridge-building units in the Punjab. Now he spoke up for the 'poor bloody infantry' (this took some courage, too). The speech, which has come down to us, can only be a rough representation of what he said, but it rings true. It is an epic moment (wonderfully dramatized in the 1943 Indian blockbuster *Sikander* which was banned by the English precisely because it depicted the mutiny of an occupying army in India). Not surprisingly Coenus began cautiously:

*Sire, we know that you have never wished to lead us like a dictator, but you say you lead us by persuasion, and if we convince you to the contrary you will not use coercion, so then*

*I shall speak not on behalf of the officers present here, but for the rank and file …
With you as our leader we have achieved so many marvellous successes, but isn't it time
now to set some limit? Surely you can see yourself how few are left of the original army
which began this enterprise … some died in battle, others were invalided out with
wounds, many left behind in different parts of Asia; but most have died of sickness, and
so of all that great army only a few survive, and even they no longer enjoy the health they
had – while their spirit is simply worn out. One and all they long to see their parents,
if they are still alive, their wives and children, and their homeland … Sire the sign of a
great man is knowing when to stop.*

His speech caused uproar; many wept openly. Alexander was furious, 'irritated at Coenus's
freedom of speech and the timidity of the other officers'. Next day he reconvened the
meeting. One line is particularly true to character. As it became apparent that his words
were falling on deaf ears, that his Prince Hal act would no longer work, he got angry and
we can hear the little boy in the man thwarted: 'All right then,' he shouted in that harsh
voice, 'I will go on myself, and I will compel no Macedonian to go against his will, I will
have volunteers only, and those who wish to go home may do so, and they can tell their
friends they came back and left their king surrounded by enemies!'. After this he retired to
his tent and, like his hero Achilles, sulked for three days waiting to see if there would be a
change of mind. There was none. Finally he emerged and asked the army seer to perform
the sacrifice for the river crossing. Predictably the signs in the entrails were bad. Ever adept
at manipulating omens, Alexander announced that he had accepted the will of the gods.
The army erupted with joy. They would turn back.

## THE MYSTERY OF THE ALTARS

Before he left the Beas, Alexander did one last thing. He divided the army into work-
brigades and ordered the construction of twelve huge altars, 'higher than the higher siege
towers', 17 metres square and 25 metres high, built of squared stone. Among the gods
honoured, according to Plutarch, was Hercules. Later sources alleged the army engineers
also dug a vast camp and the carpenters had billets made with giant couches 'to leave the
impression that the Greeks had been a race of giants'. This tale is surely a later fabrication.
The altars, though, were real enough. They were left by the bank of the Beas as memorials to the great expedition which had stopped there six years after landing on the shores
of Asia. They certainly survived for some time, too. Chandragupta Maurya, the founder of

the first Indian empire, who was said to have met the Greek king when he was a boy, is reported to have venerated the altars in later days in memory of Alexander.

Where these great constructions were built has never been discovered. A later writer, Philostratus, gives details of the inscriptions on some of these strange monuments: to 'Father Ammon and Brother Heracles and Athena of Foresight and Olympian Zeus and the Cabeiroi of Samothrace and Indus and Helios (or Indian Helios?) and Apollo of Delphi ...

A pantheon so odd and circumstantial that it may just be true. Philostratus mentions a brass obelisk or column which bore the inscription, 'Alexander stopped here'. If Philostratus was right, then the altars should perhaps be sought on an eminence overlooking the Beas river in the Siwalik hills, 'Siva's hills', where there are today many famous temples. This might connect with the testimony of a late source on Alexander, the so-called *Metz Epitome*, which says that Alexander built the altars 'where the river flowed by a town called *altusacra*'. This is meaningless and plainly needs emendation – *alta sacra,* meaning the 'holy hills', is the most obvious solution. This could, perhaps, have been applied to a range, such as the Siwaliks, by Alexander's local guides. A possible site is the ancient town of Dasuya, which certainly existed in Greek times. In Sanskrit, Dasuya means the 'high place'. But the present site of Dasuya is medieval; the town moved down from the hills as the river shifted westwards. My own guess, and it is hardly more than that, is that the altars – one of strangest monuments in the ancient world – were built somewhere in this vicinity, although my own search there in January 1996 failed to turn up any trace, or any local tradition of such a site, even though the Indian emperors are believed to have worshipped at these altars in later days. As so often, though, with Alexander's tale, close attention to the topography usually reveals more than suspected. Alexander's altars must have been built above the level of the flood plain, and it may well be that some trace remains to be found – if only we knew where to look.

## THE FLEET PREPARES

Around 21 September, after sacrifices, and gymnastic and equestrian games, the army pulled back from the Beas and headed back to the base at the newly-founded cities on the Jhelum river. Only a few days later, by the Chenab river, Coenus was taken ill and died. Some have inferred that he did not long outlive Alexander's displeasure for his 'freedom of speech' at the Beas. 'The funeral was as lavish as circumstances allowed,' says Arrian curtly. An unpleasantly catty remark is attributed to Alexander who could not resist a snipe at the man who had spoken for the troops on the Beas river: 'all for the sake of a few days – as if he was the only one of us who wanted to see home again'. In the eighteenth century, a great mound by the Chenab was pointed out as the site of the tomb of one of the companions of Sikander. Such legends are common in North India and the Punjab, but it would be interesting to know whether a genuine tradition has been preserved here.

Back at Bucephala, Alexander threw himself into the construction of the fleet and the preparations for the next stage of the campaign. Although the troops would not go further east, they still had serious campaigning to do because Alexander intended to reduce all of 'southern India' down the Indus valley to the sea, that is, today's Pakistan. There would be no easy homecoming for the army which had refused to go on at the Beas.

In the meantime, there were entertainments: Dionysian festivals, athletics competitions, and musical events; anything to keep the army's mind occupied after the Beas debacle. No doubt all these played their part in keeping morale up before the army moved south to begin the reduction of 'southern India'.

## THE CONQUEST OF THE PUNJAB AND SIND

The expedition was ready to set off again around 21 November. Just before it did, if we can trust the *Metz Epitome*, Roxanne gave birth to a son who died that autumn on the banks of the Jhelum river before the fleet sailed. Here, yet again, is possibly a very significant moment in Alexander's inner biography, on which we have no other information. All we know is that he plunged himself back into warfare: 'after the baby was buried and the religious rites performed, he set off for the Ocean'. Alexander embarked on the fleet with the light troops and the royal guard. Hephaistion took the main army with 200 elephants down the east bank. Craterus marched along the right bank with infantry and cavalry, and other mobile forces were ready to mount forays when required. The fleet included warships, horse transports, and a huge number of local river craft numbering nearly 2000 vessels. It was a spectacle which impressed all who saw it: the beating of the oars, the shouts of the bosuns, the cheers of the oarsmen, and the singing of the local Indians who, for a while, followed on the banks in sheer amazement.

Terror was now the tactic. The Greeks met resistance wherever they went and always met it with absolute ruthlessness. When Alexander reached the junction of the Jhelum and Chenab rivers, he struck out east towards the Ravi where the major centres of population were situated. The rivers have changed courses, but modern archaeology is beginning to make sense of the campaign. Alexander made a fast 80-kilometre march through the night over the open alluvial plain and hit a large town, probably marked by the ancient mound of Kot Kamalia. Taken by surprise, crammed with refugees, the place was cordoned off and overwhelmed.

After another night march, Alexander forded the Ravi at daybreak and assaulted what the Greeks called 'Brahmin towns' around Tulamba. (This was still a noted Brahmin town until the Partition in 1947.) In this countryside, at least a dozen big city mounds rise above the alluvial plain along the Ravi, some of them huge like Atari, Bagar and Kalkanwal Bir, and they can have been little different in appearance from the many rural mud-brick towns you see today, rising out of the paddy fields. It must have been an unremittingly grim winter right across the Punjab, and reading Arrian it is easy to imagine scenes matching the terrible newsreels of Partition, with long columns of refugees moving away from the line of the Greek advance.

The two most powerful peoples of the Punjab – the Mallians and the Oxydracae – both seem to have had well-ordered states. These resisted the Greeks and were subjected to massive attack, city by city. Their mud-brick defences were powerless against the Macedonian siege-engineers with their modern technology of siege-towers, catapults, sappers, mines, and mantelets. Any resistance was met by a cordon to stop all ingress or escape, then investment, followed by the ruthless application of the military conventions, namely the slaughter of all adult males and the enslavement of women and children. The crusade against Persia had become a war against the people of Asia.

## 'THE KING IS DEAD': THE SIEGE OF MULTAN

Alexander pursued those who fled along the Ravi westwards. As far as the Greeks were concerned, flight constituted resistance and was punished accordingly. Only if you stayed put and surrendered were you spared. Many from the cities fled into the forests along the Ravi. (These forests were still used as a refuge when Tamerlane assaulted the Ravi towns in the fourteenth century, and again during the British attack in the 1840s.) The Macedonians hounded them. Alexander was determined to use terror as a means of imposing his will, driving refugees across the Ravi. The chief people here were the Mallians, whose main town, according to popular belief, was the old cultural capital of the southern Punjab, Multan. The ancient citadel at Multan stands on a deep mound which has been a centre of population for at least 2000 years. Whether it is quite as old as Alexander's day, though, is not yet certain. Perhaps the chief town of the Mallians must be sought on another as yet unidentified site nearby. But here, or hereabouts, a famous incident in Alexander's story took place.

The Greek troops surrounded the town and began the attack but were showing a distinct lack of resolve in the assault. (By now they must have been heartily sick of the demands constantly made on them.) Alexander lashed out at the men for slacking and then decided to lead by example. Placing a siege-ladder against the wall he raced up on to the parapet. Three of his guards followed, but, when more forces pushed forward, the ladder broke and the four men were left standing alone on top of the wall. At that moment, instead of scrambling back down, Alexander saw 'red' and jumped inside the wall. There, he and his three companions fought off a horde of attackers until Alexander was pierced by an arrow through his right breast and fell. One of the guards, Peucestas, stood over the king's body with the shield of Achilles from Troy and desperately tried to protect him. The other two both fell. Whooping with triumph the defenders closed in for the kill.

Meanwhile, outside the walls a tremor of panic ran through the Macedonian ranks and they frantically tried to claw their way in, using battering rams against the wall and hammering metal spikes into the mud-brick. Eventually, they broke through a gate. The word now swept through the rank-and-file that the king was dead, and they went berserk, massacring the entire population of the town.

Alexander, meanwhile, was carried back to camp where the doctors assessed the wound. He was near to death, and the surgeons hesitated to cut out the arrow for fear they would kill him. The king had not yet lost consciousness and, gritting his teeth, brusquely told them to get on with it. At length one of them, Critobulos, who came from the famous medical family of the island of Kos, took a deep breath, picked up the knife and cut the arrow out. When he did so, 'blood and air' came out – the lung was punctured. The king passed out and Critobulos packed the wound and administered poultices to sterilize the wound. It was going to be touch and go.

The rumour that the king was dead had, meanwhile, swept through the whole army. Eventually it reached fever-pitch. After a week, Alexander agreed to appear in public, to show them he was still alive. Mounting a horse, he waved painfully to the assembled ranks to wild cheers. It took four more days for him to recover enough to be moved by boat down to the confluence of the Ravi and Chenab where the main armies had established their base. Here, Alexander rested until he was able to continue southwards. Only the king's iron constitution had saved him. Local Multan legend, however, adds a twist to this tale. Some say he actually died there and was buried near Multan or Uchch. The Greek high command, it is told, were too frightened to reveal his death to the army for fear the

Uchch the Holy: one of the medieval shrines on the old mound
of Uchch, south of Multan, in the southern Punjab; probably the site
of the Greek city called Alexandria at the Confluence.

whole expedition would disintegrate so far from home, so they covered up the disaster, employing a double to lead them back to Babylon. It is a pleasing thought, although no doubt erroneous, that the true grave of the conqueror is not to be sought by the southern shore of the Mediterranean but under the palm groves of the southern Punjab.

Not far south, at the confluence of the Indus with the Punjab rivers, Alexander founded another city and dockyard. He called it Alexandria at the Confluence, 'expressing the hope it would become a world famous city'. When you drive along the flat plain of the Indus for four hours south of Multan, you come to the little town of Uchch Shariff: 'Uchch the Holy'. An ancient mud-brick town on a high mound, it is surrounded by rice paddies and palm groves, and dotted with the blue-tiled shrines of Sufi saints, the ancestors of the great families who came from Central Asia in the thirteenth century. A famous centre of religion and culture in the subcontinent during the Middle Ages, Uchch was once in the middle of the confluence, because the Indus and the Chenab met below the city. It has now been left high and dry by the shifting of the Indus, which is now 50 kilometres off, and the other Punjab rivers now combine 20 kilometres away at the Panchnad. But Uchch is still a pretty country town with an annual fair much frequented by the travelling singers, poets and holy men and women who still conserve the memory of the great saints of the Indus valley. The old part of the mound is a warren of brick streets with painted shrines hung with flags and offerings. Outside one of these, I met the town's genealogist, the keeper of the family records of the descendants of the Prophet – a distinguished man with a thin weaselly face, pointed beard, and an outsized turban. Composed and quietly spoken, with intense eyes, he was nothing less than the keeper of the memory of the town.

'Uchch had many names in olden days,' he said. 'Its present name means a high place, but when the Muslims first came here it was called Iskandera or Eskanderiya because Alexander came here. He stayed for six months, and built a city 10 kilometres round – not on this part of Uchch but on the eastern mound.'

'How do you know this?

'The ancient books say so; and the tradition is handed down.'

Later, on the terrace of the Bukharis' hostel, we sat on charpoys and sipped green tea while the sun set over the palm forests. In front were the broken domes of grand tombs on the edge of the mound, their bands of blue tile luminous in the last light. It is a lovely spot, one of the most delightful in the subcontinent. Another Alexandria, and still a good place to live, too.

The Greeks pushed on southwards into what is now Sind, the burning alluvial plain which has always been the heartland of Muslim culture in India. In places, according to the Greeks, the Indus was 15 or more kilometres wide. (It is now much narrower due to the building of modern barrages and canals.) For a while we tried to follow the Greeks on the river. On the lower Indus, beneath the bridge of boats at Mithancot, all the way down to Sehwan, you see the graceful Mohanno boats. Some of them are nearly 30 metres long, flat-bottomed with huge sails and great stern rudders, their ornately carved cabins and stems decorated with marquetry, mirrors, tin and mother of pearl inlay, so their sides reflect the shimmering water as they are poled through the glassy expanses of the river in the somnolent heat of Sind. They are sailed by the Mohanno people, lower caste boat-people. Increasingly marginalized in today's Pakistan, they live on their boats, and make a scant living by carrying firewood, grain, and vegetables up and down the river. This kind of boat is depicted on Bronze Age seals from the Indus, and, although the Greeks built ships to their own design for the expedition, Arrian says they also commandeered many local craft 'which had been long plying on the rivers' whose design was ideally suited to the shallows of the Indus and its frequent squalls. (Greek triaconters, whose plans I showed to a master boat-builder on the Indus, were dismissed as being unstable for the river flow – fine for Mediterranean waters, not for the wide fast shallow water of the Indus where sudden winds can sweep you on to the shore in a jiffy, as in fact happened to Alexander's fleet.)

So like Alexander, we sailed for a while on an Indus craft. We picked up Muhammed and Mai Pathani's boat in Sukkur, where the river comes through a rocky gap by the ancient city of Rohri. Here, there is a big Mogul fort and the British railway bridge which crosses by a picturesque Hindu island temple. Close by are the ruins of Alor where Alexander was entertained at the court of King Musicanus. This region was much admired by Alexander, and was said to be the richest in this part of India.

At night, as we sailed, the women cooked on the clay fireplace in the bowels of the ship, while, on deck, their old uncle and cousin sang Sufi songs with a two-string drone and a cooking pan as a drum. Here the tradition of Alexander is not so strong, although there are still folk tales. One of the famous eighteenth-century Sufis, Sachal, told Alexander stories, such as the following, which is still current on the river, and was told me on the boat one night near Sukkur:

*Sikander went to a mystic, a fakir, and asked him, 'Tell me, is the whole world really just an idea, just imagination?' The mystic took him to a bathing ghat here on the banks of the river and both of them stripped off and entered the water for a dip. 'Now dive under water for a moment' said the fakir to Alexander. Sikander did. And what did he see in that moment? He forgot his kingly consciousness; he saw himself now a poor man with many little children starving and a wife as poor and miserable as he, all the cares of the world on them. And one day a terrible disaster happened to him … But he gave a start and look! There he was back again as a king at the bathing ghat, dripping wet along with the fakir. He was struck with wonder. Of this tale Sachal said this: 'Sikander thought many years had passed, but it was merely the history of a moment'. So he said: 'You see, you are merely an idea'.*

The Sachal story is a late version of tales which seem to go back to real meetings. At Taxila, Alexander had met the Indian holy man Calanas who was sufficiently intrigued by Alexander to come with him all the way back to Babylon, where he then died self-immolated on a funeral pyre in ritual suicide when he realized he was suffering from an incurable disease. Evidently, then, Alexander did have the opportunity to discuss some of the famous conundrums of Indian philosophy with the sceptics, rationalists, and material-ists to be found in contemporary Indian thought; and he may well have been intrigued by the similarities with early Greek thought. For example, the assertion that there was a natural law in the universe, which they, of course, maintained even he, Alexander, could not transgress.

The journey down the river took Alexander nine months. Resistance was often fierce. King Musicanus, who initially submitted to Alexander, was only buying time and rose in revolt as soon as the Macedonians had gone through. They then turned back, crushed him and crucified him in his own citadel of Alor. In the region south of Musicanus, there were ferocious punitive reprisals. According to one ancient source 80,000 Indians were killed on the lower Indus. Whatever the exact numbers, there was clearly a frightful toll. The Greeks were puzzled and disturbed by the fierceness of the resistance, especially by the hold the Brahmins seemed to have on the warrior aristocracy who led the revolts. So, where they could capture them, they killed them. (Musicanus's Brahmin advisers, for example, were also crucified with him.) In one famous story, Alexander interrogated some before execution and they saved their lives by the cleverness of their answers. This tale is late, but there may just be some substance in it, though the Greeks were immediately taken with the touristic aspects of Indian religion, snake-charmers, naked fakirs, suttee and so on. This was all material with which Greek writers engaged as readily as modern travel writers.

According to Plutarch, however, the only remark which one sage made at their meeting was this: 'Why did Alexander come all this way to India?'

---

For their long journey down the Indus to the ocean, the
Macedonians commandeered many local boats like this one.

## AT THE SOUTHERN OCEAN

In the summer of 326 BC Alexander reached Patala (modern Hyderabad). This was then the apex of the Indus delta, for modern research has shown that most of the delta has silted up since Greek times. Alexander established a naval base at Patala and mounted expeditions down both arms of the river. On the east he crossed open water, now the saline flats of the Rann of Kachch which today only flood in the monsoon; he landed at the ancient site of Lakhpat in Kachch (back inside present-day India) and crossed over to the seaboard somewhere near Rampur, evidently on reconnaissance for a harbour site.

Sailing down the western arm of the river he reached open sea just beyond present-day Thatta, then sailed on southwards, well out of sight of land, and sacrificed a bull in the deep sea to mark the end of his Indian campaign. Then coming back inshore he landed on a small island where he left altars to Ocean and the primal Earth. Copies of these altars turned up as votive offerings in York of all places, left by a traveller in Trajan's day. They commemorated Alexander's departure from the end of the earth and his return to civilization. With the York plaques in hand, we can be tolerably sure of Alexander's inscriptions: TO OKEANOS AND TETHYS.

The site of the 'island in the sea' has never been found, although it must be well inland now, somewhere in the salt-encrusted flats of the delta, south of Thatta, near the Hyderabad-Karachi road. One balmy evening as the summer heat was coming on, I journeyed out there from Karachi with French archaeologist Monique Kervran. Monique has excavated at many of the great Near Eastern sites (she found the great Egyptian-style statue of Darius at Susa), and is now engaged in a survey of the Indus delta. She, if anyone, would know where the lost island could be. Hugh Lambrick, my tutor at Oxford, who had been census officer here in Sind, identified the island with a hill called Aban Shah. But, in all Monique's searches, even with Lambrick's directions and the Survey of India maps in hand, she has never found such a hill and had begun to wonder whether he had made a mistake. In the meantime, however, she had been able for the first time to establish the layout of the delta in Greek times. Even better, she had located the sites where the Greek fleet anchored along the western arm of the river.

Using the day-log of Alexander's admiral Nearchus (which Arrian published in a separate book, the *Indica*), Monique was able to trace the fleet along an old course of the Indus which led into the flat plain near Gujo. Now salt flats, thorny scrubland and waving elephant grass, this was once sea at the point where the estuary opened out into the ocean. Here, Nearchus says, he stopped at a place which he called 'Alexander's Harbour'. Monique thinks this must be Tharro island, just off the Karachi-Thatta road. Here, there are crumbling cliffs, silted up bays, and a fine sheltered anchorage between the former island and the ancient shore. On top, 10 metres above the old beach, are medieval Muslim graves and a ruined sixth-century Hindu temple made of beautiful golden coloured stone. Local Muslims still describe an old Hindu pilgrimage route down this lost arm of the Indus.

Nearchus says he stayed for twenty-three days on the island, and built defensive walls. He also describes his men eating oysters for the first time since they left the Mediterranean. We scrambled up the still steep cliffs. On top, two lines of rubble-stone defences were clearly visible, and, sure enough, scattered all over the surface were also great middens of oyster shells. Oysters are virtually indestructible in the archaeological record, and, as shellfish are not eaten by Muslims, these shells are very likely to be the remains of Nearchus's feast. Picking up the weathered but still shiny shells from the heaps which lay on the surface of the 'island', I had the uncanny feeling of standing on a site hardly disturbed since Nearchus weighed anchor here in autumn 325 BC. Only the sea had gone.

But where was the little island where Alexander built his last altars? Standing on Tharro, looking out at sunset time, we could make out a flat-topped rock, another former island, less than a kilometre away. Two eagles circled (Alexander would have seen that as an omen!). As we walked out to it through mimosa and elephant grass, our guide, a local policeman, told us a story. The rock, he said, was called the Boat; local legend spoke of a holy man living on the island who repulsed a great invasion which came by sea: 'Many boats came, but he prayed to God and they were turned to stone. This is one of them.'

The island lay just off the old estuary shore. Two hundred metres long, its sides had been eroded by ancient waves. On top were Muslim graves, which are often found on ancient sites, but the only inhabitant now was a great King Cobra. We sat on the cliff edge, facing the sunset, which, as Nearchus remembered, had set exactly on the Greek fleet's homeward path. Monique broke my reverie: 'This is the last land. Southwards from here we are sure was all sea in Greek times. If the Greeks came down the western arm of the river, then this was the last island'. So, after sailing out into the open sea, to check there really was no more land, perhaps Alexander came back to this little rocky platform where he left his altars to Earth and Ocean.

As the red disc of the sun disappeared below the horizon, I picked over the rubble heaps round the Muslim graves, but there was no trace of reused ancient stones. The altars marked the true end of the *anabasis,* the 'expedition up country'; the altars matching those Alexander had left at the Dardanelles, at Alexandria the Farthermost in Central Asia, and at the Beas river. Now the time had come for the *nostos,* the return home.

# PART SIX

# NOSTOI:
## the RETURNS

# PAKISTAN, IRAN AND IRAQ
## 326 – 325 BC

*Journey through the Makran; mass marriage in Susa;*
*mutiny at Opis; nemesis: 'This is how it ends…';*
*death of Hephaistion; we'll say our goodbyes in Babylon;*
*Alexander's last days; after Alexander's death; Alexander's legacy;*
*what if Alexander had lived?*

THE CONSTRUCTION OF THE ALTARS to the Ocean and Earth drew a line under the story of the great expedition. That autumn Alexander's army set off from somewhere near Karachi on the long journey back to Babylon, which was now the centre of his world. Craterus took another three phalanx brigades with 10,000 demobbed veterans who were past service, along with other units – upwards of 20,000 men all told, with 200 elephants – from the Indus valley into Iran over the Bolan Pass. They seem to have managed this journey without undue discomfort. For Alexander, though, it would be a very different story.

Alexander had decided to lead the main force back through the Makran, the inhospitable desert which lies along the Arabian Sea between Iran and Pakistan. His numbers are disputed. Maximum estimates suggest over 80,000 infantry and 18,000 cavalry, plus a huge baggage train and an unknown number of non-combatants, which some have put at as much as 50,000. These are almost unbelievable figures, but clearly it was a huge army which left India.

The full truth of what happened next will never be known. To get to the Bampur region of southern Iran entailed a march of about 1000 kilometres from the region of Karachi. The first part of the road along the shore past the sacred Hindu site of Hingol, and then inland to Bela, is relatively straightforward. After that, the terrain becomes increasingly harsh. From the air you can see what a terrible landscape it is, with long serrated ridges between tracts of barren gravel desert. The main route into Iran, however, was a well defined road which should not have been too much trouble, running between the Central and Coastal Makran Ranges along the Kech river to Turbat.

But, even before Turbat, Alexander ran into serious problems. In the winter season the Kech valley is notorious for tremendous flash-floods which can strike with little warning. Even today, it is quite common for unwary travellers to be drowned in their vehicles when crossing or when camped in the wide stream-beds where the floods come down from the mountains. Two French tourists were killed just before we came through. 'Don't camp in the stream-beds' we were warned by the local Baluchi tribes people. 'Sometimes they are so wide you don't realize you are in one. You get half an hour warning for the big ones: if you know how to listen you will hear the noise.' Whole villages have gone even in recent years. This happened to Alexander's army. One midnight a deluge swept the camp;

---

Previous pages, left: In the Makran Desert. Right: Second-century BC copy of a portrait by Lysippos. The lined features suggest an older man in whose face some have seen 'a disillusioned Alexander exhausted from war and mutiny and ill with excessive drinking'.

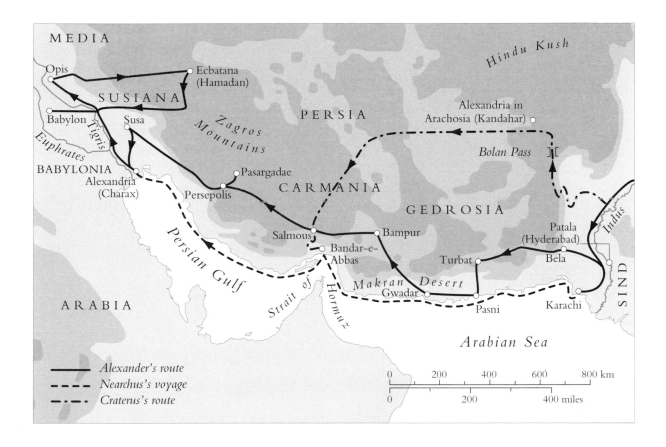

much of the baggage train was destroyed; many of the non-combatants were swept away, and some of the weapons and fighting equipment of the army was also lost. Worse was to follow.

## JOURNEY THROUGH THE MAKRAN

At the fertile and extensive oasis of Turbat, Alexander could draw breath, find good water and supplies, dates and grain. Here French archaeologists have identified the dramatic site of Mir Qalat as the key fortress and settlement on the route west. From the summit of the great mound the road can be seen going straight west towards Iran. But, for some reason, Alexander did not go that way. Instead, he moved southwards and headed for the sea. Why is still a great mystery. The journey from Turbat to Pasni on the coast is not too long – 140 kilometres – but it goes through a dreadful terrain of eroded hills and blistering gravel desert without a trace of vegetation. It took us twelve hours by four-wheel drive

211

(stopping to film, admittedly). There was little water, just one good spring after about 40 kilometres. At one point, I left the cars with a local guide to trace the ancient caravan route through a desiccated range of hills. These are still used by Baluchi nomads and smugglers, but the route was a barely visible depression through parched grey screes of shale.

Why did Alexander come this way? What was he doing? Did all the army go or just Alexander with part of the force? We simply do not know. Most modern attempts at an explanation centre on the fleet. Nearchus, so the argument goes, was on the way to the Persian Gulf with the fleet, and Alexander's fear was that they would come to grief through lack of food and water. So worried was he about their supply, that he went down to the sea to dig wells for them along the shore, and to make contact with the ships. Perhaps more likely though, was Alexander's long-term concern with opening up a sea-route between his Indian empire and the Persian Gulf. This would have involved the creation of harbours and the sinking of wells, so quite possibly the journey down to the sea was in part a reconnaissance to see whether colonies could be planted along the coast. If this was the reason, he would soon have been disappointed.

He also failed to meet up with the fleet. But, then, instead of turning back the way he came, he pushed on along the coast towards Gwadar, a journey of three days and nights by camel train, according to experienced drivers, but much longer for an army. From Gwadar, today's camel handlers reckon another four days and nights to the Iranian border; with perhaps a further week to the Bampur valley in Iran. But, somewhere, Alexander made a miscalculation. His army ran into serious difficulties, ran out of water and could not find any more on the way. The suffering from heat and thirst became intolerable, and our sources speak of horrendous losses, especially among the non-combatants. It was on this stretch of the journey, according to Arrian, that Alexander made one of his 'noblest gestures'. Although himself very distressed from thirst, he poured a precious helmet full of water into the sand in front of his men, rather than drink when they could not.

Our own experience gave us an inkling of what they went through. Following in Alexander's footsteps we joined a camel train at Pasni going straight though the desert to Gwadar. On the first day we passed along a burning seashore with no shred of shade, then entered a landscape of high dunes which pulled the feet at every step. We camped in the open desert and cooked a goat under the night sky. Next day we entered a ferocious salt-desert, rimmed with lunar peaks and ridges, which seemed to reflect the heat back on to

--------

Previous pages: The Makran coast near Gwadar. 'The king dug wells along the beach and discovered drinkable water, so he stuck to the shore for seven days before pulling back into the interior' (Strabo).

us. Further on, the path led for kilometre after kilometre over dismal salt-flats, then through broken ranges of hills until, after 100 kilometres, it enters a surreal landscape of wildly eroded ridges covered with what looks like a snowfall of white dust. Finally, at the gigantic natural rock outcrop of Sur Bandar, a straggle of straw huts by the sea where hundreds of small fishing boats ride at anchor and donkey carts off-load fish, we reached what the Greeks aptly called the 'land of the Fish Eaters'.

We had taken our own water with us, as none would be forthcoming between Pasni and Gwadar, but we miscalculated on the length of marches and, on one occasion, we did not eat between one evening and the following midnight. Fortunately, we had enough water to keep going, on our short expedition, but it was easy to understand how the Greeks had run into trouble. Why they did, though, is still a mystery. Was the disaster as bad as it is made out in our texts, or was it dramatized for the public back home – the world conqueror's final heroic battle with nature itself?

They arrived at Bampur in Iran sixty days after entering the Makran. Alexander's propaganda portrayed the Makran journey as a feat of heroic endurance, showing the leader's courage and selflessness, despite the suffering. What it did not say was whether the disaster was due to the leader's foolhardiness. The truth is never likely to emerge. But, as we toiled with our camels through the blazing sun west of Pasni, the thought did cross the mind that, subconsciously, Alexander had wanted to punish his army for not following him across the Beas river. Impossible? With Alexander's weird psychology we can never be sure.

Once again, it was the tireless Aurel Stein who traced Alexander's return track through southern Iran, from Gwadar up today's Highway 13 as far as Iranshahr, then turning west along the old road through Bampur and on across the desolate wastes of Sistan to Salmous, the ancient mound of Tepe Yahya a little beyond Kahnug. There were later stories that the weary troops were allowed seven days' rest and recreation in this fertile spot, and spent it in orgiastic and Dionysian revels.

Plutarch tells an extraordinary tale of Alexander and his leaders travelling on a great carriage dressed up in fancy costume, paralytically drunk on wine. As so often with Alexander, such tales were dismissed out of hand by gentleman-scholars of the imperial age as unseemly and improbable in the great man, an officer and a gentleman. They could not accept that the Macedonian officers, with their staggering constitutions, their unrestrained appetite for booze, sex and violence, were so unlike their own public-school classically-educated British generals! Harder men, though, can seldom have lived. The Macedonians themselves had learned a different lesson from reading Homer. Why should they, for all their admiration of Homer's heroes, feel embarrassed about letting it all hang

out among their own? We, who have lived through the amazing revelations of the tawdry and unrestrained private lives of great modern tyrants, such as Mao, cannot be so quick to disbelieve such stories. But what lay behind the Greeks' licentious behaviour? Could it have been sheer relief at having got through? Or did, perhaps, Alexander already sense his star had deserted him?

Suitably replenished, they then moved down to the Strait of Hormuz in the vicinity of Bandar-e-Abbas. Here, Alexander met Nearchus in the famous 'recognition' scene described by Arrian from Nearchus's own journal. A sun-burned, bearded, long-haired figure in tattered clothes, Nearchus had lost a lot of weight because of his austere diet, and, on seeing him, Alexander burst into tears: 'What happened to the fleet? Are you all that is left?' He then heard the astonishing news that the fleet, unlike the army, had come through

Our Makran journey on the second day's march between Pasni and
Gwadar, where the dunes give way to a desolate salt-encrusted
plain. 'Alexander was in great distress for the whole journey because
he was marching through such a dreadful terrain' (Strabo).

unscathed. In its own way, it had been an impressive feat of exploration. When Alexander
was on his death bed, Nearchus would sit with him retelling the tale.

In January 324, Alexander set out for the last leg, about 800 kilometres to Persepolis.
His route followed the modern road north as far as Sirjan; then went westwards on the old
minor road to Neiriz, and on to Persepolis and Pasargadae. Picking over the burnt shell of
Persepolis, it is said that, with hindsight, Alexander regretted what he had done.

217

## MASS MARRIAGE IN SUSA

By late February 324, Alexander was back in Susa, just over six years since after he had left it to go east. Soon there was more unrest among the officers and troops. There was disquiet at the growing orientalizing; the favouritism shown towards the new Persian brigades; the piling on of Persian protocol and Persian dress; and the increasingly despotic character of Alexander's behaviour. By now, surrounded by a tightly-knit bunch of cronies and flatterers, Alexander believed his own publicity. Macedonia had been forgotten. The centre of gravity of Alexander's world – both psychological and political – had shifted to Babylon. He showed no sign of ever contemplating a return to Greece. A new world was in the process of creation, a beast slouching towards Babylon waiting to be born.

All this climaxed in the splendid mass-marriage ceremony in the great audience hall in Susa, where between eighty and a hundred Macedonian officers took Persian or Median brides – Persian style. Alexander and Hephaistion married the daughters of Darius, who, having been taken in the royal tent at Issus, had now received a Greek education. Ten thousand troops from the ranks were also forced to take the plunge, a deliberate attempt, it was said, to bring the two nations closer together. (More likely, it was to create a new ruling class in Iran whose loyalties lay there, not back in Macedonia. The mass marriage has been remembered with bitterness down to the present-day Zoroastrians in Iran, where it is commonly said that the hated Alexander 'forced our boys and girls to marry against their will'.) Provisions were also made for the education of no less than 10,000 children born to the troops by captive women during the expedition.

Meanwhile, Alexander's favourite Hephaistion was growing ever more deeply unpopular. The office of grand vizier had been revived for him and he was lavish in his patronage, favouritism and bribery. The second most powerful man in the empire, and the most likely successor to Alexander, he had come to be hated by the old-school Macedonian officer corps. Alexander attempted to defuse the antagonisms by paying off over 10,000 of his veterans and sending them home. In his eyes it was better to get rid of them than court more dissenting voices. At the same time he sent a weird letter to the cities of the Greek league, announcing he wished to be recognized as a god. (This provoked derision, fear and loathing in Athens.)

Time was running out. In February 324, he left Susa for southern Iraq, where he founded a new city – an Alexandria at the top of the Gulf. Then he was rowed and punted back up the Euphrates through the 'great Babylonian swamp', the marshes which have now been deliberately drained by the present tyrant of Baghdad. Alexander sailed by the ancient city of Uruk, in whose countryside stood the tombs of Nebuchadnezzar and the last native Babylonian dynasty. (Now in a windswept desert, one of the huge star-shaped brick tomb mounds still stands 30 metres high opposite the immense ruin field of Uruk, the ancient Babylonian city which was a Greek *polis* in the days of Alexander's successors.)

At Opis, north of Babylon, an army mutiny was narrowly averted, and angry confrontations with his long-serving veterans provoked threats from Alexander to raise his new army only from Iranians. Bitter exchanges open old wounds. ('If it hadn't been for the old guard, men like Arrhaidaeus, you'd still be camped outside Halicarnassos!' one of them bawled at him.) At a great public meeting a raging Alexander jumped off the platform into the crowd and pulled out the ring-leaders, despatching them to instant execution. In high summer, with discontent still simmering, Alexander then moved up from the heat of the plains from Susa via Bisitun to Hamadan (Ecbatana), the Great King's summer retreat. Here fate started to close in.

As it stands in our texts, the atmosphere was increasingly unpleasant and factional. One strange fragment from this time, which reveals something of Alexander's state of mind, was recorded by his secretary Eumenes of Cardia (although why Eumenes should have recorded such things is open to speculation). The fragment is dated October. Alexander was on a journey, perhaps the seven-day march from Bisitun to Hamadan:

> *On the fifth day of the month he drank with Eumaeus; on the sixth he slept after drinking, reviving only in what was left of the day enough to discuss the next day's march with his commanders: saying they should set off early. On the seventh he feasted with Perdiccas and drank again so that he slept through the eighth. On the fifteenth of the month he drank in the same fashion and passed the next day as he usually did after drinking. On the twenty-fourth he dined with Bagoas* [possibly the beautiful Persian eunuch with whom the king had intimate relations]. *Bagoas' house was a mile from the palace* [by now we are evidently in Hamadan]; *then till the twenty-sixth he rested* [after this drinking bout he was still sleeping two days later]. *One of two conclusions may be drawn from this: either that Alexander did himself great damage by drinking in so many days of the month, or that those who wrote these things were liars, that is* [the secretary] *Eumenes of Kardia.*

> AELIAN

This picture is confirmed from other sources, some of which speak of prodigious drinking contests – after one of which a number of Alexander's companions actually died. The king was now as often drunk as sober, and his sleeps after these bouts became longer and

more frequent. As Plutarch said: 'After drinking he would bathe and often sleep till midday; sometimes even spending the entire day asleep.' This kind of information came from intimate notes from people inside Alexander's circle, who recorded the events of his last year – and must be true. It is not the picture of a man who is fighting fit – or in control of his destiny. His doctors must have been increasingly worried. After all the punishment his body had taken over the years, the king's megalomania and manic depressive tendencies were now being fuelled by drink and alcohol psychosis. The deep strain of insecurity which seems to have run in the king's character was never assuaged by power; indeed we might guess that such power only made it worse.

Above: A contemporary bronze head, now damaged,
of Alexander's closest friend Hephaistion.

Opposite: Alexander in the guise of the god of war, Ares, marries
Stateira who is shown as Aphrodite, the goddess of love; a Roman
copy of a lost Greek original, from Pompeii.

## NEMESIS: 'THIS IS HOW IT ENDS ...'

At Ecbatana it all came to a head. This is where, remember, Alexander had secretly engineered the murder of his old stalwart Parmenio, his father's right-hand man. (There were those among the old guard who would never have forgotten this.) Ecbatana, Iran's highest big city at 200 metres, was on the main caravan route, later the Silk Route, from Central Asia to the Mediterranean. Ancient writers describe a city of fantastic splendour, temples with silvered roofs, palaces adorned with gilded cedar wood, massive walls and wonderful gardens. Here, in Hamadan in October or November, fate – or Alexander's enemies – turned against him.

After more quarrels, a grand junket with athletics contests was held at the army camp outside the city; then an epic drinking party. Afterwards Hephaistion fell ill, having drunk 'immoderately' or 'inappropriately'. (By now, the imagination boggles at what constituted inappropriate drinking.) He disobeyed his doctor's instructions and went back on the drink. He was dead before Alexander returned from the games. The king's grief knew no bounds: an agony of grief, fed, no doubt, by boyhood memories; and youthful emulation of the Homeric heroes. For a day and a night Alexander lay on Hephaistion's body, weeping and moaning. He cut off his hair, just as his hero Achilles did for his beloved Patroclus in the *Iliad*. Even the horses' tails were shorn. The unfortunate doctor Glaucias was crucified. The temple of the physician god Asclepius, in Ecbatana, was destroyed (even the gods were punished).

What does this mean? No doubt Alexander recalled Achilles's words in Homer: 'My dear companion whom I honoured above all others, and in like measure to my own person, is dead'. Perhaps he also knew Aeschylus, in whose words the relationship of Achilles and Patroclus was overtly erotic, shot through with intense personal passion. Perhaps it is Aeschylus' Achilles who takes us closest to Alexander and Hephaistion: 'Weep for me the living, rather than for him, the dead; for I have lost my all ... I am not ashamed to say it ... No care did you have for the chaste consecration of our thighs o thou most ungrateful for my many kisses ... and the devout union of our thighs!'

We simply do not know the nature of Alexander's relationship with Hephaistion, but perhaps those lines of Aeschylus can help us better to understand Alexander's feelings for Hephaistion. A pious heroic, homo-erotic bond of friendship remains the likeliest possibility. The epic theme of the Homeric heroes, which they had played out since boyhood, had come true, even if Hephaistion's death had hardly been a hero's. The choice between long inglorious life and an early glorious death had long since been made. And Alexander's alter ego was now dead.

A vast, five-storey funeral pyre was planned for Hephaistion in Babylon. Fluttering with flags, adorned with glittering eagles and serpents, stuffed with larger than life-size warriors and the gilded beaks of 240 quinqueremes (galleys), it would cost 10,000 talents. Alexander even sent to Siwa, asking whether Hephaistion could be worshipped as a god. But this was too much for Ammon, who, politely but firmly, said no. (A hero cult, he said, would be quite sufficient.) The grand hecatomb was never constructed, but the remains of a funeral pyre were uncovered by archaeologists in the north-east quarter of Babylon. The great brick platform, covered with burned debris, lay near the Greek theatre in an open part of the city used in Greek times for dumping building rubbish. The area is now a desolate and overgrown suburb of Saddam's megalomaniacal reconstructed city. It would somehow be fitting if this were Hephaistion's last resting place. One of the least sympathetic characters in the story, Hephaistion had never lost Alexander's affection. According to one tradition, the reason was simple. 'Others loved me because I am king. Hephaistion loved me for myself.'

A strange tailpiece to the story perhaps casts some light on Alexander's passion for Hephaistion, and on his inordinate grief. There is no evidence Alexander ever particularly coveted sexual relations with women. Memnon's widow Barsine is said to have been his first sexual experience with a woman. But Roxanne, who was possibly a very young girl, had by all accounts attracted him by her beauty, and he had married her in the teeth of scorn and disapproval from his companions. In the month after Hephaistion's death, Roxanne became pregnant by Alexander, and the son she subsequently bore was Alexander's sole legitimate heir. As Plutarch wrote: 'It was sleep and sexual intercourse, he used to say, which more than anything else reminded him that he was mortal.'

After the protracted period of mourning for his friend, Alexander roused himself. In midwinter he marched against the Cossaeans, a nomadic tribe in the Zagros Mountains: 'to lighten his sorrow, as if tracking down and hunting live human beings might console him', says Plutarch in a terrifying passage, 'and he massacred the entire male population from the youths upwards'. A human sacrifice to the spirit of Hephaistion, just as Achilles had killed Trojan youths over the grave of Patroclus. Blood for the ghosts.


## 'WE'LL SAY OUR GOODBYES IN BABYLON'

At the end of the year, Alexander moved westwards once more from Iran to Babylonia, 'by easy marches, stopping all the time to rest the army', says Diodorus. Reading between the lines, we might detect the same story as the secretary Eumenes records: late starts, missed

days, long sleeps after extended drinking sessions. And now (as we read it in the pages of
Arrian, Curtius and Plutarch) the story acquires a fateful momentum; at least that is how,
with hindsight, the Alexander historians have crafted the tale in the literary form which
has come down to us.

Perhaps that is just hindsight? Did it actually appear that way at the time? Or did his
return to Babylon in the eyes of his contemporaries merely signal a brief reorganization
before new plans? Ambassadors had come from the West; there was talk of exciting new
projects, of expeditions to Carthage and Rome and the conquest of the western
Mediterranean. Perhaps he had even heard news of a Greek captain's voyage of exploration to the Baltic and Iceland, circumnavigating the British Isles. Would he have taken a
new expedition, drawing on the manpower of the old Persian empire, back to the Beas
and on to the Ganges? The fact is that we don't know and cannot know.

This last year, then, could have been a time of optimistic planning. Equally, though,
it is certain that sometimes in the tide of history, fortune may seem abruptly to ebb away;
luck will apparently desert a lucky general, and a series of events can take place which
suddenly seems to conform to a pre-destined course. And none was more open to such
ideas about fate and destiny than Alexander and his inner circle. Indeed, during the early
years of their meteoric rise, they had been adept at the manipulation of favourable omens,
from Delphi to Gordion and Siwa. But this necessarily made them all the more suscepti-
ble to contrary forces. Looked at in that light, then, from the mutiny at the Beas river,
events could be made to fit an ominous pattern despite the propagandists' energetic efforts
to make the Makran disaster fit the old template of manifest destiny. The king's star, it may
be, was no longer in the ascendant.

Even before he left Iran there had been strange omens. The Indian saddhu Calanus,
now seventy-three, had accompanied Alexander, but had become ill. Realizing death was
near, he announced he would immolate himself alive in Indian fashion on a funeral pyre.
The spectacle was never forgotten by the Macedonian high command who stood by.
Before he ascended the funeral pyre, Calanus had said goodbye to Alexander's companions, but to the king himself had remarked darkly: 'We'll say our farewells in Babylon'.
Then (or so it was said later) before the king reached Babylon, he was met by Chaldean
wise men, astrologers who drew him aside and begged him to go no further because their
god Bel had said that for the king to enter the city at this time would be fatal to him.
'Don't go westwards', they urged, 'turn round and go back to the east.'

After dithering for a while Alexander by-passed Babylon and camped beyond the
city at Borsippa 15 kilometres to the south. (Borsippa was an ancient city, famous among
Greek historians as a place of Chaldean astrologers. Remains of its great ziggurat still stand,

a great eroded finger of mud-brick towering over the Euphrates plain.) All this, however, smacks of uncharacteristic indecision: the man who had acted with such speed at the Persian Gates or Aornos suddenly cannot make up his mind whether to enter his capital city.

There was a debate with his entourage, who tried to persuade him to ignore the warning and, more to the point, to rebuild his self-esteem once again. The sceptic and atheist Anaxagoras, who had justified the murder of Cleitus, got right to the point telling the king to ignore all omens as meaningless mumbo-jumbo. Fortified by Dutch courage, Alexander then resolved to enter Babylon. He was not, however, allowed to put the omens out of his mind. No sooner had he entered the city, than ravens were seen fighting over the walls, an infallible sign of divine disapproval. Then a sacrifice for the king's health yielded no lobe on the victim's liver, a threatening prodigy, as the diviner admitted when Alexander tried to force the truth out of him. Suddenly the signs were not capable of being twisted round.

Then came the most disturbing occurrence, and this is how the Greeks told it: one day when the king came in stripped for athletics after playing games, an unknown young man, apparently half mad, was found sitting in silence on the king's throne; he was wearing the royal robes and diadem. Interrogated in the presence of the king he said nothing for a long while, then when he came to his senses he said he had been brought from the coast in chains for some unspecified crime; 'then the god Serapis had loosed his chains and told him to come here and do these things'. When Alexander heard the story, he spoke to his seers and all agreed the young man should be put to death.

What does this sinister tale mean? Recently it has been put in a Babylonian context, whose dark meaning later Greek writers failed to divine. Shortly before the king's death, it is argued, the omens were so dire that the priests of Babylon set in motion the archaic ritual of the Substitute King. In order to stave off disaster, the ruling king temporarily abandoned his throne for a stand-in, a scapegoat, a convicted criminal who took on the bad karma of the real king and, having ruled for a short period stipulated by the astrologers, was then put to death. The fact that Alexander is said to have ratified the death sentence on the young man, his surrogate, suggests he understood and approved the implementation of the ritual.

If we have read it right, this astonishing tale only intensifies the feeling of a cloud of superstition and darkness descending on Alexander's inner circle in the last days. Many parallels could be cited from our own time of rulers so corrupted by power that they become completely divorced from reality. As a result of the young man's death, says Plutarch, 'the king's confidence now deserted him, he began to believe that he had lost the favour of the gods, and he became increasingly suspicious of his friends'. There were insane eruptions of anger, with Alexander, at one point, banging a companion's head against the wall, now 'so obsessed by his fears of the supernatural, so overwrought and apprehensive in his mind that he interpreted every strange or unusual occurrence no matter how trivial, as a portent, with the result that the palace was filled with soothsayers, sacrificers, purifiers and fortune tellers'.

## ALEXANDER'S LAST DAYS

Nothing, including the fact that Roxanne was about to give birth, stopped Alexander's binges. Indeed, perhaps it drove him further to drink to forget himself. That May he held a splendid banquet for Nearchus and, after two days of drinking, he began to feel feverish. He developed a raging fever and, in his thirst, drank more and became delirious. The journal of his last days is given by Arrian, with dates by Plutarch. It has all the marks of a contemporary record, laconic, circumstantial, and intimate, in such marked distinction to the self-glorifying official records. According to Plutarch it comes 'almost word for word from the royal diaries'. It is one of the most dramatic historical records from the ancient world:

*On 29 May he slept in the bathroom because he was feverish. Next day after taking a bath he moved into the bedchamber and spent the day playing dice with Medius. He took a bath late in the evening, offered sacrifice to the gods, dined and remained feverish throughout the night. On the 31 May he again bathed and sacrificed as usual and while he was lying down in the bathroom he was entertained by listening to Nearchus' account of his voyage and his exploration of the great sea. On 1 June the fever grew more intense: he had a bad night and all through the next day his fever was very high. He had his bed moved and lay in it by the side of the great plunge bath; there he discussed with his commanders the vacant posts in the army and how to fill them with top calibre officers. On the 4 June his fever was still worse and he had to be carried outside to do sacrifice. He then gave orders to his senior commanders to remain on call in the palace courtyard and to his company commanders to spend the night outside. On June 5th he was moved to the palace on the other side of the Euphrates, and there slept a little, but the fever did not abate. When his commanders entered the room he was speechless and remained so through June 6th. The Macedonians now believed he was dead and crowded the doors of the palace; they began to shout and threaten the Companions, who at length were forced to let them in. When the doors had been thrown open they all slowly filed past his bedside one by one, wearing neither cloak nor armour.*

(Arrian adds a vivid detail here which rings true: 'Nothing could keep them from seeing him a last time and the motive in almost every heart was grief and a sort of helpless bewilderment at the thought of losing their king. Lying speechless as the men filed by, he yet struggled to raise his head, and in his eyes there was a look of recognition for each individual as he passed.')

> *In the course of this same day* [Plutarch continues], *Python and Seleucus were sent to the temple of Serapis to ask whether Alexander should be moved there. The god replied that they should leave him where he was. On the twenty-eighth day of the month of Daesius* [10 June 323 BC] *towards evening he died.*

Alexander was not yet thirty-three.

> *At the time* [says Plutarch], *no one had any suspicion that he was poisoned, but it is said that five years afterwards some information was given on the strength of which his mother Olympias put many men to death and had the ashes of* [the cupbearer] *Iolas, Antipater's son, scattered to the winds on the supposition that he had administered the poison. According to some writers it was Aristotle who advised Antipater to arrange the murder and entirely through his efforts that the poison was provided …*

Not surprisingly, tales circulated in plenty in the aftermath of the death of the man who had ruled most of the known world. The story that Iolas was the poisoner was known in Athens soon afterwards, where he was proposed a public vote of thanks by the orator Demosthenes. Extremely circumstantial stories have come down to us which might support the idea that Alexander and Hephaistion did not die by natural causes. One is told of a Macedonian army officer who was present at that time at both Hamadan and Babylon. On Alexander's return from India, fearing he might fall victim in the expected next round of purges, he consulted a soothsayer. What should he do? He was told not to worry; both Hephaistion and Alexander would soon be dead. Hephaistion died within days, Alexander within the year, both from inexplicably high fever after drinking unmixed

Overleaf: The south palace in Babylon, scene of Alexander's last illness. Top right is the Ishtar Gate. Lower centre, clearly visible as an open rectangle, is the throne room where the sinister episode of the Substitute King took place (see page 225).

wine. (A doctor's comments on the pharmacology suggests slow strychnine poisoning is the best bet; coincidentally or not, Aristotle's botanist friend Theophrastus describes its uses and dosage, saying that 'the best way to disguise its bitter taste is by administering it in unmixed wine'.)

There were also later stories that Aristotle himself had been responsible, realizing that he had helped create a monster, but the most Plutarch will say is this: 'At first Alexander greatly esteemed Aristotle, and became more attached to him than to his father … but in his later years he came to regard him with suspicion. He never actually did him any harm, but his friendship lost its original warmth and affection, a clear proof of the estrangement which developed between them'. As so often with Alexander, we will never know the truth.

The symptoms of liver failure through alcoholism and poisoning, of course, are not dissimilar. Most scholars today do not accept the poisoning story, although some would not dismiss the idea that he and Hephaistion were removed in this way. There are other possibilities: pleurisy, inflamed by the wound he received at Multan; typhus, helped by alcohol abuse; excessive grief even. All or any could have fatally undermined his immune system. But, as always, we interpret evidence to suit the concerns of our own time. For us, it is not such an unlikely scenario that Alexander was poisoned by a junta of exasperated and disillusioned senior officers. Many of the king's erstwhile friends and companions had by now become appalled by what they had seen, by the orientalizing extravagances, the murderous rages, and, worst of all perhaps, by the claims to divinity. For them, he had become a tyrant, arbitrary, and unpredictable. As Alexander's tutor Aristotle himself had said: 'No one freely endures such rule'.

For the Macedonians, 'he accomplished greater deeds than any, not only of the kings who had lived before him, but also of those who were to come later down to our time' (Diodorus, writing in the first century BC). Fortunes had been made, empires built, half a world conquered. Elsewhere, though, there can have been few who lamented his passing. When the news of his death reached Athens, the public orator Demades exclaimed: 'Alexander dead? Impossible: the whole world would stink of his corpse.'

What of Alexander himself? What were his own thoughts before the end? We will never know what lay behind the self-destructive course of the last months. For all we know, it may have been the simple fact, recorded by Plutarch, that the king was now 'at an utter loss to know what he should do with the rest of his life'.

## AFTER HIS DEATH

Who would be Alexander's successor? The generals crowded the deathbed to ask. It was said that the king regained the power of speech, if only of a few words, before the end. We can imagine them all there in that room overlooking the Euphrates, the blistering summer heat subsiding over the plains of Babylon; the towering brick walls of the palace throbbing with heat; a slight breeze coming up over palm forests in the royal gardens below the window and gently gusting down the wind-catchers. Intent eyes were upon him, the eyes of Ptolemy, Seleucus, Nearchus and the other generals. The one key question now he was obviously going to die was: To whom should the empire go? The fevered answer, whispered through the death-rattle so they all had to stoop over the bed to hear: to *kratisto*, to the strongest. Of course. What else should we have expected from him?

The body was embalmed, but the funeral car to Macedonia was hijacked by Ptolemy who wanted it in Egypt, which had fallen to him in the carve-up of the empire which followed the king's death. Alexander had apparently asked to be buried with his 'father' at Siwa, but his first burial was at the old capital in Memphis. Later the coffin was moved to the Sema, the central crossroads of the new city of Alexandria in Egypt, where it was visited by many pilgrims over the years. (The recent suggestion that it has been found at Siwa is a complete fabrication.) Last recorded in the fourth century AD, the site of the tomb has never been located. Traditionally, the site of the Sema was close to the later mosque of Daniel 'the two-horned prophet' where the sarcophagus of the last pharaoh Nectanebo, which is now in the British Museum, was found being used as a water trough. (Some have suggested that Alexander's coffin was placed inside this.) Remarkable new underwater excavations in the eastern harbour, however, have suggested the palaces and royal tombs should be placed much further east. In which case the beautiful alabaster fragment of a Hellenistic mausoleum, which stands next to an unkempt Greek cemetery in the eastern quarter of the city, may well mark Alexander's last resting place. Fitting, perhaps, that some trace should remain in this first Alexandria, which to Greeks will always remain, as the poet Constantine Cavafy put it, 'the capital of memory'.

As for the other characters in the tale, many of course had left their bones on the long road between the Balkans and India, as Coenus said on the banks of the Beas river. (He himself would be one of them, along with Darius, Parmenio, Bessus, Callisthenes, and so many others.) Others died in the murderous feuds which followed. The fate of the king's mistress Barsine and her son Heracles is unknown; Roxanne and her son survived till 313, when they were murdered; Alexander's second wife Stateira, the daughter of Darius, had already been killed by Roxanne. The king's redoubtable mother, Olympias, perished too in civil war in Macedonia. Some, though, made undreamed-of fortunes. Ptolemy became king in Egypt, creating a dynasty which ended with Cleopatra, last of the Greek-speaking rulers of Egypt. Seleucus ruled a great kingdom from Babylon with his Bactrian wife Apama. They and their successors were restorers of the glories of old Babylonia. Further out in Bactria and north-west India, kings of Greek descent survived for 300 years, minting coins as maharajahs. The conquistadors had become dynasts.

## ALEXANDER'S LEGACY

On one level Alexander's is a tale of blood and horror but, as so often in history, war unleashed tremendous energies, stirring lives up, accelerating the pace of change. In the centuries which followed, Greek culture enjoyed an amazing afterlife in east Asia and India. Galvanized by these tremendous events, new worlds opened up, linked by new land and sea routes. The theorem of Pythagoras, for example, reached China within a few decades of Alexander's death.

Nearer home, the cities of the Near East entered a period of great prosperity under Alexander's successors. Uruk, for example, had the greatest and densest period of habitation in its whole history. Immense temples were built by patrons with mixed Greek and native names, who controlled enormous financial resources stimulated, perhaps, by the growth of trade between the Mediterranean, the Gulf and India. Egypt, too, under the Ptolemies enjoyed a late flowering with magnificent temples and rich urban life, especially in Alexandria which would become the 'first city of the world'. Indeed in conservative Egypt, generations of Greek settlers went native, the very thing Alexander had hoped for in founding cities as far away as Tajikistan and the Punjab.

Nor did the Greek expansion stop with Alexander's death. In the second century BC the Hellenistic general Menander, who had been born in Afghanistan, led an expedition down the Ganges where he sacked Kosambi, Benares, and Patna, gaining in some eyes the reputation of being 'even greater than Alexander'. Menander, though, was conquered by India in the end, becoming a Buddhist. But the Greek kingdoms in the North-West Frontier and Afghanistan lasted into the late first century BC, long after Macedon itself had been defeated by the Roman empire. By then, Greek sailors had mastered the timing of the monsoon routes across the Indian Ocean from the Red Sea, and, in the early Roman empire, Alexandrian merchants were the middlemen who brought Indian hardwoods, perfumes and spices to the West, along with Chinese silk and south Indian pepper to fill the pepper barns on the Tiber. At that time, Greek merchants' manuals log all the harbours as far as the Ganges mouths, and Tamil poems in south India mention Greek merchants, mercenaries, and even Greek sculptors, in the streets of Madurai. It is as if Alexander's era saw an explosion of energy, like a nebula, which left behind new universes reforming in its aftermath.

Hellenism, Greek culture, became the bedrock of the culture of the Near East. It was, by its nature, a cosmopolitan civilization, and it is no accident that, in the centuries which followed, three great world religions (that is, Christianity, Manichaeism and Islam) all arose in the Hellenistic culture zone of the Near East; all of them drawing on a mixture of Greek, Egyptian, Jewish and Iranian themes. The fact that Hellenism was one of the cultural bases of Islam is often overlooked. But, for long into the Muslim period Muslims were a minority in the lands that they had conquered. Egypt was Christian till the tenth century; Iraq, too, had strong Christian and Jewish elements, all of which shared Greek culture. The change-over to Islam was long and slow. Hellenism remained one of the roots of educated culture in the Near East up until the great period of translation of Greek texts into Arabic in tenth-century Baghdad. This was achieved by translators in Arabic who were Christian and Jewish, as well as Muslim. Hellenism even penetrated into Arabia where Greek-style art is still found after the Prophet's lifetime. In Jordan, as elsewhere, Greek was still used as the official language into the eighth century; the last inscription bearing Greek from Taxila, in Pakistan, is from the same time. Hellenistic modes of thought were so powerful that they endured long after their rule had gone, helping to give a certain unity to the whole region between the Mediterranean and the Indus. It is, perhaps, no coincidence that the land-borders of the Muslim conquests in the east, up to the eighth century, were coterminous with Alexander's empire.

And, all along, as we have seen, Alexander's legend in art and story spread over the entire ancient world from the Atlantic to the borders of China, and from the central Asian steppe south to Ethiopia. The verdicts on the man, though, are still divided. By the banks of the Ganges in Benares, the veteran Indian historian A.K. Narain told me he felt that following Alexander's path was 'going in the footsteps of violence' and that in the end, 'the Greeks came and saw, but India conquered'. In Taxila in the North-West Frontier of Pakistan, Ahmed Dani, doyen of the subcontinent's archaeologists, saw it differently:

*Out of this great exchange between east and west, Greek knowledge, science, poetry, art and philosophy entered the ancient culture of the Indian subcontinent. There was destruction and loss of life, to be sure, but great things occurred which advanced the history of humanity. This is the nature of history. In this sense this is the legacy of Westerners and Europeans but also of Muslims and Indians. Alexander belongs not only to Greece but to the Islamic world, and to Pakistan and India. For this it is one of the greatest events in the history of the world.*

## WHAT IF HE HAD LIVED?

There were plans, it was rumoured. There was, for example, an astonishing document, which came into the hands of Diodorus Siculus, listing them. This document probably owed its origin to the secretary Eumenes. (Perhaps it was noted down during the king's last moments of lucidity that sweltering June in Babylon, in the times the fever abated?) These were Alexander's plans:

First military: the conquest of Arabia; the building of 1000 extra large warships for a campaign to take Carthage and the western Mediterranean; the building of a military road all the way across North Africa from Alexandria to Gibraltar with harbours, bases and arsenals. None of this is implausible, much of it widely attested in the tradition. Alexander certainly planned to conquer the West, perhaps 'even as far as the Britannic Isles', as Arrian said.

Then there were to be new city foundations, with the transplantation of populations between Europe and Africa, eerily echoing a strange and possibly forged letter of Aristotle to Alexander which advocates the transportation of the Iranian ruling class to Europe, a necessary preparation for the forthcoming Greek world state.

Finally, there were gigantic building projects: the completion of Hephaistion's pyre; the erection of six colossal temples, wonders of the world, in Macedonia and Greece, including a renewed temple of Athena of Troy to make it 'a famous attraction throughout the world'. Most intriguing in a Freudian sense was Alexander's plan for a pyramid tomb for his father Philip to rival, and out-do, the Great Pyramid of Giza. So the architect of the Macedonian world empire would be honoured by the most impressive monument in the world. (Was the son finally giving due credit to his greatest rival – to the father he had claimed had not given him credit for what he did, and bore him 'ill-will and jealousy'?)

The 'last plans' are so weird that it is hard to disbelieve them – and there is surprising unanimity about them in the ancient tradition. Clearly, Alexander did have such enormous ambitions of further conquest. Nor need we doubt that, in the last years, his concept of his own greatness had become obsessive. His intention was not merely to surpass what had gone before, but to leave posterity no hope of equalling him.

Whether architectural or military, Alexander's achievements were to be unsurpassable by succeeding generations and kings. (They take us into the realms of the thousand-year

Reich and Albert Speer's plans for his master to rebuild Berlin.) Pyramids greater than Giza, the biggest temples in the world, the conquest of the West. And, with the manpower and resources of east Asia behind him, Alexander could well have succeeded.

Beyond that, the what-ifs are fruitless. In a great *jeu d'esprit*, Arnold Toynbee made Alexander recover from his illness in Babylon, conquer the West and India, then burst in on the warring states of China in 314, to unite the whole of the Old World. Toynbee imagined a united world order from the Hellenistic age to the present, with the steam-engine invented in Alexandria in the first century, and a contented 1950s' world under Alexander XXXV! If only history were so clear cut. But Toynbee's fantasy contains one essential truth. For Alexander, the last plans were intended to be unsurpassable by all generations which came after. Fragmentary and tantalizing as they are, they survive to bemuse later ages. Like Shelley's monument of Ozymandias, they say: 'Look on my deeds and despair.'

The real Alexander or just the Alexander for our age?
A detail from the Issus mosaic. The big nose, prominent forehead,
brown hair swept off the brow, bulging eyes and thick neck are all
attested in our sources. Perhaps this is as near to him, and
his *pothos*, his driven-ness, as we can hope to get today.

# EPILOGUE

OUR JOURNEY IN ALEXANDER'S FOOTSTEPS WAS OVER. It had taken us more than 30,000 kilometres on land, by bus, Jeep, train, camel, horse, mule, and on foot. On the way back from Alexandria I stopped over in Naples for one last rendezvous. I went to the Naples Museum, the lumber-room of the Hellenistic Age, full of statues and images looted from Greece to adorn rich houses in Pompeii. Walking its halls is rather like wandering through the bric-a-brac of the British Empire after it had gone. There are portraits of stern generals and local governors, stiff upper-lipped district officers, corpulent sensual satraps, Macedonian officers looking very dashing in their cavalry helmets and billowing scarfs - like World War I fighter aces. Here, too, are war memorials, weird cult images, and the popular statuary of the time.

Looking at these one could almost see an age like ours: cosmopolitan, internationalist, self-aware; fascinated by the possibilities of mimetic art, by sex and violence, and the grotesque. Their most extreme art has its modern apotheosis in Hollywood; the bulging muscles and extreme passion of the mythic struggles on the Pergamon altar find parallels in violent late twentieth-century action films with their muscle-bound heroes, space-age weaponry and the same aura of heroic invincibility.

Finally, there is the great mosaic of the battle of Issus: one of the most powerful of all depictions of war, and, as we see it now, the central image of the age of Alexander. Fear and pain are written all over the Persian faces. Darius reaches out unable to save his friend. Alexander strains forward, spurring his horse, eyes bulging, hair streaming, driven by his demon, his *pothos*. Copied from a painting done within living memory, this image is probably the truest representation we have of his looks, and, more important, of his spirit.

A hero he may be to generations in the West, but to the people of Asia, the Persians, Central Asians and Indians, he is a bringer of death, a 'long haired demon of the race of wrath'. I could not help but think how history repeats itself: Alexander's deeds, for example, a model for the West. Empires, even when their rulers have gone, leave chains; their thought-worlds persist, their images too powerful and seductive to be rubbed out.

Our search was over. I left the claustrophobic fear of the Issus mosaic for the sunlight over the bay of Naples.

As for our own adventures in the footsteps of Alexander, we had seen the past still alive; we had seen things hardly believable at the end of the twentieth century – the last vestiges of the ancient world Alexander and his army had known, the traditional

237

civilizations on which he had made war. We had ridden with the Turkomans and sailed with the Mohannos; we had sacrificed the goat, and drunk wine with the Black Pagans of the Hindu Kush. We had walked with the camel-drivers of the Makran and had seen the nomads of Luristan smear mares' milk on Cyrus's Tomb. We had seen the sacred tree of Cham, and the holy flame of Adur Farnbagh before which Darius himself had prayed. We had held the lost books of Galen and Theophrastus, and had knelt before the mummy of Spitamenes. We had heard the singing of the *Avesta* and had met the last descendants of the Macedonian army by a clump of violets under the sacred peak of Tirich Mir.

In the hands of the scholars, history is one thing; in the hands of the people who were our eye-witnesses all along our journey, it is another. It is a communal event which exists forever in the retelling, an event which has permeated the culture until now. As the mermaid says:

*Great Alexander Still Lives. And Rules.*

Deified as Zeus, Alexander sits on the globe between
Poseidon and Heracles (Hercules). The stuff of his dreams?

# TABLE OF DATES

'Capital of memory'. This magnificent mosaic depicts a
personification of Alexandria as mistress of the sea, crowned with a
headdress in the shape of a ship's prow. For a while 'first city of the
civilized world', Alexandria was one of Alexander's longest-lasting
legacies. Greco-Roman Museum, Alexandria, third century BC.

# CAST OF CHARACTERS

ACHILLES: legendary hero of the Trojan War, claimed by Alexander as an ancestor.

ALEXANDER III 'THE GREAT': King of Macedon, born 356, ruled 336–323 BC; also known in legend as Iskander or Sikander, 'the Great', 'the Two Horned' and 'the Accursed'.

AMBI: (Omphis according to Curtius) King of Taxila in North-West India (now Pakistan); sided with Alexander when he invaded India.

ANAXAGORAS: sceptical philosopher in Alexander's entourage. Justified Alexander's murder of Cleitus on the grounds that, by definition, all the king's acts were just.

ARIOBARZANES: Persian general defeated by Alexander at the Persian Gates.

ARISTANDER: Macedonian army seer who interpreted signs and omens for Alexander.

ARISTOBULUS: early historian of Alexander; served with Alexander and wrote his history about 300 BC.

ARISTOTLE OF STAGIRA: 384–322 BC; philosopher, tutor of Alexander, with whom he corresponded while the expedition was in Asia. Spiritual father of the Hellenistic Age.

ARRIAN (Flavius Arrianus, c. AD 95–175): Greek historian from Nicomedia in West Turkey. Wrote the best account we have of Alexander; and in his *Indica* the story of Nearchus's voyage home with the fleet.

BARSINE: Persian lady, daughter of Persian nobleman Artabazus; married successively to the Rhodian mercenary brothers Mentor and Memnon (by whom she had children), then mistress of Alexander to whom she bore a son Heracles.

BESSUS: satrap or governor of Bactria; plotted against and killed Darius III, and assumed the royal title. Pursued by Alexander into Central Asia, he was captured and subsequently executed at Hamadan.

CALANUS: Indian saddhu (holy man) accompanied Alexander back from India to Iran.

CALLISTHENES: Alexander's official historian, and nephew of Aristotle. Wrote an eye-witness account of Alexander's expedition down to 328 BC, by which time he had become a critic of the growing despotism in Alexander's court. Executed by Alexander in Afghanistan.

CLEITUS: commander of the 'royal squadron' of Alexander's cavalry; saved Alexander's life at the Granicus; murdered by Alexander in 327 BC after a drunken quarrel in Samarkand.

COENUS: phalanx commander at the battles of Issus and Arbela; spoke up for the mutinous troops at the Beas river in India in 326 BC, but died soon after.

CRATERUS: phalanx commander, Alexander's best general; killed in 321 BC in internecine fighting after Alexander's death.

CRITOBULOS of Kos: doctor of Alexander's father Philip; went with the army to India where he treated Alexander's near-fatal wound at Multan.

CURTIUS (QUINTUS CURTIUS RUFUS): Roman politician and historian. Wrote the earliest surviving and most detailed history of Alexander in the AD 30s. Died AD 53.

CYRUS 'THE GREAT': (born c. 590, ruled c. 559–530 BC) founder of the Persian empire.

DARIUS I 'THE GREAT': (ruled c. 522–486 BC) King of Persia, invaded Greece in 490.

DARIUS III: (born c. 380 BC) King of Persia 336–330 BC, defeated by Alexander; murdered by conspirators led by Bessus.

DIODORUS SICULUS, i.e., of Sicily: Greek historian (c. 80–20 BC); wrote a forty-book world history called *The Library of History* – valuable for details unrecorded elsewhere.

DIONYSUS: Greek god of possession, ecstasy, and wine. Much beloved of Alexander!

EUMENES OF CARDIA: Alexander's secretary in his last days.

FIRDOWSI (from Tus, in eastern Iran): wrote the *Shahnama*, 'Book of Kings' (completed AD 1010) using written and oral traditions in the sections on Alexander.

HEPHAISTION: favourite and beloved friend of Alexander. Handsome and charming, but of doubtful military ability. Commanded part of the army in Central Asia; died after a drinking bout in Hamadan 324 BC. Married Drypetis, daughter of Darius III.

HERCULES (HERACLES): Greek demi-god, whose Twelve Labours earned him immortality. Beloved of Alexander who attempted to emulate him.

HERODOTUS: Greek historian of Halicarnassos (now in South-West Turkey); his *History* written around 450 BC is our main account of the Great Persian War.

MEMNON: Rhodian mercenary commander, married to Barsine; fought for the Persians against Alexander in West Turkey. Died summer 333 BC.

NEARCHUS: childhood friend of Alexander. Commanded the Greek fleet on its return from the Indus to the Euphrates.

OLYMPIAS: (born c. 375 BC) princess of Epirus, wife of Philip and mother of Alexander, who wished her to be deified after her death. Murdered 316 BC.

OXYARTES: Sogdian baron, father of Alexander's wife Roxanne.

PARMENIO: Macedonian general, number two under Philip and Alexander. Father of Philotas, Hector and Nicanor, all of whom died or were killed during Alexander's reign. Murdered by Alexander at Hamadan in 330 BC, aged about seventy.

PATROCLUS: legendary hero of the Trojan War and intimate of Achilles.

PERDICCAS: leading commander and trusted friend of Alexander at Issus, Tyre and Arbela; fought in central Asia and India. Before his death Alexander gave Perdiccas his signet ring, and

Perdiccas supported Alexander's son by Roxanne as successor. Murdered by his own officers in 321 BC.

PHILIP II: (c. 382–336 BC) father of Alexander and founder of the Macedonian empire.

PHILOTAS: son of Parmenio, Companion cavalry commander at Arbela and the Persian Gates; tried and executed by Alexander after the assassination plot at Fara in 330 BC.

PLUTARCH: of Chaeronea, historian and essayist (c. AD 46–126); wrote a short brilliant anecdotal account of Alexander, which is full of intimate personal detail.

PORUS: rajah of the lands between the Jhelum and the Chenab rivers in the Punjab. Defeated and reinstated by Alexander.

PTOLEMY: general and friend of Alexander; later became King of Egypt (305–283 BC) and founded the Ptolemaic dynasty which ended in 30 BC with the famous Cleopatra. Wrote the key history of Alexander's expedition which is lost but used by Arrian.

ROXANNE: daughter of Oxyartes of Sogdia. Married Alexander in Balkh in 327; a son, born of the union after Alexander's death, became his heir; mother and boy were murdered in 314.

SPITAMENES: from Sogdia (now Uzbekistan-Tajikistan), a noble of royal birth. Led Sogdian revolt against Alexander in 328–7 BC; murdered by his own side (or, as Curtius claims, by his wife).

STATEIRA: sister and wife of Darius III. Captured at Issus in 333 BC, died before Arbela in 331 BC; her daughter by Darius, also called Stateira, married Alexander in 324 BC.

XERXES: King of Persia 486–465 BC. Invaded Greece in 480 BC, destroyed Athens, but was defeated at Salamis. Alexander's crusade against Persia was, in part, planned as revenge for Xerxes's sacrilegious acts in Greece.

# SOURCES AND BIBLIOGRAPHY

The custom of writing memoirs did not start with the generals of Desert Storm and the Falklands! Just as would happen today, many of the participants in Alexander the Great's story published their versions of the tale in the decades after his expeditions; among them Ptolemy, Aristobulus, the fleet admiral Nearchus, the helmsman Onesicritos, and Baeton from the bematists (surveyors). Other eye-witness accounts included Callisthenes of Olynthos and Cleitarchus. None of these primary narratives survives save in fragments (these are translated in a fascinating compendium, C. A. Robinson, *The History of Alexander the Great I*, 1953; see, too, L. Pearson, *The Lost Histories of Alexander the Great*, 1960).

Our sources for Alexander in the late twentieth century are people who wrote later with access to these lost works. The chief texts are four, all of which are easily available in translation. Arrian, a Greek civil servant and military man from Western Anatolia in the second century AD, has pride of place, although, as an admirer of Alexander, he has tailored his sources to that end. Arrian's *Campaigns of Alexander* is translated in Penguin Classics; P. Brunt's Loeb edition, with Greek and English texts and copious notes, is especially useful, and includes the *Indica*; A. B. Bosworth's *Commentary on Arrian* (two volumes so far, Oxford 1980 and 1985) is indispensable for detailed research. Quintus Curtius, the earliest (mid first century AD), is translated in Penguin Classics with helpful notes by W. Heckel, and with parallel Latin text in Loeb. Curtius gives us much material, not in Arrian, which probably came from good sources and is important, for example, for the Central Asian part of the story. Diodorus of Sicily wrote a world history in Greek in the first century BC with valuable material on Alexander from the tradition used by Curtius (*Library of History* Book 17, Loeb edition volume VIII; Alexander's last plans are in Book 18, Loeb volume IX). Plutarch's life of the king is in *The Age of Alexander* (Penguin, 1973) with a detailed commentary by J. R. Hamilton *Plutarch: Alexander. A Commentary* (Oxford, 1969). Other valuable and otherwise unattested information is contained in the historian Justin and in the so-called *Metz Epitome;* both these Latin texts are in the Teubner series; no

---

The medieval Alexander carried to heaven in a chariot pulled
by griffons. His tale was so extraordinary that, in later centuries,
it became a metaphor for the human need to reach beyond itself,
to exceed the boundaries of what is possible, or even desirable.

anom ambra laquelle cite il
assegea mais ceulz dedans se
deffendirent moult vigoureu
sement et nafferent moult
de ceulz de lost de tarreaulx
et de sautes Mais sembla a
alixandre en avision que le
dieu amon lui venoit denant
en semblance de mercurine
et lui monstroit herbes et
lui disoit filz alixandre done
cestes herbes a tes nafsies
et lunenu ne lui greneva
pas Alixandre se sueilla
maintenant du songe et
trouva lerbe denant lui Si
la fist destremper et a plu
senrs en donna a boure et a tous
ses thena here et furent main
tenant gueris des plaies
et du venin maintenant
quil vit ses gens gueris
il fist assaillir lacite et la
prinst par force darmes Et
quant il lot prinse si la fist
abatre jusques aux fodeme
Comme alixandre se fait por

Comme alixandre prinst lacite
du roy ambira et lafist abatre

vant alixandre ot des
confit leroy ambira
et ses gens et il ot sacite prinse
et abatre si sen parti atant
delisle auec tout son host
et sen ala sur lamer rouge
et sellerguer se logerent
Pres dela dela herbe vue vic
si y auoit vng mont si hault
et si grant quil sembloit
quil surmontast les nuee
Adont alixandre monta sur
ce mont et lui sembla quil
estoit jusques au ciel main
tenant se pense il en son cuer
quil seroit faire vng engin
par quil les oyseaulx thir so
le porteroient jusques au
ciel pour ce quil vouloit veoir
quelles choses il y auoit au
ciel amont et de quelle forme
la terre estoit par dessus lore
tes en leur aux trestons

translation is available for either. Much relevant material is also to be found in the Greek geographers, notably Strabo and Pliny (both in Loeb Classical Library).

As for secondary sources, in a work of this kind there is no need to cite a long bibliography: the literature is truly vast, as may be seen from the bibliographies published by E. Badian (*Classical World* 65, 1971) and J. M. O'Brian *Alexander the Great: The Invisible Enemy* (1992). In this section, I have tried to be selective with a bias towards recently written works. Modern studies include A. B. Bosworth's lucid, sceptical, severely factual but very rewarding *Conquest and Empire* (1988); N. Hammond *Alexander the Great* (1981) reflects a great mastery of the sources, deep knowledge of the terrain and is informed by personal experience of war; P. Green *Alexander of Macedon* (Pelican ed. 1974) is a terrific read; Robin Lane Fox's *Alexander the Great* (1973) is a youthful *tour de force* attacked by some scholars for what one called its 'Boys Own' approach to the king. Older works include the still great U. Wilcken *Alexander the Great* (new ed. 1967), and, for those with German, the magisterial F. Schachermeyr *Alexander der Grosse* (1973). A famous British work was W. Tarn *Alexander the Great* (1948). Tarn's theories about Alexander's conception of the unity of mankind were critically exposed by E. Badian in *Historia* 7 (1958) (reprinted in *Alexander the Great: The Main Problems*, edited by G. T. Griffith 1966). For interesting symposia: *Alexander the Great* in *Greece and Rome XII* (1965); *Alexandre le Grand: Image et Réalité* (Fondation Hardt, 1974) which contains Badian's fascinating 'Some Recent Interpretations'; *The Image of Alexander* (Rome, 1995).

On the Macedonian background: E. Borza *In the Shadow of Olympus* (1990); see, too, *Macedonia and Greece* (edited by B. Barr-Sharrar), and E. Borza *Studies in History of Art 10* (Washington, 1982). On Alexander and the Near East: S. K. Eddy *The King is Dead* (Lincoln, Nebraska, 1961). On Alexander's logistics: D. Engels *Alexander the Great and the Logistics of the Macedonian Army* (1978). On Alexander in India: A. B. Bosworth *Alexander in the East* (1996, gripping analogies with conquistadors). Older classics include: A. K. Narain *The Indo-Greeks* (1957); W. Tarn *The Greeks in Bactria and India* (second ed. 1951); M. Wheeler *Flames over Persepolis* (1968). On Ptolemaic Egypt: there is the beautifully illustrated A. Bowman *Egypt after the Pharaohs* (1986); N. Lewis *Greeks in Ptolemaic Egypt* (1986); P. M. Fraser *Ptolemaic Alexandria* (three volumes 1972). On Iraq/Babylonia: S. Sherwin White and A. Kuhrt *Hellenism in the East* (1987), and *From Samarkhand to Sardis* (1993); Joan Oates *Babylon* (1986 ed.); D. J. Wiseman *Nebuchadnezzar and Babylon* (1985). On Iran there are many works, for a general survey, R. Ghirshman *Iran* (1954); a short introduction, John Curtis *Ancient Persia* (1989); and two brilliant compilations *The Legacy of Persia* edited by A. J. Arberry (1953) and *L'Ame de L'Iran* (Paris 1951) (reprint prefaced by D. Shayegan 1990); the periodical *Iran*, the journal of the British Institute of Persian

Studies, is full of interesting material. On individual sites: D. Wilber *Persepolis* (1969); D. Stronach *Pasargadae* (1978); *The Royal City of Susa* (Metropolitan Museum, New York, 1992). Important material on Zoroastrians in Alexander's day can be found in the works of Mary Boyce, especially her *History of Zoroastrianism III* (1991), and *Zoroastrians* (1979). Finally on Iran, a valuable new periodical *Achaemenian History* contains essays on many aspects of politics and culture, which challenge old assumptions about Persian rule. On Alexander's cities: see now P. M. Fraser *Cities of Alexander the Great* (Oxford, 1996). On Sogdia and Bactria: most new work is in Russian. For references, see S. Sherwin-White and A. Kurht; and F. Holt *Alexander the Great and Bactria* (Leiden, 1985) supplemented by Holt's contributions to the periodical *Ancient World*.

On the art of Alexander's age: J. J. Pollitt's *Art in the Hellenistic Age* (1986) is superb; C. M. Havelock *Hellenistic Art* (1971); R. R. R. Smith *Hellenistic Sculpture* (1991). There are several excellent exhibition catalogues of Macedonian treasures: *The Search for Alexander* (National Gallery, Washington, 1980); *Alexander the Great* (Archaeological Museum of Thessaloniki, 1980); *Alessandro Magno* (Rome, 1995).

For broad sweeps on Hellenism: P. Brown *The World of Late Antiquity* (1971); A. Momigliano *Alien Wisdom* (1975); G. Bowerstock *Hellenism in Late Antiquity* (1990); L. H. Martin *Hellenistic Religions* (1987); B. H. Fowler *The Hellenistic Aesthetic* (1986). A. J. Toynbee's great what-if essay (see page 235) is in his *Some Problems of Greek History* (1969).

On the legend in art and literature: G. Cary *The Medieval Alexander* (1956); D. J. A. Ross *Alexander historiatus: a guide to medieval illustrated Alexander literature* (Warburg, 1963); Victor Schmidt *A Legend and its Image* (Groningen, 1995) with fascinating bibliography on the medieval legend. The *Greek Alexander Romance* is translated in Penguin Classics (1991).

Guide Books: for conditions *en route* before modern times I used the old Admiralty Intelligence Guides and the works of many earlier travellers, such as Aurel Stein, G. le Strange, Percy Sykes, Freya Stark, Masson, Yule, Burnes, Elphinestone and Olufsen. As for modern guide books: *The Blue Guides* to Greece, Egypt and Turkey are all excellent; there are detailed guides to the classical antiquities of Western Turkey by G. Bean *Aegean Turkey*; *Turkey Beyond the Maeander*, *The Southern Coast of Turkey* and *Lycia*. There is no new good guide to Iran; easily the most valuable to the traveller is still Sylvia Matheson *Persia An Archaeological Guide* (Faber, 1976 ed.) which should be updated and reissued. Afghanistan: Nancy Dupree *Afghanistan* (1977 ed.), can be got from libraries, likewise her catalogue to Kabul Museum which includes the Begram treasure. *The Light Garden of the Angel King* by Peter Levi (1972) is a luminous portrait of that land on the eve of its fall.

On Central Asia: there is much interesting new work, but E. Knobloch's *Beyond the Oxus* (1972) is still an indispensable guide to the archaeology and architecture, although it needs revision in the light of important new discoveries especially in Tajikistan. For traveller's guides: *Central Asia* (Lonely Planet, 1995) is useful. On Pakistan: there are two good recent guide books, Isobel Shaw *Pakistan Handbook* (1989) and J. King and D. St Vincent *Pakistan* (Lonely Planet, 1993). For India: there are numerous good guides but the old John Murray books are best for the North-West areas; the most useful resource is the district gazetteers, produced under British rule, which are full of local archaeological detail for present-day Pakistan and India; my search for the lost altars, for example (see page 196) began with the Hoshiarpur District Gazetteer.

For those interested in more detailed questions on Alexander's exact route, I found the following useful: F. Stark *Alexander's Path* (south-west Turkey); Aurel Stein *Old Routes of Western Iran* (1940); J. Hansman in *Iran* (X, 1972) (on the Persian Gates in Iran); K. Fischer in *Bonner Jahrbuch* (CIXVII, 1967) (on the Herat-Kandahar-Ghazni route in Afghanistan); A. Foucher *La Vieille Route de l'Inde de Bactres à Taxila* (Paris, 1942) (a magnificent book with fascinating photos). On the Passes of the Hindu Kush, 'Crossing the Hindu Kush', by Felix Howland in *Geographical Review* (1940); F. von Schwarz *Alexanders des Grossen Feldzüge in Turkestan* (1906) covers the Uzbek-Tajik part of the journey but needs revision. For the North-West Frontier: Aurel Stein *On Alexander's Track to the Indus* (1929). For the Jhelum river crossing: A. Stein *Geographical Journal* (80, 1932, 31–46), and *Archaeological Reconnaissances in North-West India and South-East Iran* (1937, 1–26). On the Makran: A. Stein 'On Alexander's route into Gedrosia' *Geographical Journal* (102, 193–227). On Alexander's route in India there has been no detailed work since A. Anspach *De Alexandri Magni Expeditione Indica* (3 fascicles, Leipzig, 1901–3) which is still useful for those who can read Latin.

For maps on our journey, we used Geo Centre Maps, and for detail US Airforce TPCs (1:500,000 with excellent detail on terrain, on public sale at a modest price).

A last word, on fictions. Many fabulous tales have been told of Alexander, from the Greek Romance to Mary Renault and Hollywood. One particularly wonderful story is by Robert Graves in a poem 'The Clipped Stater', dedicated to Lawrence of Arabia. In this, Alexander does not die in Babylon, but leaves his old identity behind and wanders in the wilderness. Finally, far to the east, he enlists in an army out on the frontiers of Mongolia and serves as a common soldier in lands whose existence he never dreamed of. One day he is paid off and recognizes his own profile on a rubbed silver coin struck from the bullion seized after the battle of Arbela, when he was Alexander of Macedon. As Jorge Luis Borges remarked, this fable deserves to be very ancient!

# ACKNOWLEDGEMENTS

As might be expected, in a project of this scope which covered seventeen countries and thirty weeks of recce and filming, my debts are unusually great.

In particular, I would like to thank David Wallace, who directed the films which lie behind this book, for bringing these ideas to life with inspiring skill, commitment and good humour – even when under arrest! Years ago, David and I travelled up the Congo together on another great journey for the BBC, and it would be hard to think of a better companion for such testing trips. Rebecca Dobbs, the producer of the series, was the anchor on which all our expeditions relied; without her brilliant organizing skills – and her powers of persuasion – we might never have got beyond the Near East; she was a galvanizing presence both in the planning and the cutting stages. Steve Singleton, our editor, shaped a huge mass of material with heroic patience and great sensitivity; as always it was a joy to work with him. My thanks, too, to Leo Eaton our good friend and co-producer across the Atlantic for his constant support and good counsel. Kathy Quatrone was our mainstay at Public Television (the prime movers in this project) and I would also like to thank Jennifer Lawson and Don Marbury who originally backed the project with typical generosity of spirit. The main film crew was Peter Harvey, Lynette Frewin and John Anderton, to whom my gratitude goes back over many years now, and over many adventures. Peter Jouvenal and Tim Fraser shot Afghanistan and Central Asia; great companions under not the easiest conditions. I would also like to thank all at Maya Vision: John, Sally, Chris, Christine and Paula; Chris Woods for his research in Egypt, Lebanon and Gaza, and Peter Sommer for his sterling work in Turkey and Central Asia. At the BBC my thanks to Alan Yentob, Sheila Ableman, Laurence Rees, Debbie Manners and Steve Nam for their support, and a special thanks to John Triffitt for his generous advice during the preparation of these programmes.

Many scholars gave freely of their time and help: Gabby Gaballah and Mustafa El-Abbadi, S. M. Ansari, A. K. Narain, Ahmed Dani, Brian Bosworth, Nick Hammond, Ken Sams, Ken Harl, Roland Besevan, Monique Kervran, Marie-Henriette Gates, Nina Jidejian, Peter Kuhlman, Gene Borza, Machin Khan, W. Siddiqi, M.Kiani, W. Kleiss, E. Rutveladze and Elizabeth Baynham. Brian Bosworth was especially generous in providing us with the proofs of his *Alexander in the East* which provided much food for thought as we journeyed down the Indus. Our main fixers for the films comprised a real-life magnificent seven without whom the whole project would have been impossible: Cem Yücsoy (Turkey), Zoreh Majidian and Ali Akbar Neysari (Iran), Muhiddein Ganiev (Central Asia),

# ACKNOWLEDGEMENTS

Hanif Sharzat (Afghanistan), Asad Ali (Pakistan), and Romany Helmy (Egypt). My thanks, too, to Hasnaim Ghulham (Pakistan), Harbreet Singh in the Punjab, Louise Ferouz (Iran), Saud Abu Ramadan (Gaza), Engineer Khan in Chitral, and to Maria Powell once again in Greece; I would also like to thank Tira Schubart for so generously setting us on the right path in Iran, and Elizabeth Winter who did likewise in Afghanistan. Among our long-suffering drivers, I should single out Mustafa in Turkey, Bandar and Abbas in Iran, and Boris and Shiref in Uzbekistan. Among the many and various lodgings we found during our journey, I would particularly like to thank the staff of Quduz's guest house in Kabul for their many kindnesses. Several airlines helped us beyond the call of duty, but I must especially single out PIA for its tremendous help in the making of these films. The Pakistan Navy was also most generous. In Turkey, Nebahat Baydar smoothed the way for our filming at Incirlik airbase.

Along the road we received incomparable hospitality in too many places to mention here, but I would like to thank the Gardezi family in Multan, Pakistan, especially Sultan and Hur; General Shafgat Ahmed Seyed for his participation in the films and for our memorable days in Jalalpur; in Iran, Zavareh Shojaei and his family in Mulla Susan put us up with much kindness over three visits. The Zoroastrian community in Iran was most welcoming, especially the Yazdani family in Yazd; and the Belivani family in Sharifabad; I am indebted in particular to Shahriar Mahanni for his many kindnesses in Yazd and for our magical visits to Pir i Sabz, Taft and Mobareke. Thanks, too, to Ali Reza Haggighi who got us out of numerous scrapes in Iran. In Pakistan, my thanks to the Fisherman's Union of the Mohanno Boat People. In Afghanistan, The Halo Trust, which does heroic, devoted and unsung work clearing mines, gave freely of its valuable time; Terence White in Kabul, Seyyed Jaffar and Haroun Nadiri in Pul-i-Kumri all helped us on our way. I would like to thank the UN in Lebanon for its generous assistance in filming around Tyre, and also in Afghanistan for being available when we needed help. Our special thanks also are due to the Red Cross, which is always so generous to journalists despite taxing obligations to a more important cause: Jaques Villettaz in Kabul and Jean-Paul Jacquod in Mazar made our journey possible. Back home, a special thanks to Barbara Nash who edited this book during a short and hectic period when I was pulled between Tajikistan and South Lebanon; and to Martha Caute, Linda Blakemore and Frances Abrahams at BBC Books.

My last, and greatest debt, is to Rebecca and our daughters Jyoti and Mina who put up with my absence for the large part of more than one year in the making of these films; communication was at best by phone and fax, and often non-existent, but they were always in my heart. To them, as always, my deepest thanks and my love.

# INDEX

*Page numbers in italics refer to the photographs*
*Alexander's name is abbreviated to A*

251

# PICTURE CREDITS

*BBC Books would like to thank the following for providing photographs and for permission to reproduce copyright material. While every effort has been made to trace and acknowledge all copyright holders, we would like to apologize should there have been any errors or omissions.*

Page 2 Staatliche Glypothek, Munich/E.T.Archive; 3 David Wallace; 6 Bibliothèque Royale, Brussels/Bridgeman Art Library, London; 10 *top* Michael Wood, *bottom* British Museum, London; 14 *both* Maya Vision; 19 *left* Erich Lessing/AKG London, *right* Pella Museum, Greece/E.T.Archive; 20 British Museum, London/ Michael Holford; 23 *left* Bibliothèque Nationale, Paris/AKG London, *right* Kunsthistorisches Museum, Vienna; 26–7 *left* Kunsthistorisches Museum, Vienna/ AKG London; 27 *right* Museo Nazionale, Rome/ E.T.Archive; 30–1 Pella Museum, Greece/E.T.Archive; 34 National Museum, Athens/Scala; 35 Pella Museum, Greece/E.T.Archive; 38 Robert Harding Picture Library; 42–3 *both,* 46–7 & 50 David Wallace; 55 Michael Wood; 58–9 National Musem, Naples/Scala; 62 David Wallace; 63 Museum of Fine Arts, Brussels/E.T.Archive; 65 Michael Wood; 68–9 British Museum, London/Michael Holford; 73 Peter Clayton; 77 David Wallace; 80–1 Georg Gerster/Comstock; 84 Robert Harding Picture Library; 85 Acropolis Museum, Athens/ E.T.Archive; 89 Archaeological Museum, Naples/E.T.Archive; 93 & 97 Georg Gerster/Comstock; 100 & 101 Louvre, Paris/Bridgeman Art Library, London; 104 & 112 *left* David Wallace; 112–13 *right* Zefa Picture Library; 116 & 120 Michael Wood; 124 Bodleian Library, Oxford; 132 Robert Harding Picture Library; 133 Collection of the J. Paul Getty Museum, Los Angeles, California; 140-1 David Wallace; 145 Michael Wood; 148–9 *left* Robert Harding Picture Library; 149 *right* David Wallace; 156 Robert Harding Picture Library; 157 Michael Wood; 165 David Wallace; 168 British Library, London/Bridgeman Art Library, London; 169 Fitzwilliam Museum, Cambridge/E.T.Archive; 172 Thessalonika Museum/Greek Ministry of Culture; 176–7 Robert Harding Picture Library; 180 & 184 Michael Wood; 185 *both* British Museum, London; 188 David Wallace; 189 Michael Wood; 193 British Library, London; 201 & 205 David Wallace; 208 Michael Wood; 209 Archaeological Museum, Istanbul/AKG London/Erich Lessing; 212–3 Georg Gerster/Comstock; 216–17 Michael Wood; 220 Archaeological Museum, Naples/E.T.Archive; 221 Prado, Madrid/E.T.Archive; 228–9 Georg Gerster/Comstock; 236 National Museum, Naples/Scala; 238 Gregorian Museum, Rome/E.T.Archive; 240 Graeco Roman Museum, Alexandria/David Wallace; 245 Musée Condé, Chantilly/Lauros/Giraudon.